UNCANNY X-MEN

OUR EXPOSE | EXCLUSIVE:

poptopia

TOP 8
MUTANT SUSPECTS!

1. **WRITER**
Joe Casey

2. **PENCILERS**
Ian Churchill with Sean Phillips
and Mel Rubi, Ashley Wood, Tom
Raney and Tom Derenick

3. **INKERS**
Mark Morales, Art Thibert, Norm
Rapmund, Danny Miki, Scott Hanna
with Lary Stucker and Sandu Florea

4. **COLORISTS**
Avalon Studios and Hi Fi Design

5. **LETTERERS**
Richard Starkings & Comicraft

6. **EDITORS**
Mark Powers and Pete Franco

7. **EDITOR IN CHIEF**
Joe Quesada

8. **PRESIDENT**
Bill Jemas

8 MEANEST AUTOGRAPH SIGNERS

1. **COVER ART:**
Ian Churchill

2. **DIRECTOR:**
PUBLISHING
OPERATIONS:
Bob Greenberger

3. **COLLECTIONS
EDITOR:**
Ben Abernathy

4. **ASSISTANT
EDITOR:**
Matty Ryan

5. **MANUFACTURING
REPRESENTATIVE:**
Stefano Perrone Jr.

6. **BOOK DESIGN:**
Camille Murphy

7. **DIGITAL
ASSISTANT:**
Jessica Schwartz

8. **SPECIAL THANKS**
Cory Sedlmeier

CAUGHT ON FILM!
NAMES VERIFIED!

MUTANT MANIA!

Nightcrawler

Cyclops

Iceman

Wolverine

"I GAVE BIRTH TO A MONSTER."

TEEN SUPERSTAR, SUGAR KANE, SPOTTED AT HIDE-OUT OF MUTANT, A.K.A. "CHAMBER"

UNCANNY X-MEN® POPTOPIA. Contains material originally published in magazine form as UNCANNY X-MEN #s 394-399. First Printing, October 2001. ISBN # 0-7851-0801-7. GST. #R127032852. Published by MARVEL COMICS, a division of MARVEL ENTERTAINMENT GROUP, INC. OFFICE OF PUBLICATION: 10 EAST 40th STREET, NEW YORK, NY 10016. Copyright © 2001 Marvel Characters, Inc. No similarity between any of the names, characters, persons, and/or institutions in this publication with those of any living or dead person or institutions is intended, and any such similarity which may exist is purely coincidental. This publication may not be sold except by authorized dealers and is sold subject to the conditions that it shall not be sold or distributed with any part of its cover or markings removed, nor in a mutilated condition. X-MEN (including all prominent characters featured in this publication and the distinctive likenesses thereof) is a trademark of MARVEL CHARACTERS, INC. Printed in Canada. PETER CUNEO, Chief Executive Officer; AVI ARAD, Chief Creative Officer; GUI KARYO, Chief Information Officer; BOB GREENBERGER, Director – Publishing Operations; STAN LEE, Chairman Emeritus.

PLAYING GOD

PART ONE:
UNCANNY X-MEN #394

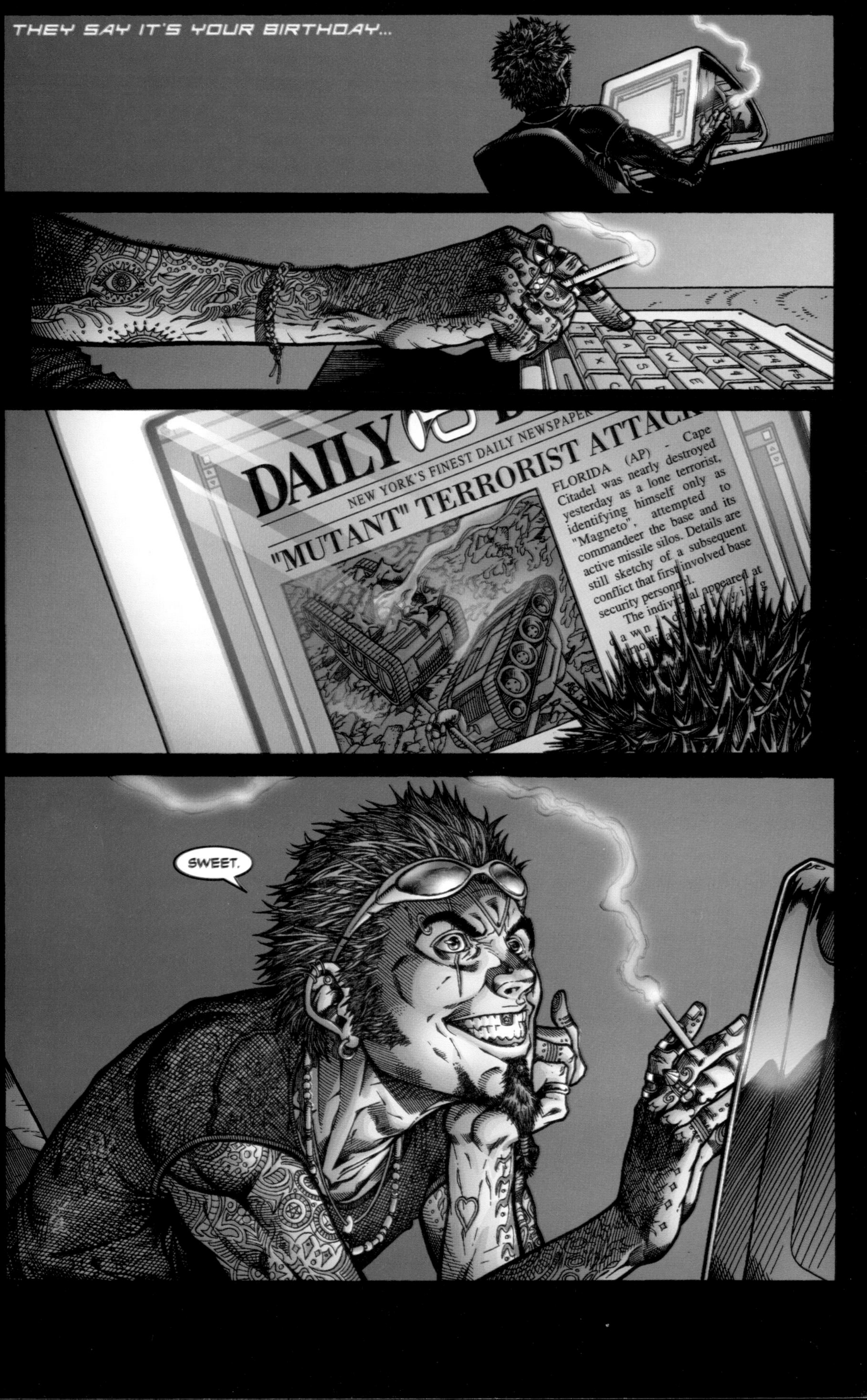
THEY SAY IT'S YOUR BIRTHDAY...
DAILY
NEW YORK'S FINEST DAILY NEWSPAPER
"MUTANT" TERRORIST ATTAC
FLORIDA (AP) - Cape Citadel was nearly destroyed yesterday as a lone terrorist, identifying himself only as "Magneto", attempted to commandeer the base and its active missile silos. Details are still sketchy of a subsequent conflict that first involved base security personnel.
SWEET.

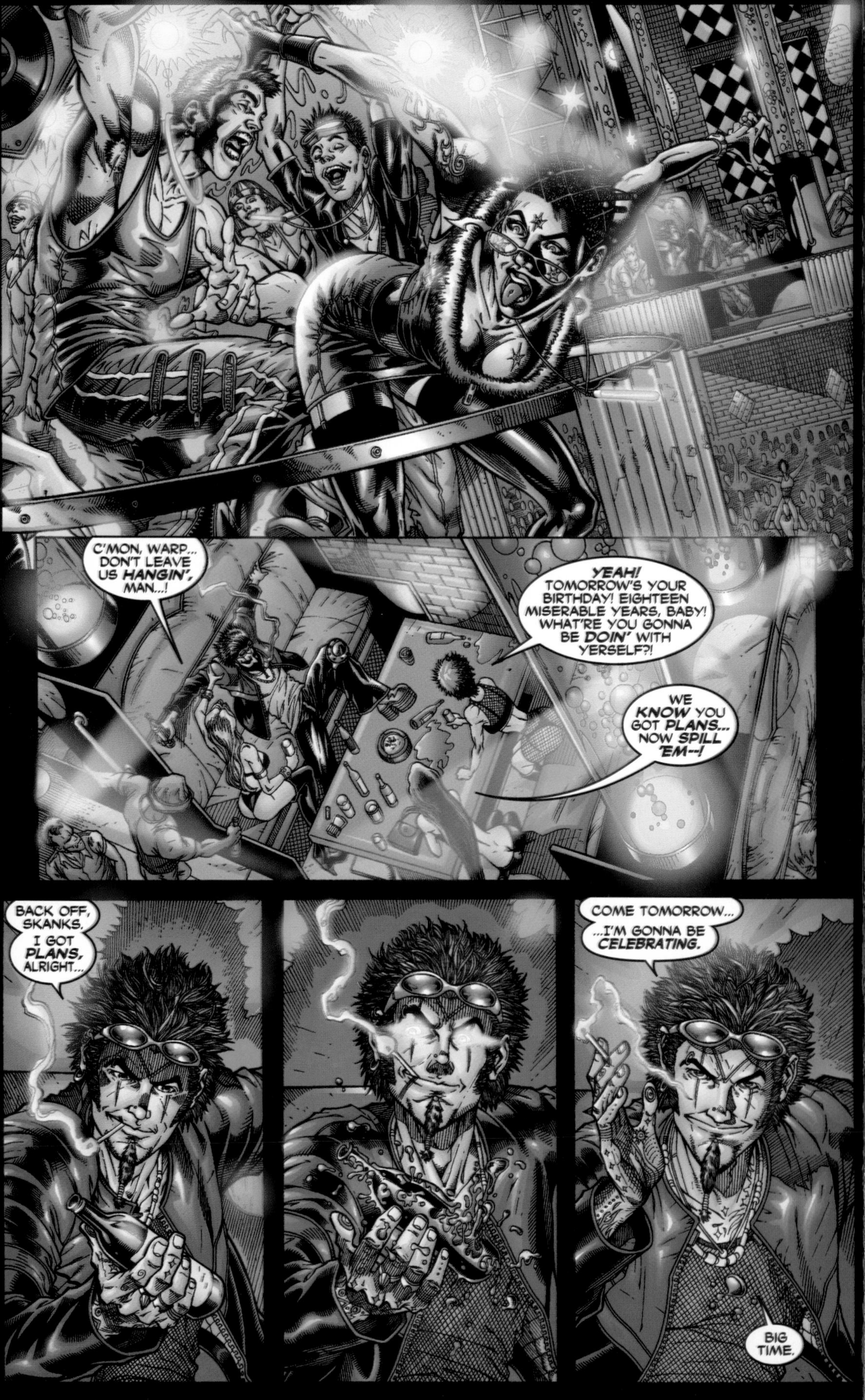
C'MON, WARP... DON'T LEAVE US HANGIN', MAN...!
YEAH! TOMORROW'S YOUR BIRTHDAY! EIGHTEEN MISERABLE YEARS, BABY! WHAT'RE YOU GONNA BE DOIN' WITH YERSELF?!
WE KNOW YOU GOT PLANS... NOW SPILL 'EM--!
BACK OFF, SKANKS, I GOT PLANS, ALRIGHT...
COME TOMORROW...
...I'M GONNA BE CELEBRATING.
BIG TIME.

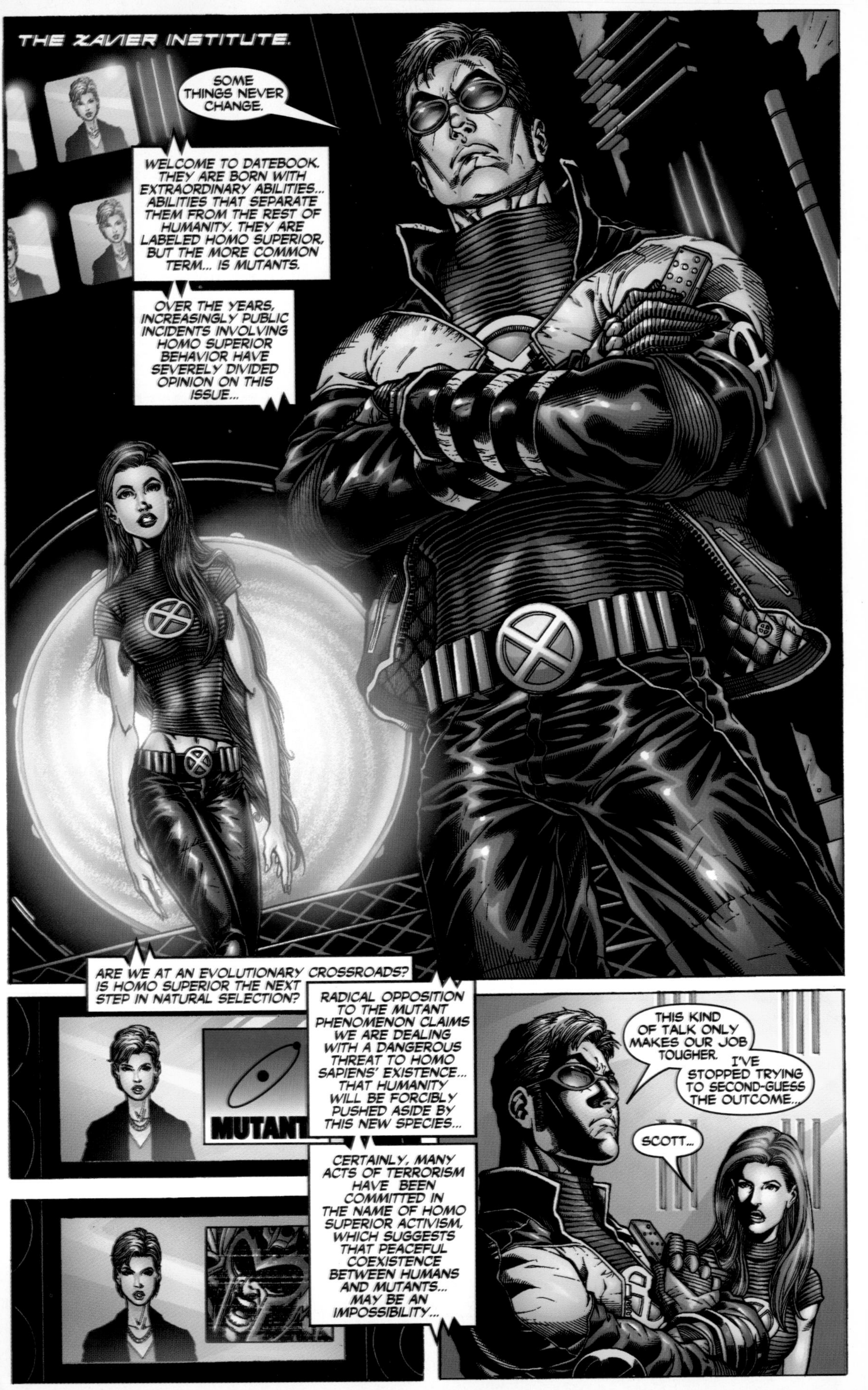
THE XAVIER INSTITUTE.
SOME THINGS NEVER CHANGE.
WELCOME TO DATEBOOK. THEY ARE BORN WITH EXTRAORDINARY ABILITIES... ABILITIES THAT SEPARATE THEM FROM THE REST OF HUMANITY. THEY ARE LABELED HOMO SUPERIOR, BUT THE MORE COMMON TERM... IS MUTANTS.
OVER THE YEARS, INCREASINGLY PUBLIC INCIDENTS INVOLVING HOMO SUPERIOR BEHAVIOR HAVE SEVERELY DIVIDED OPINION ON THIS ISSUE...
ARE WE AT AN EVOLUTIONARY CROSSROADS? IS HOMO SUPERIOR THE NEXT STEP IN NATURAL SELECTION?
MUTANT
RADICAL OPPOSITION TO THE MUTANT PHENOMENON CLAIMS WE ARE DEALING WITH A DANGEROUS THREAT TO HOMO SAPIENS' EXISTENCE... THAT HUMANITY WILL BE FORCIBLY PUSHED ASIDE BY THIS NEW SPECIES...
CERTAINLY, MANY ACTS OF TERRORISM HAVE BEEN COMMITTED IN THE NAME OF HOMO SUPERIOR ACTIVISM, WHICH SUGGESTS THAT PEACEFUL COEXISTENCE BETWEEN HUMANS AND MUTANTS... MAY BE AN IMPOSSIBILITY...
THIS KIND OF TALK ONLY MAKES OUR JOB TOUGHER.
I'VE STOPPED TRYING TO SECOND-GUESS THE OUTCOME...
SCOTT...

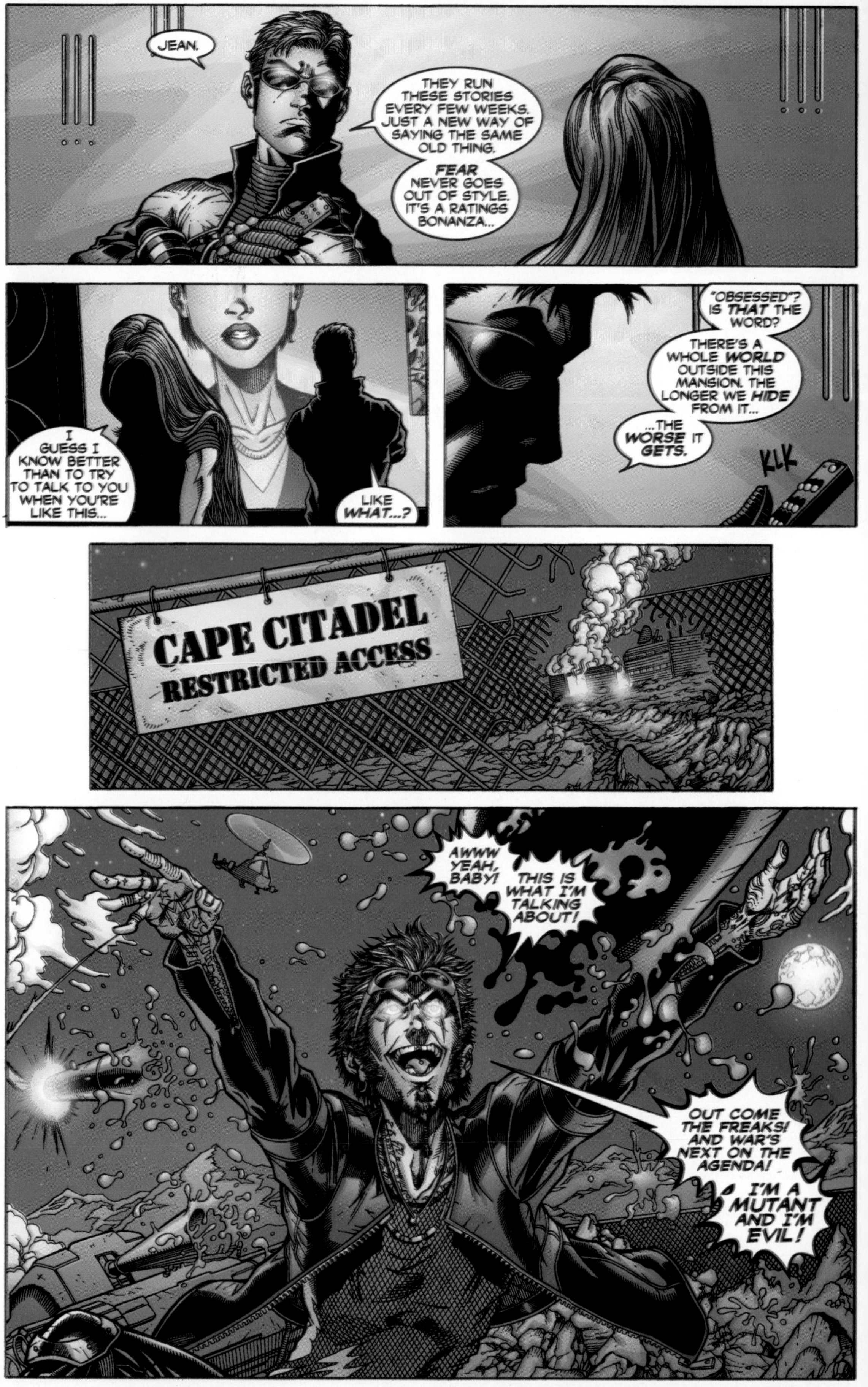
JEAN.
THEY RUN THESE STORIES EVERY FEW WEEKS. JUST A NEW WAY OF SAYING THE SAME OLD THING.
FEAR NEVER GOES OUT OF STYLE. IT'S A RATINGS BONANZA...
I GUESS I KNOW BETTER THAN TO TRY TO TALK TO YOU WHEN YOU'RE LIKE THIS...
LIKE WHAT...?
"OBSESSED"? IS THAT THE WORD?
THERE'S A WHOLE WORLD OUTSIDE THIS MANSION. THE LONGER WE HIDE FROM IT...
...THE WORSE IT GETS.
KLK
CAPE CITADEL
RESTRICTED ACCESS
AWWW YEAH, BABY!
THIS IS WHAT I'M TALKING ABOUT!
OUT COME THE FREAKS! AND WAR'S NEXT ON THE AGENDA!
I'M A MUTANT AND I'M EVIL!

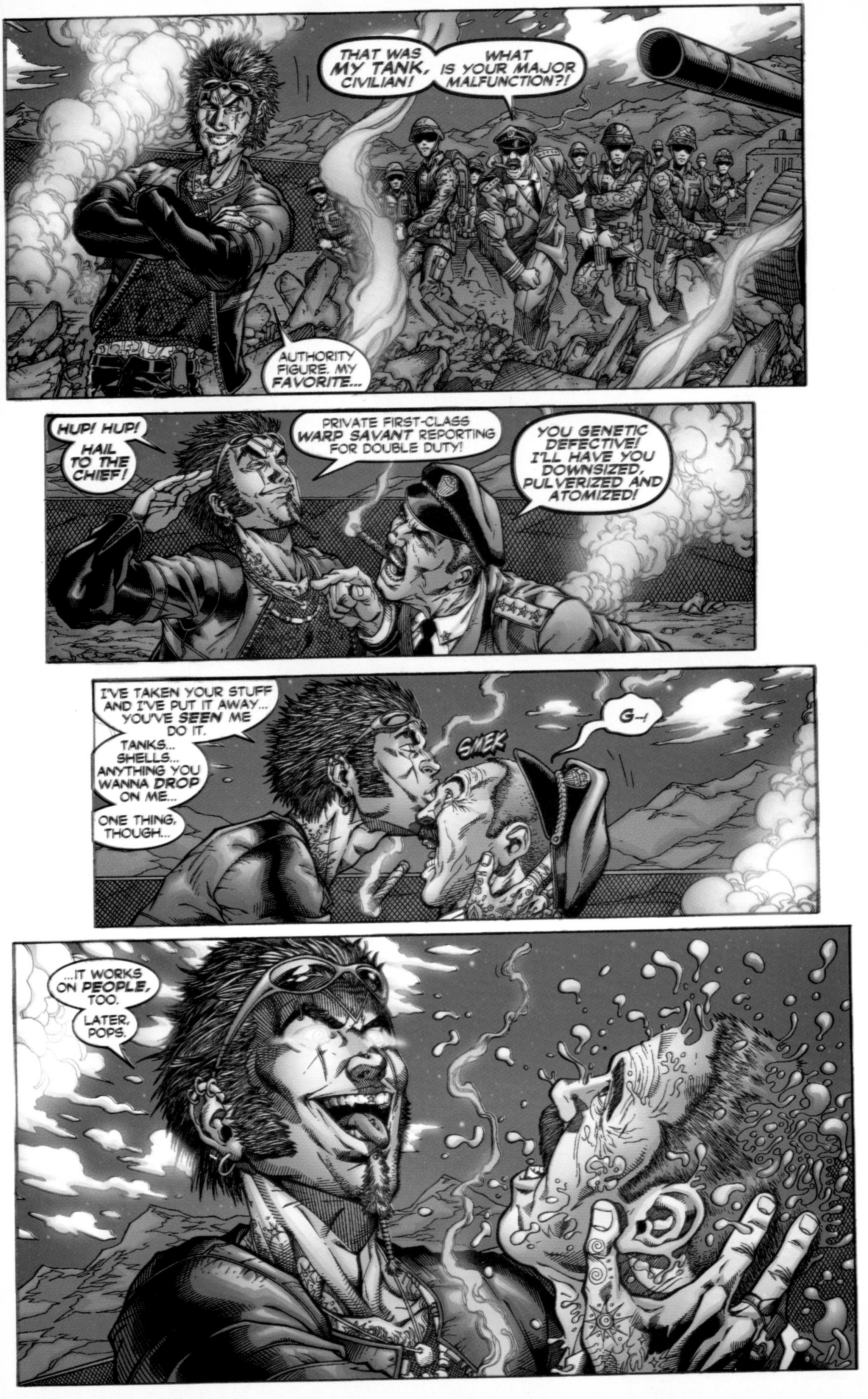
THAT WAS MY TANK, CIVILIAN!
WHAT IS YOUR MAJOR MALFUNCTION?!
AUTHORITY FIGURE. MY FAVORITE...
HUP! HUP! HAIL TO THE CHIEF!
PRIVATE FIRST-CLASS WARP SAVANT REPORTING FOR DOUBLE DUTY!
YOU GENETIC DEFECTIVE! I'LL HAVE YOU DOWNSIZED, PULVERIZED AND ATOMIZED!
I'VE TAKEN YOUR STUFF AND I'VE PUT IT AWAY... YOU'VE SEEN ME DO IT.
TANKS... SHELLS... ANYTHING YOU WANNA DROP ON ME...
ONE THING, THOUGH...
SMEK
G--!
...IT WORKS ON PEOPLE, TOO.
LATER, POPS.

YOU RANG?

TROUBLE IN FLORIDA. MCCOY'S IMPROVEMENTS ON *CEREBRO* CONFIRMED IT. STRAIGHT FROM OUR GENE POOL...

ANYONE WE *KNOW?*

I DON'T THINK SO. NO MATCHES IN CEREBRO'S MEMORY FILES.

ANOTHER NEW KID ON THE BLOCK. *WE'LL* TAKE HIM TO SCHOOL.

ARE WE IT TONIGHT?

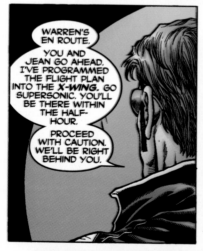

WARREN'S EN ROUTE.

YOU AND JEAN GO AHEAD. I'VE PROGRAMMED THE FLIGHT PLAN INTO THE *X-WING.* GO SUPERSONIC. YOU'LL BE THERE WITHIN THE HALF-HOUR.

PROCEED WITH CAUTION. WE'LL BE RIGHT BEHIND YOU.

LOVE YOU, SCOTT.

LOVE YOU, WIFE.

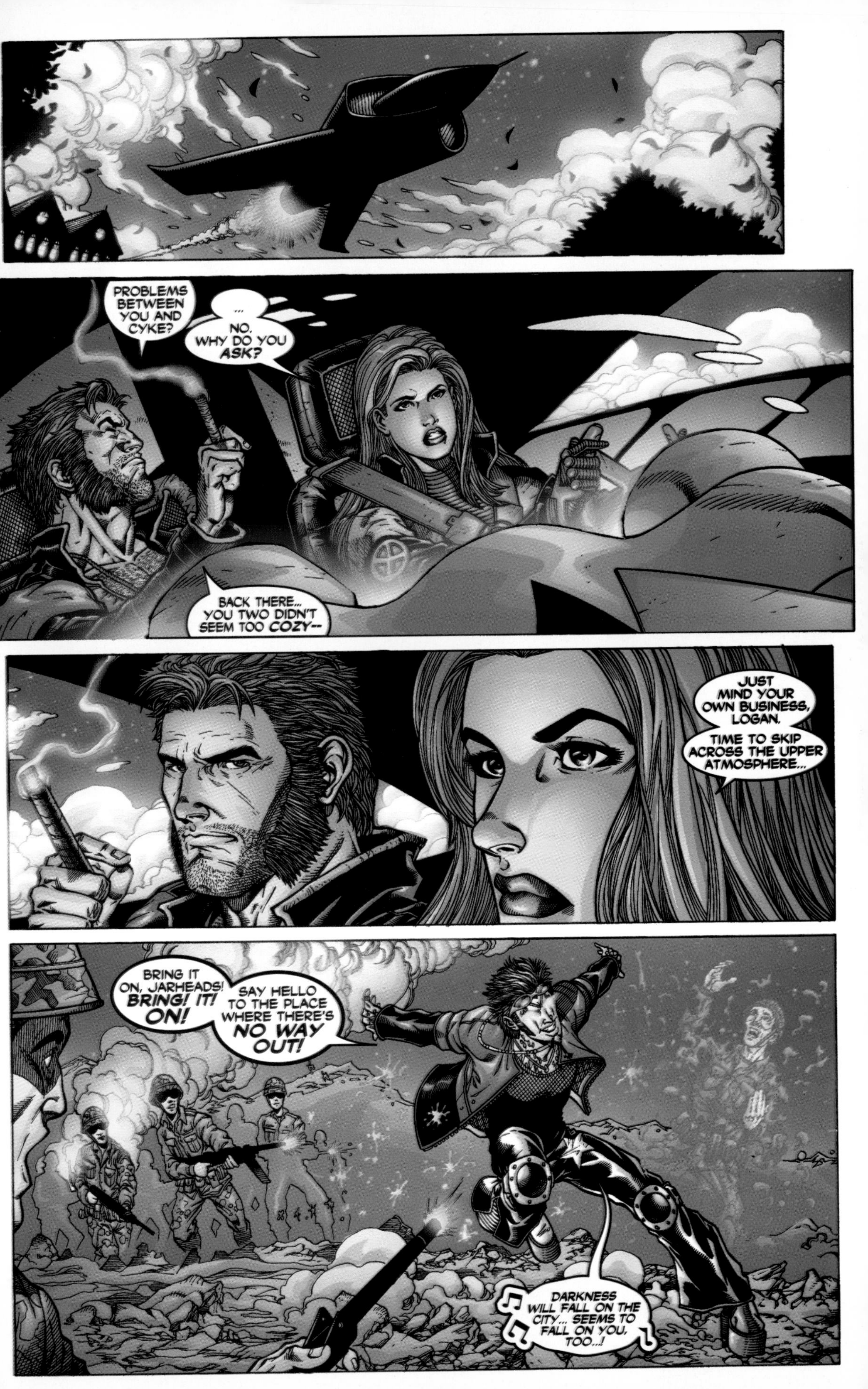
PROBLEMS BETWEEN YOU AND CYKE?
...
NO. WHY DO YOU ASK?
BACK THERE... YOU TWO DIDN'T SEEM TOO COZY--
JUST MIND YOUR OWN BUSINESS, LOGAN.
TIME TO SKIP ACROSS THE UPPER ATMOSPHERE...
BRING IT ON, JARHEADS! BRING! IT! ON!
SAY HELLO TO THE PLACE WHERE THERE'S NO WAY OUT!
DARKNESS WILL FALL ON THE CITY... SEEMS TO FALL ON YOU, TOO...!

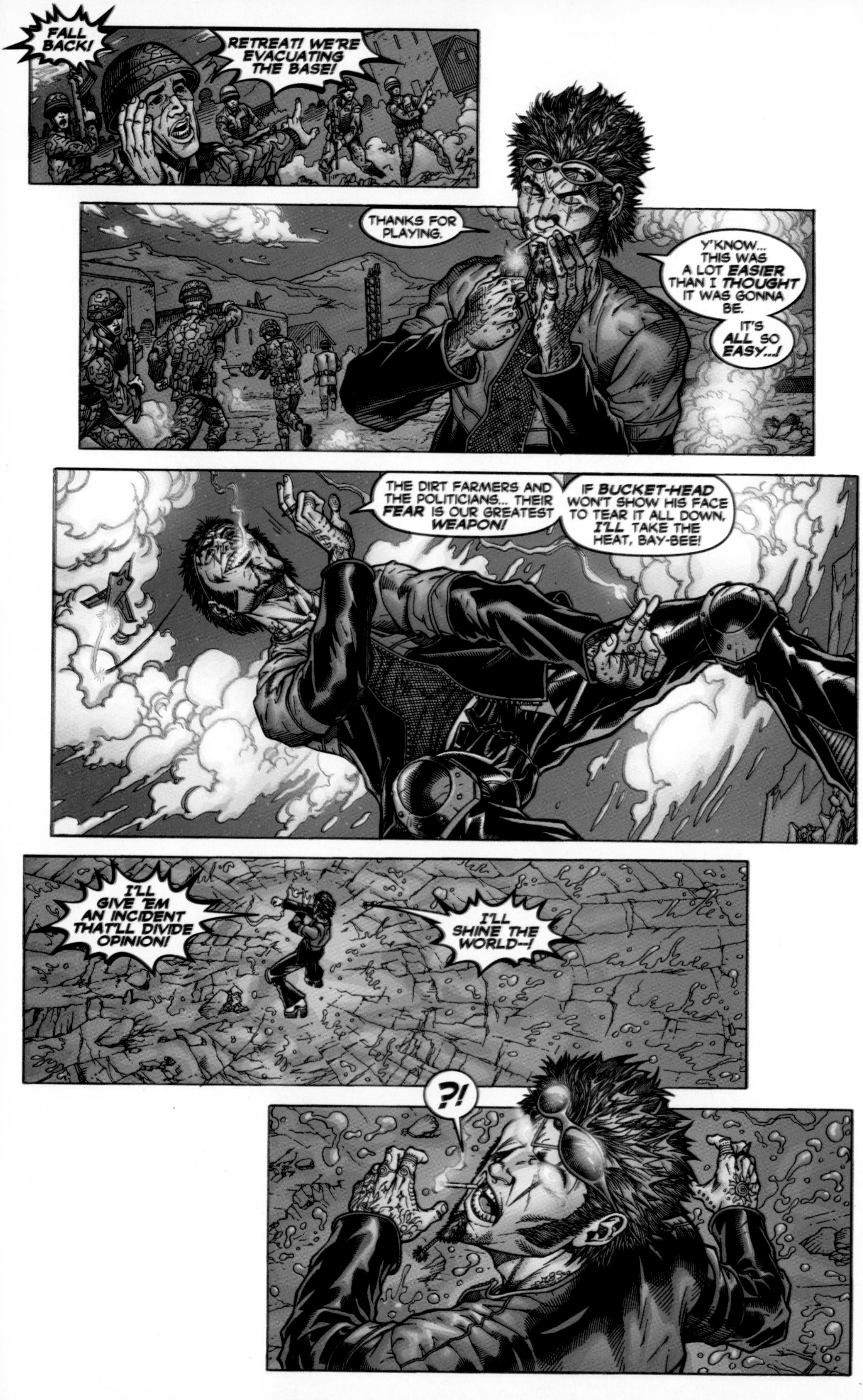
FALL BACK!
RETREAT! WE'RE EVACUATING THE BASE!
THANKS FOR PLAYING.
Y'KNOW... THIS WAS A LOT EASIER THAN I THOUGHT IT WAS GONNA BE.
IT'S ALL SO EASY...!
THE DIRT FARMERS AND THE POLITICIANS... THEIR FEAR IS OUR GREATEST WEAPON!
IF BUCKET-HEAD WON'T SHOW HIS FACE TO TEAR IT ALL DOWN, I'LL TAKE THE HEAT, BAY-BEE!
I'LL GIVE 'EM AN INCIDENT THAT'LL DIVIDE OPINION!
I'LL SHINE THE WORLD--!
?!

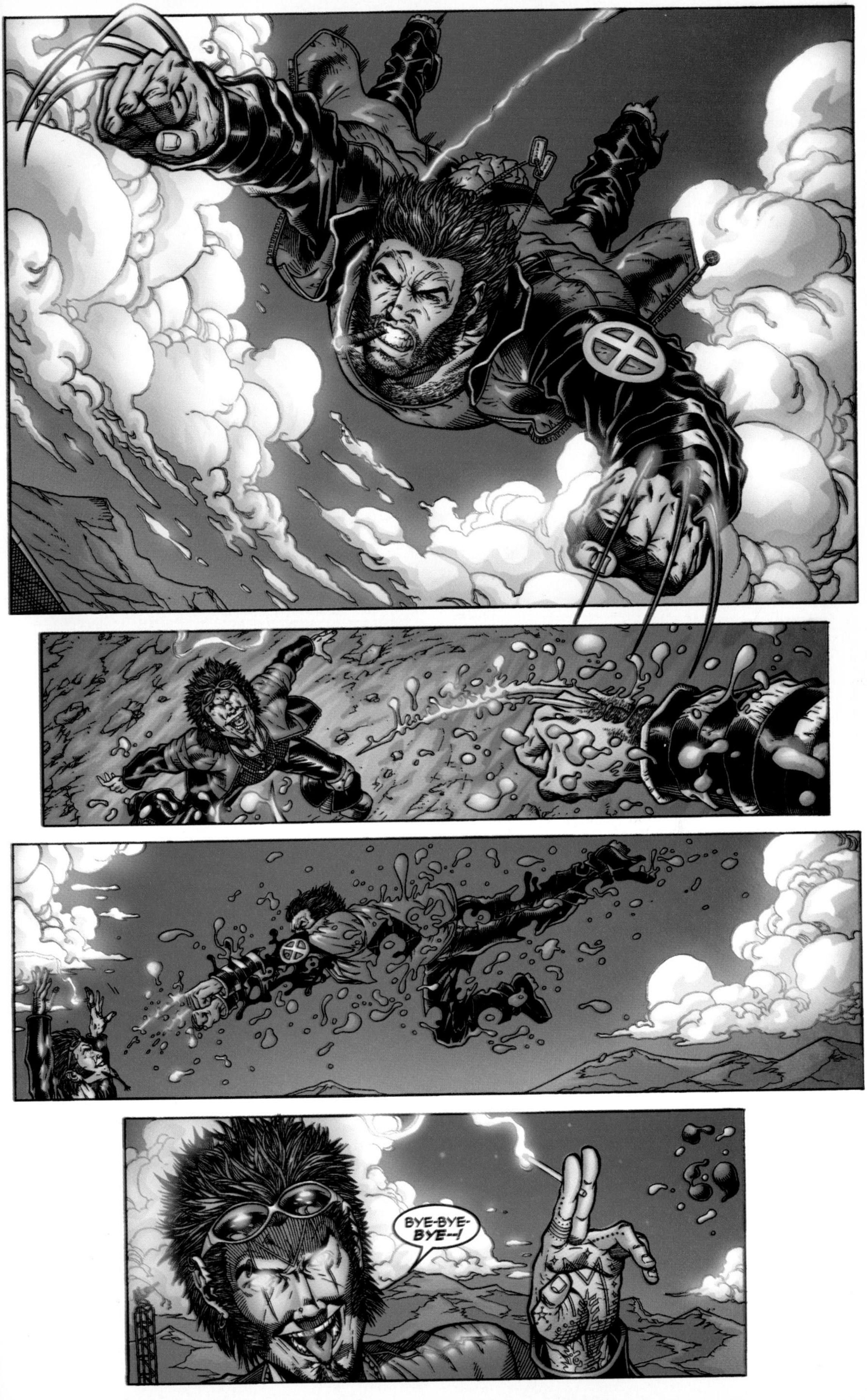
BYE-BYE-BYE--!

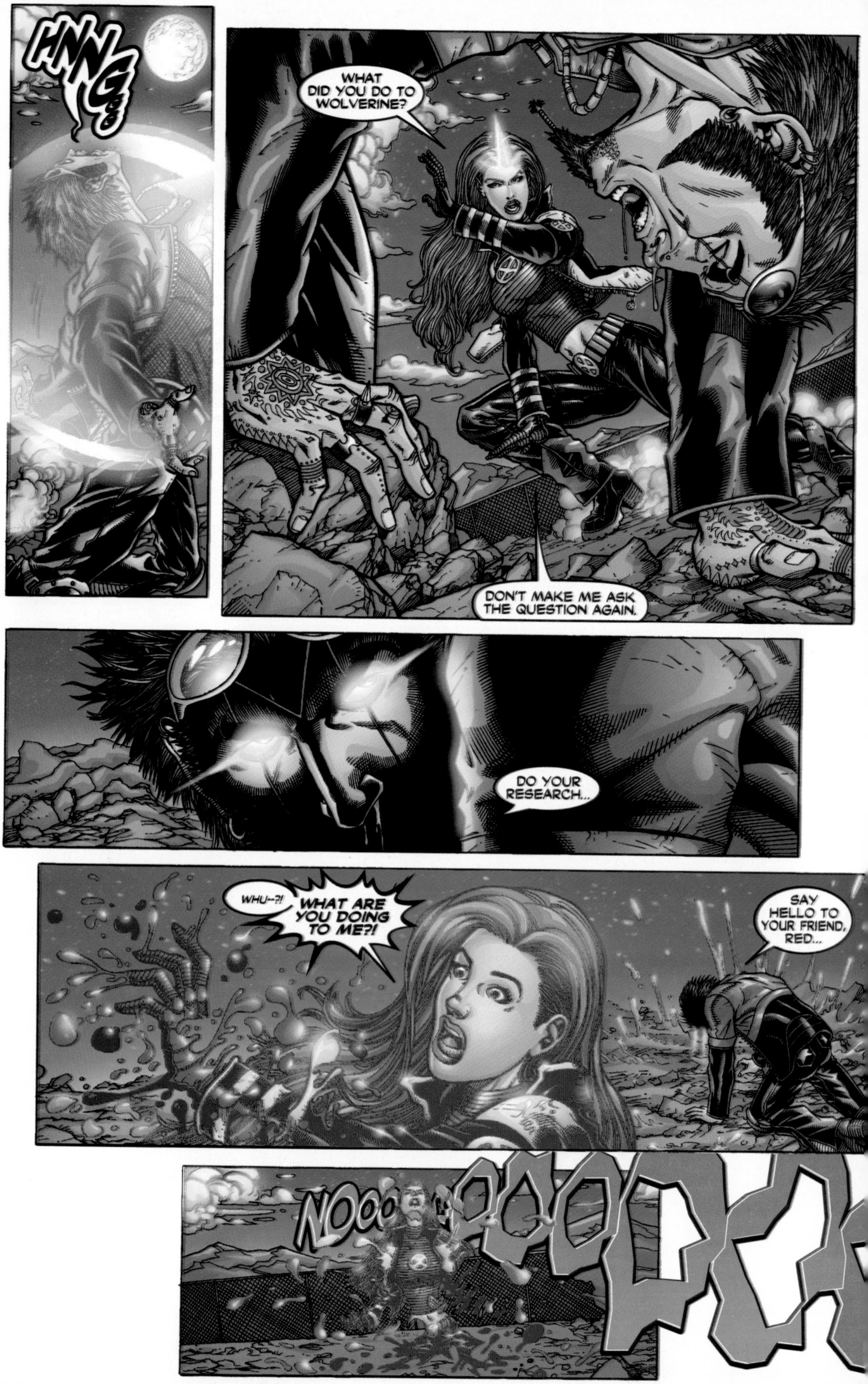
HNNGGG
WHAT DID YOU DO TO WOLVERINE?
DON'T MAKE ME ASK THE QUESTION AGAIN.
DO YOUR RESEARCH...
WHU--?!
WHAT ARE YOU DOING TO ME?!
SAY HELLO TO YOUR FRIEND, RED...
NOOOOOOOOOO

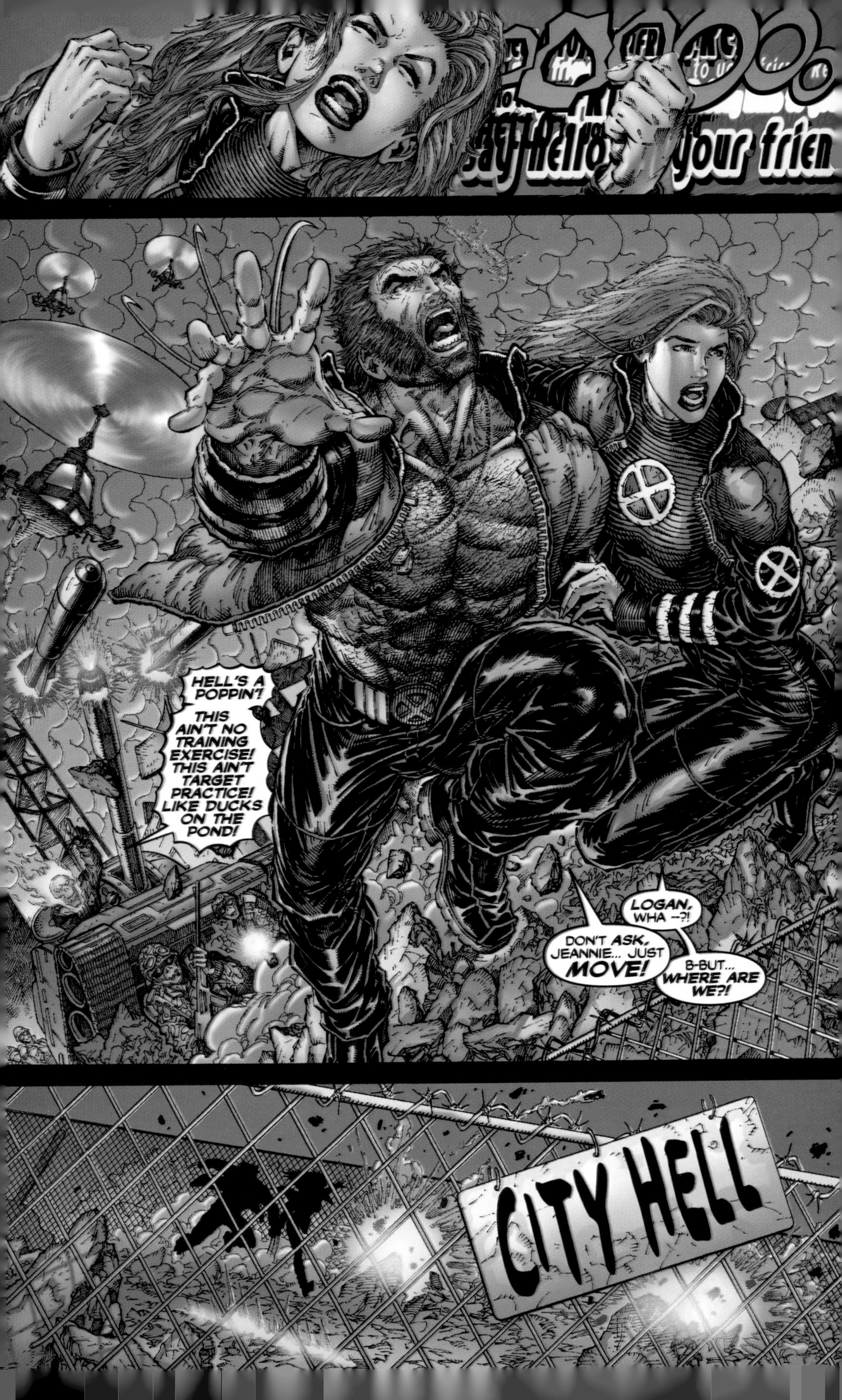
say hello
your frien
HELL'S A POPPIN'!
THIS AIN'T NO TRAINING EXERCISE! THIS AIN'T TARGET PRACTICE! LIKE DUCKS ON THE POND!
LOGAN, WHA --?!
DON'T ASK, JEANNIE... JUST MOVE!
B-BUT... WHERE ARE WE?!
CITY HELL

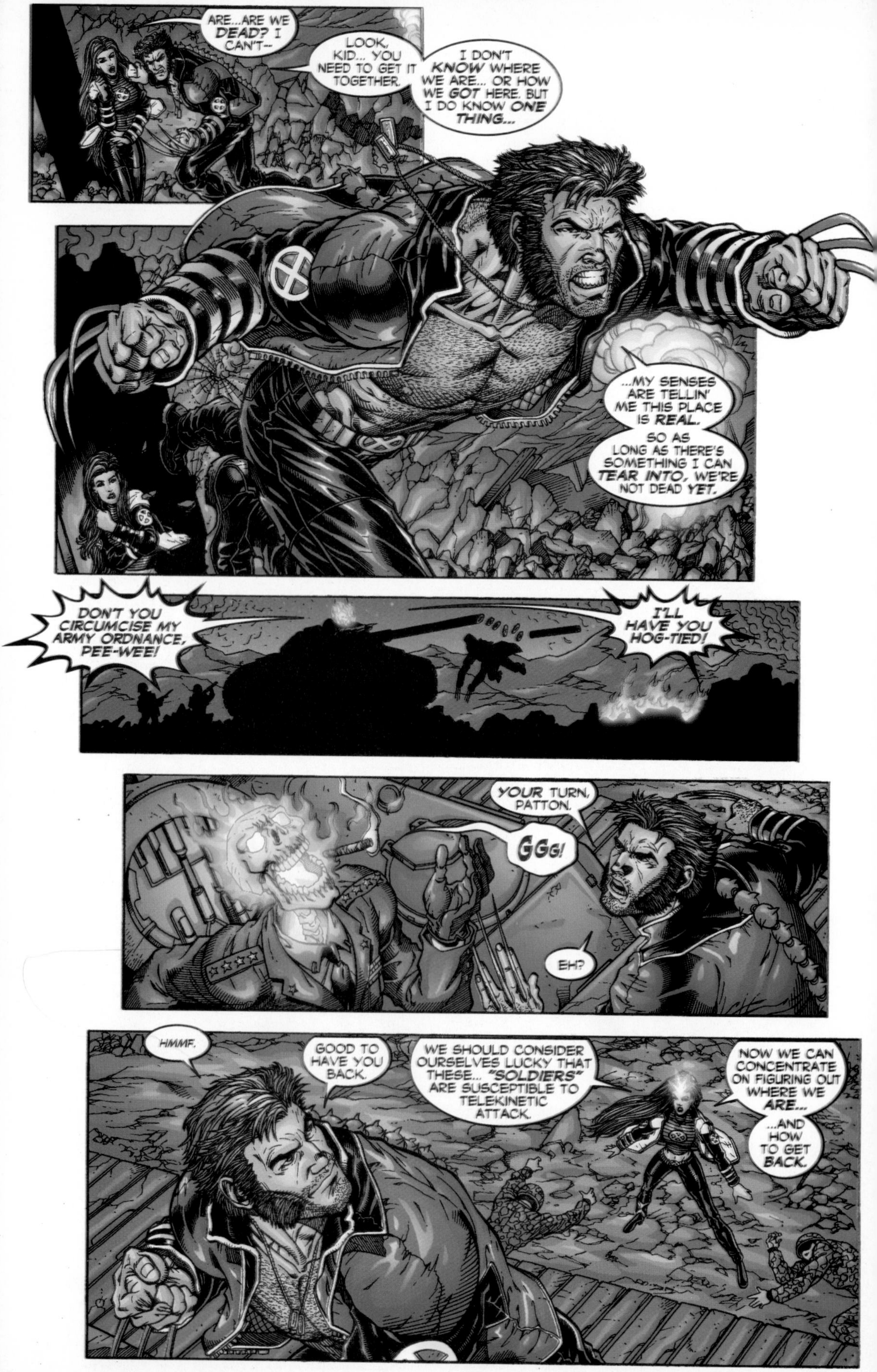
ARE...ARE WE DEAD? I CAN'T--
LOOK, KID... YOU NEED TO GET IT TOGETHER.
I DON'T KNOW WHERE WE ARE... OR HOW WE GOT HERE. BUT I DO KNOW ONE THING...
...MY SENSES ARE TELLIN' ME THIS PLACE IS REAL.
SO AS LONG AS THERE'S SOMETHING I CAN TEAR INTO, WE'RE NOT DEAD YET.
DON'T YOU CIRCUMCISE MY ARMY ORDNANCE, PEE-WEE!
I'LL HAVE YOU HOG-TIED!
YOUR TURN, PATTON.
GGG!
EH?
HMMF.
GOOD TO HAVE YOU BACK.
WE SHOULD CONSIDER OURSELVES LUCKY THAT THESE... "SOLDIERS" ARE SUSCEPTIBLE TO TELEKINETIC ATTACK.
NOW WE CAN CONCENTRATE ON FIGURING OUT WHERE WE ARE...
...AND HOW TO GET BACK.

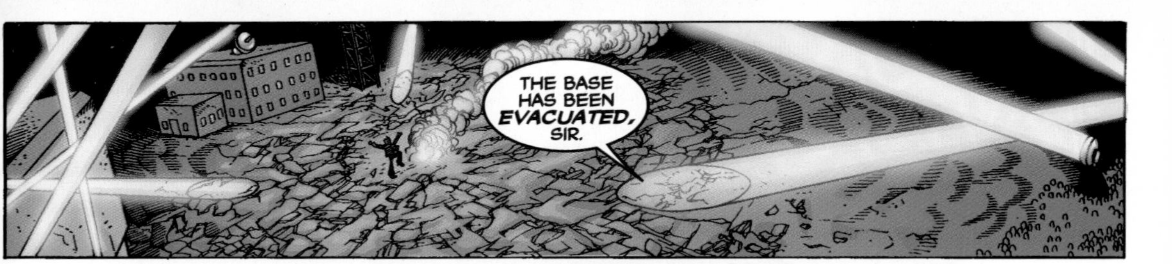
THE BASE HAS BEEN EVACUATED, SIR.

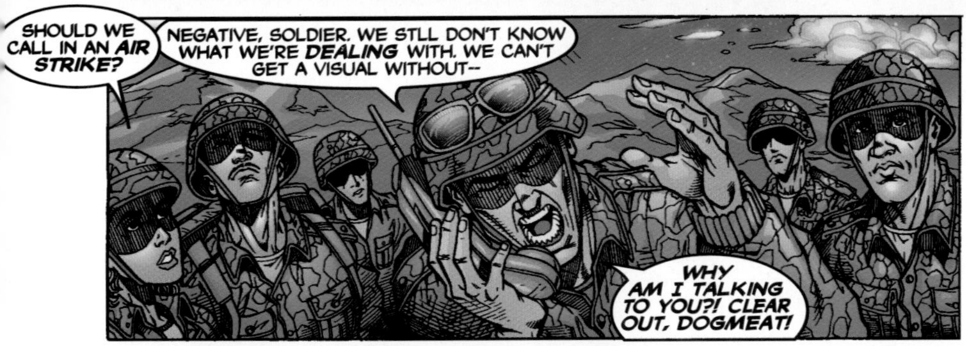
SHOULD WE CALL IN AN AIR STRIKE?
NEGATIVE, SOLDIER. WE STLL DON'T KNOW WHAT WE'RE DEALING WITH. WE CAN'T GET A VISUAL WITHOUT--
WHY AM I TALKING TO YOU?! CLEAR OUT, DOGMEAT!

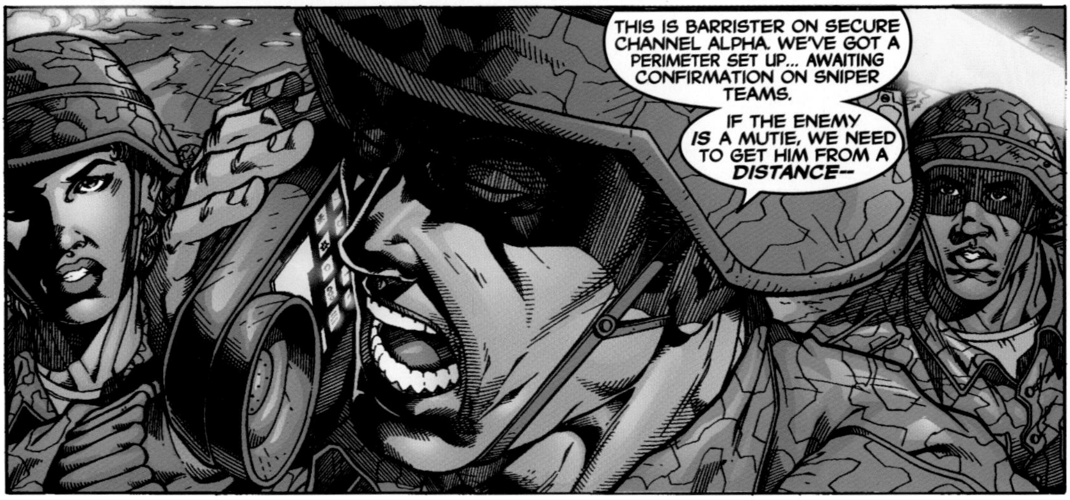
THIS IS BARRISTER ON SECURE CHANNEL ALPHA. WE'VE GOT A PERIMETER SET UP... AWAITING CONFIRMATION ON SNIPER TEAMS.
IF THE ENEMY IS A MUTIE, WE NEED TO GET HIM FROM A DISTANCE--

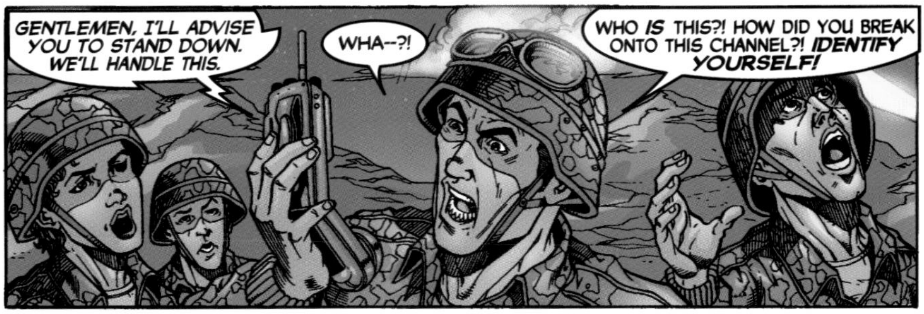
GENTLEMEN, I'LL ADVISE YOU TO STAND DOWN. WE'LL HANDLE THIS.
WHA--?!
WHO IS THIS?! HOW DID YOU BREAK ONTO THIS CHANNEL?! IDENTIFY YOURSELF!

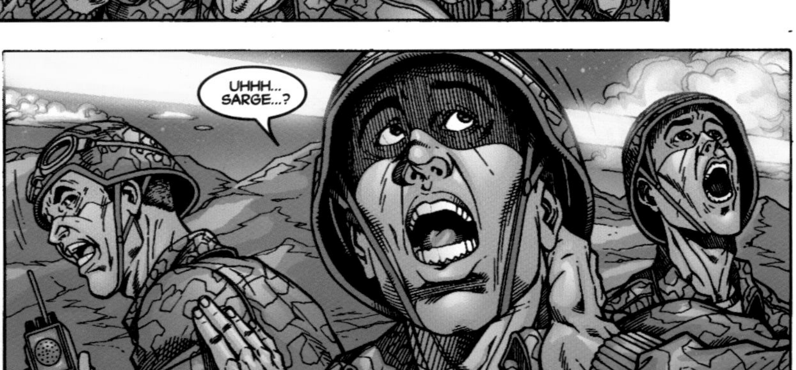
UHHH... SARGE...?

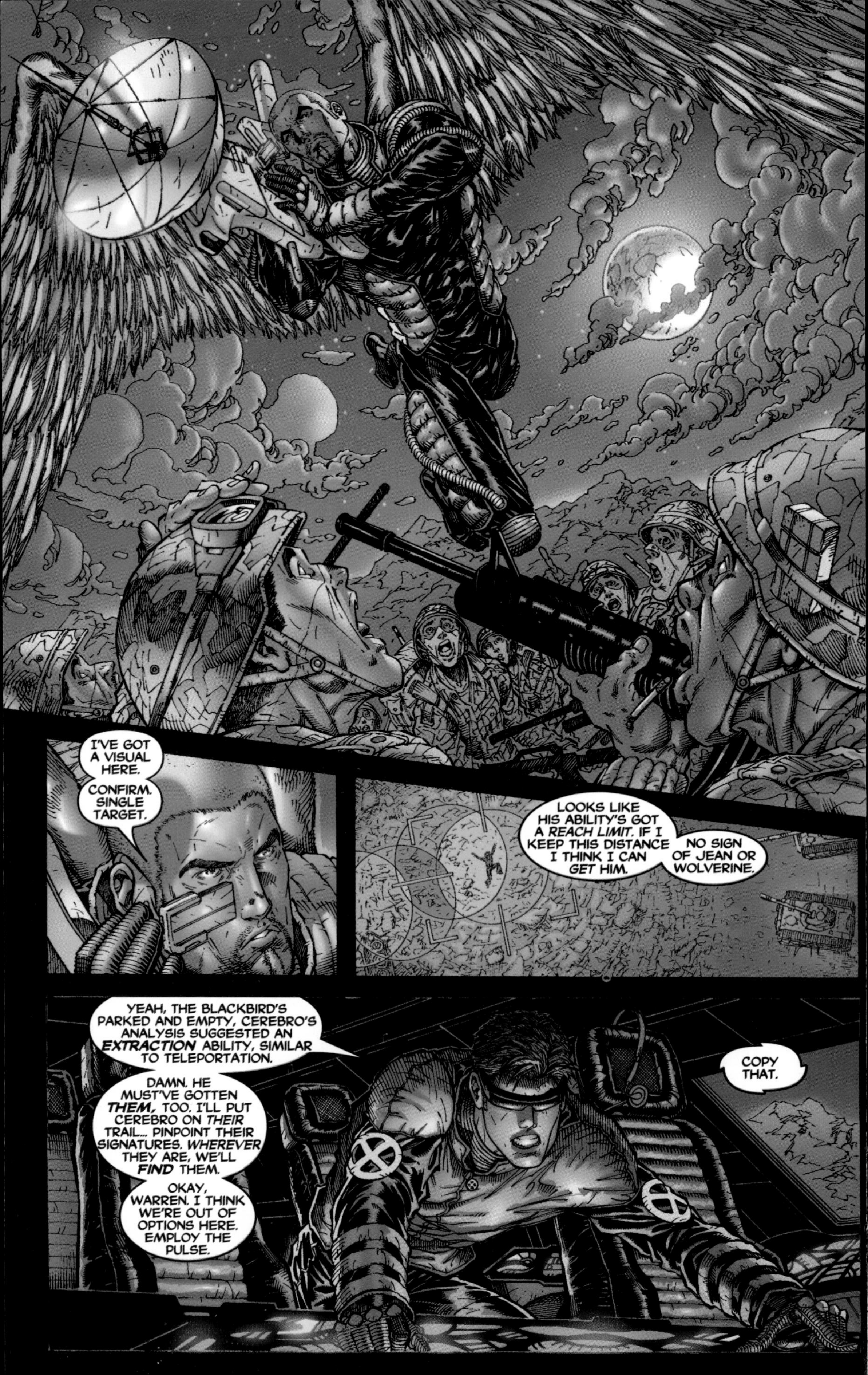
I'VE GOT A VISUAL HERE.
CONFIRM. SINGLE TARGET.
LOOKS LIKE HIS ABILITY'S GOT A REACH LIMIT. IF I KEEP THIS DISTANCE I THINK I CAN GET HIM.
NO SIGN OF JEAN OR WOLVERINE.
YEAH, THE BLACKBIRD'S PARKED AND EMPTY. CEREBRO'S ANALYSIS SUGGESTED AN EXTRACTION ABILITY, SIMILAR TO TELEPORTATION.
DAMN. HE MUST'VE GOTTEN THEM, TOO. I'LL PUT CEREBRO ON THEIR TRAIL... PINPOINT THEIR SIGNATURES. WHEREVER THEY ARE, WE'LL FIND THEM.
OKAY, WARREN. I THINK WE'RE OUT OF OPTIONS HERE. EMPLOY THE PULSE.
COPY THAT.

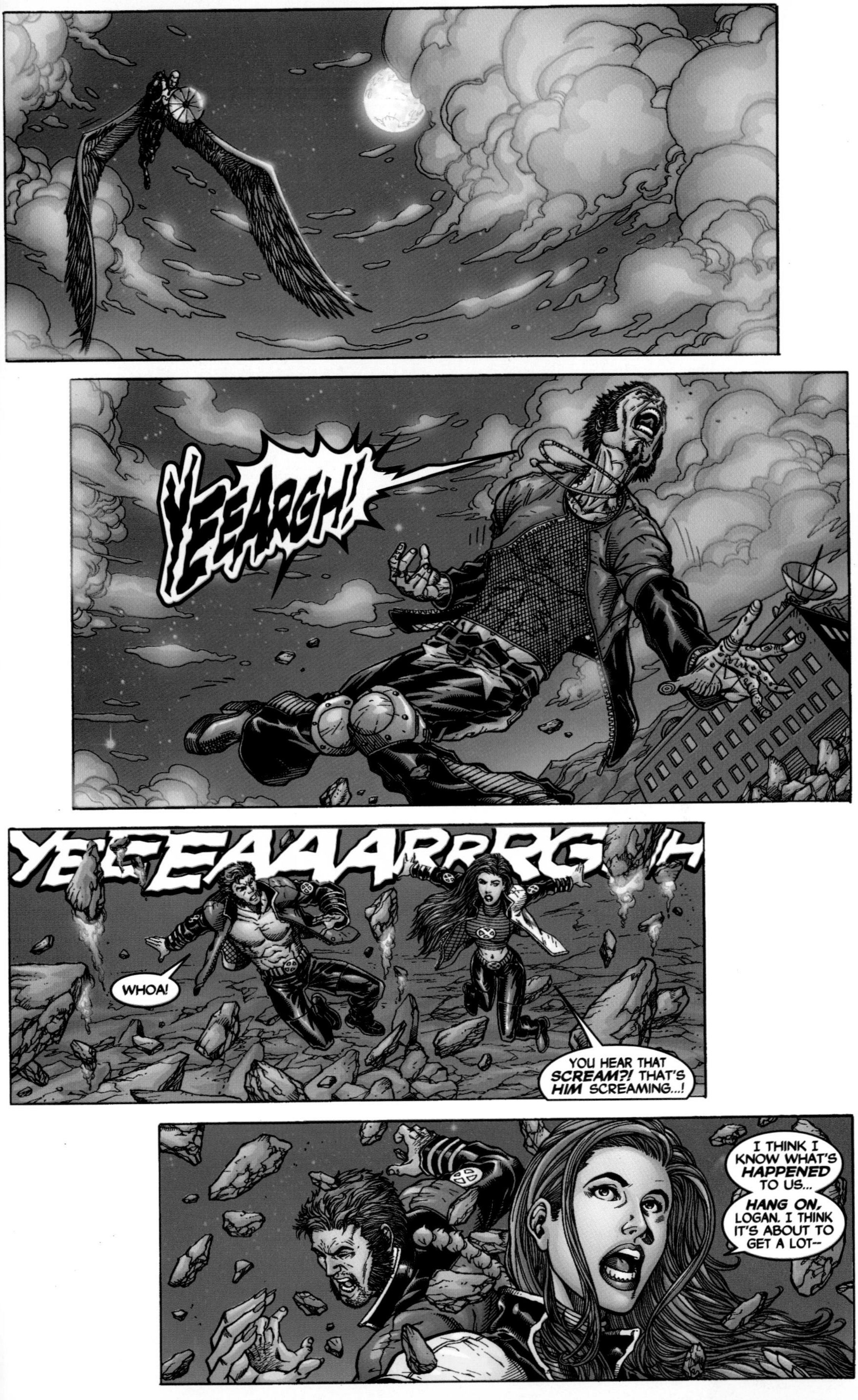
YEEARGH!
YEEAAARRRGH
WHOA!
YOU HEAR THAT SCREAM?! THAT'S HIM SCREAMING...!
I THINK I KNOW WHAT'S HAPPENED TO US...
HANG ON, LOGAN. I THINK IT'S ABOUT TO GET A LOT--

—WORSE...?

SNNF
SNNF

SMELLS KINDA LIKE A KID'S ROOM. BUT THERE'S SOMETHING ELSE HERE...

WELL, I GIVE THE KID SOME CREDIT... ...HE KNOWS HOW TO TREAT A GUEST RIGHT.

WHA—?! WAIT...THE MONSTER UNDER THE BED... THE CREATURE IN THE CLOSET...

...THIS PLACE IS A LIFELONG PSYCHOSIS PERSONIFIED! NOT AN ASTRAL PROJECTION... WE'RE INSIDE THE BRAIN!

SOMEONE NEEDS TO SHUT THIS KID DOWN— —IN THE REAL WORLD!

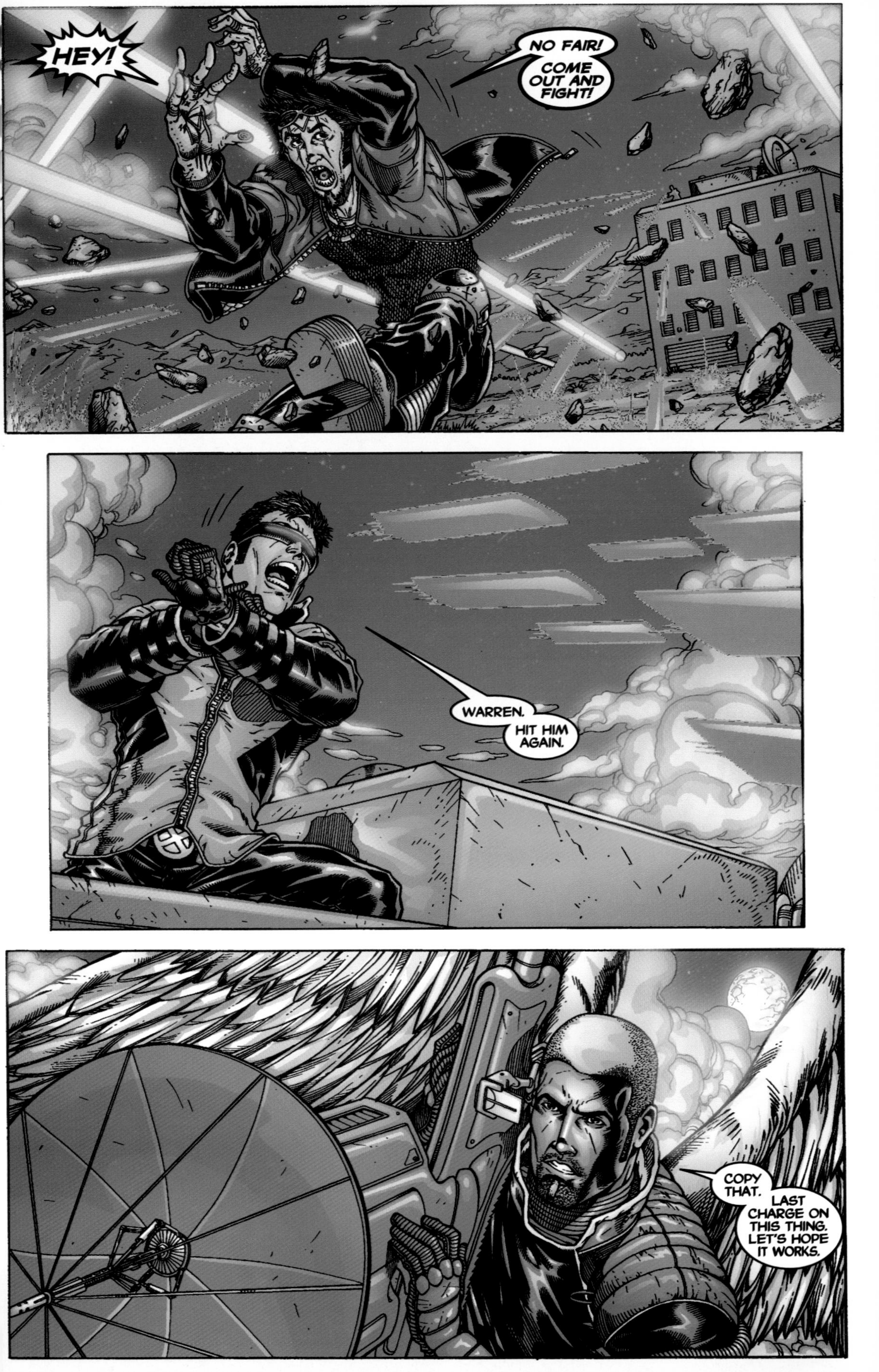
HEY!
NO FAIR! COME OUT AND FIGHT!
WARREN.
HIT HIM AGAIN.
COPY THAT.
LAST CHARGE ON THIS THING. LET'S HOPE IT WORKS.

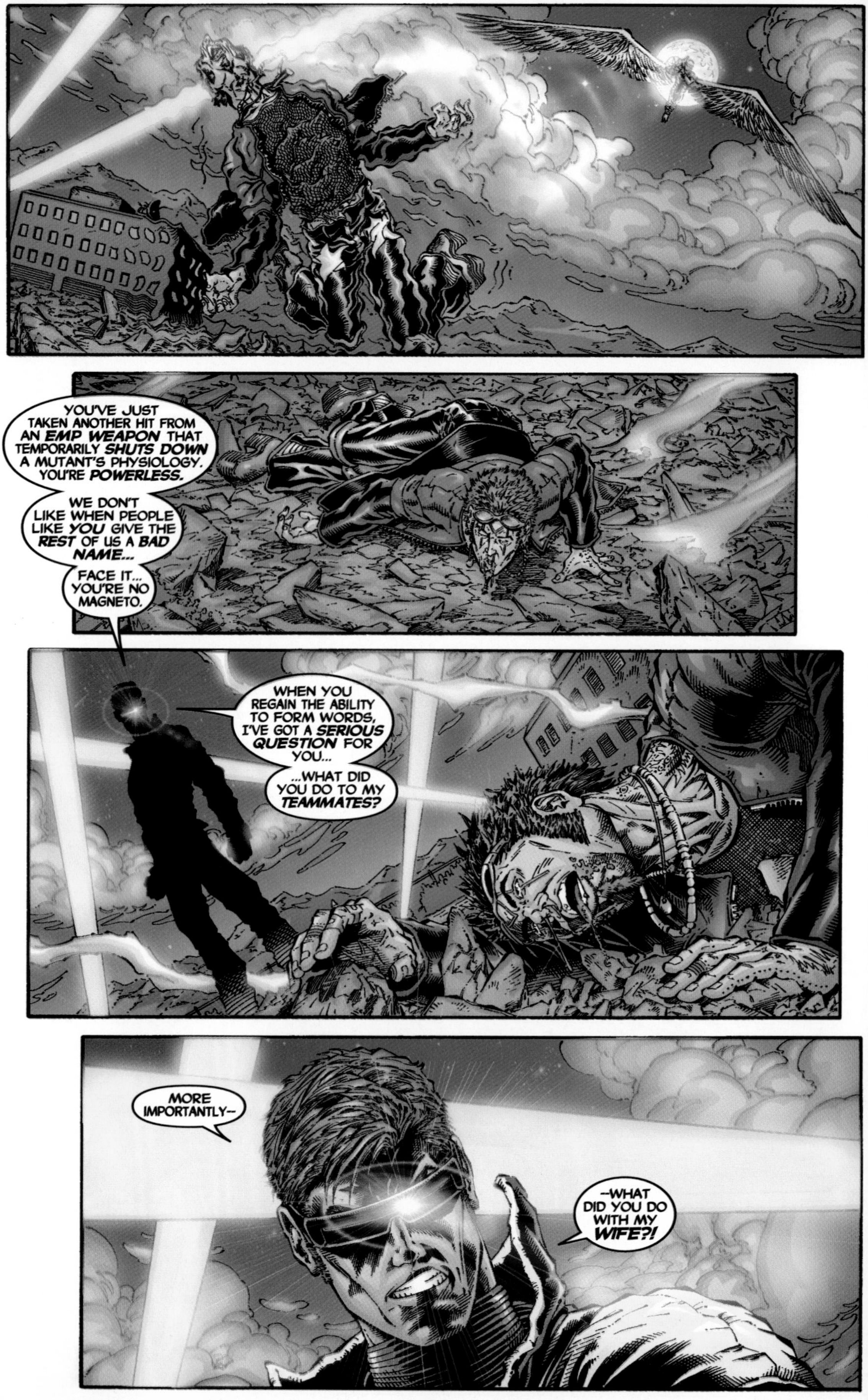
YOU'VE JUST TAKEN ANOTHER HIT FROM AN EMP WEAPON THAT TEMPORARILY SHUTS DOWN A MUTANT'S PHYSIOLOGY. YOU'RE POWERLESS.
WE DON'T LIKE WHEN PEOPLE LIKE YOU GIVE THE REST OF US A BAD NAME...
FACE IT... YOU'RE NO MAGNETO.
WHEN YOU REGAIN THE ABILITY TO FORM WORDS, I'VE GOT A SERIOUS QUESTION FOR YOU...
...WHAT DID YOU DO TO MY TEAMMATES?
MORE IMPORTANTLY--
--WHAT DID YOU DO WITH MY WIFE?!

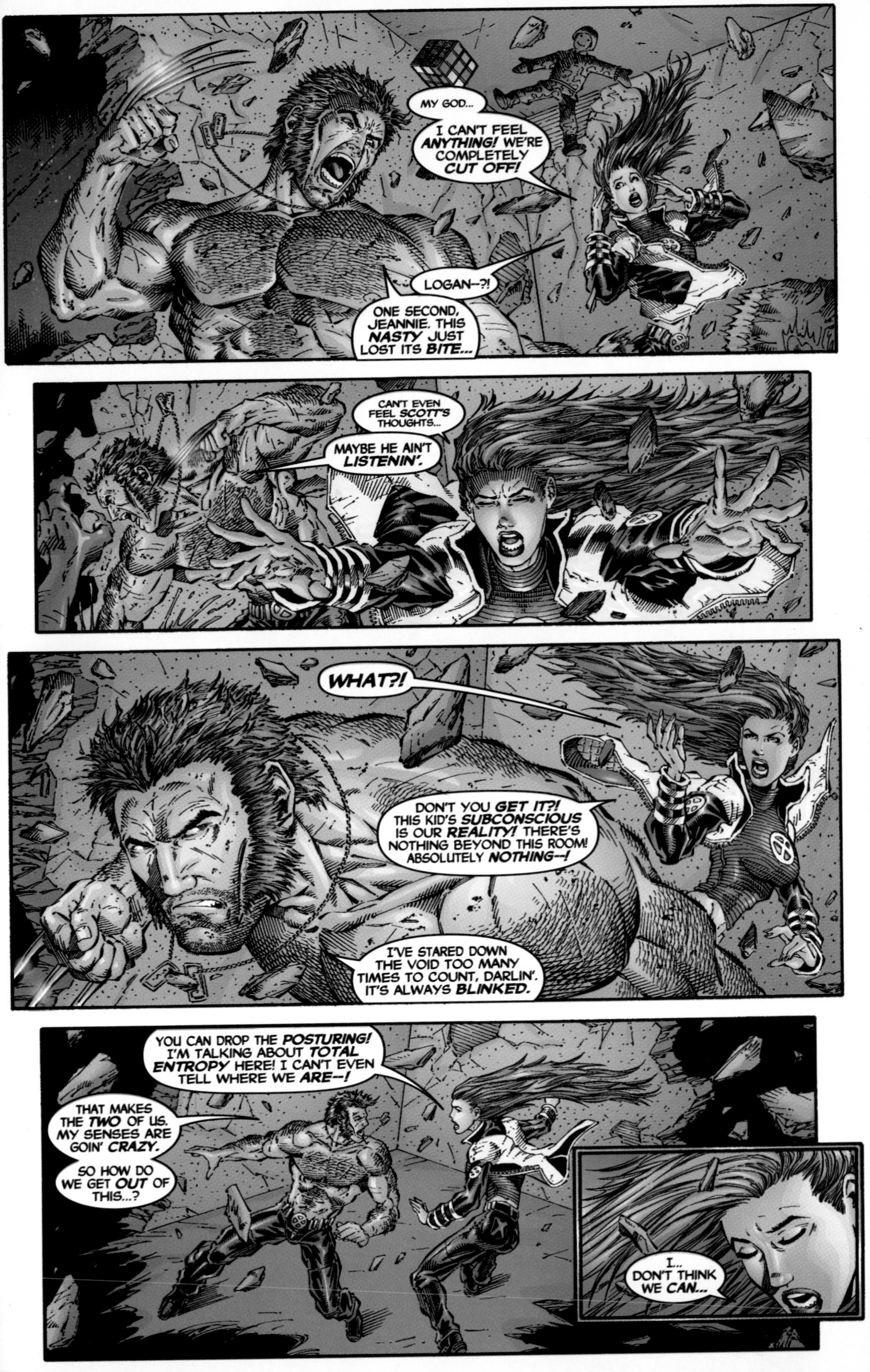

MY GOD...
I CAN'T FEEL ANYTHING! WE'RE COMPLETELY CUT OFF!
LOGAN--?!
ONE SECOND, JEANNIE. THIS NASTY JUST LOST ITS BITE...
CAN'T EVEN FEEL SCOTT'S THOUGHTS...
MAYBE HE AIN'T LISTENIN'.
WHAT?!
DON'T YOU GET IT?! THIS KID'S SUBCONSCIOUS IS OUR REALITY! THERE'S NOTHING BEYOND THIS ROOM! ABSOLUTELY NOTHING--!
I'VE STARED DOWN THE VOID TOO MANY TIMES TO COUNT, DARLIN'. IT'S ALWAYS BLINKED.
YOU CAN DROP THE POSTURING! I'M TALKING ABOUT TOTAL ENTROPY HERE! I CAN'T EVEN TELL WHERE WE ARE--!
THAT MAKES THE TWO OF US. MY SENSES ARE GOIN' CRAZY.
SO HOW DO WE GET OUT OF THIS...?
I... DON'T THINK WE CAN...

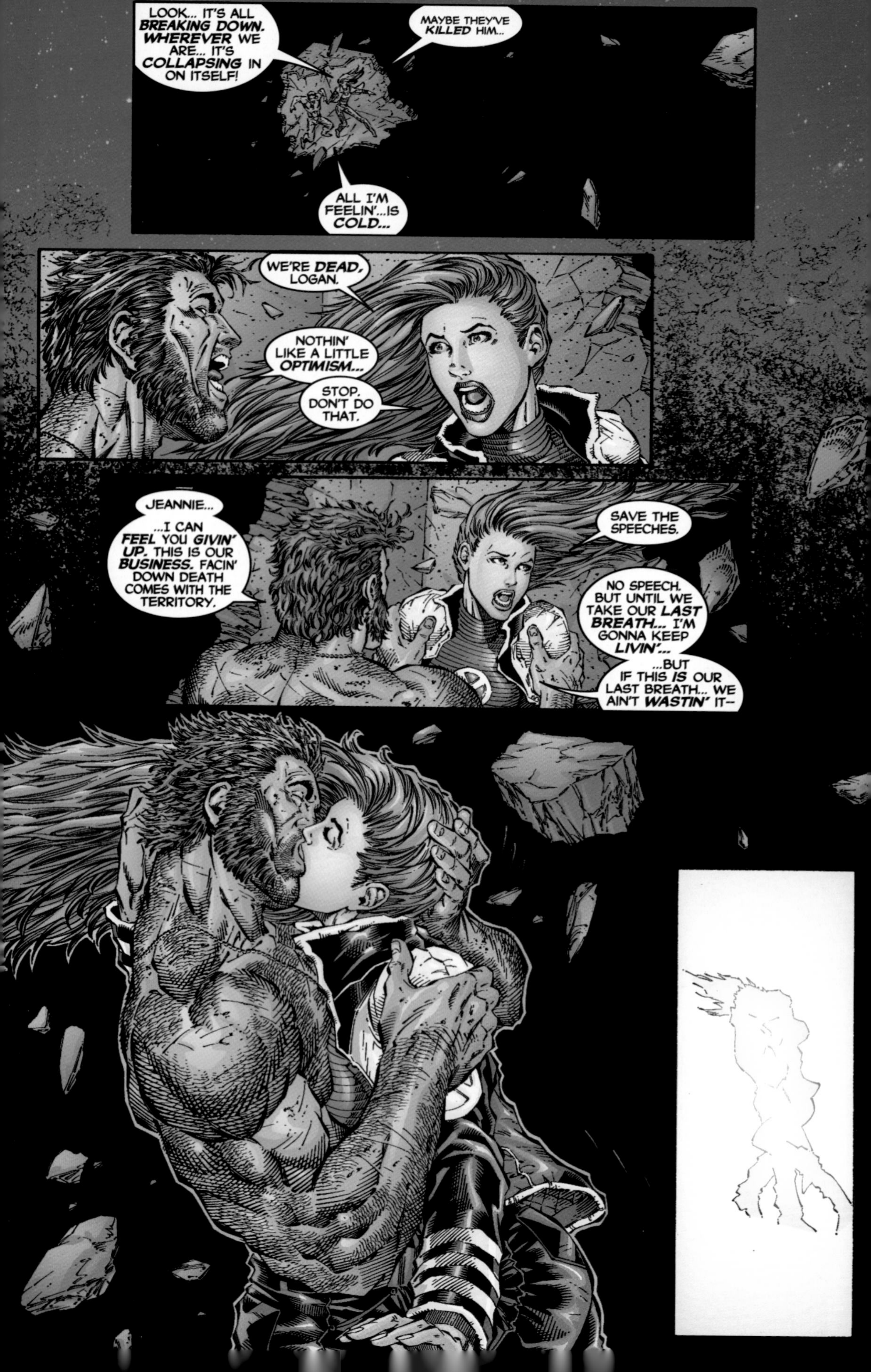
LOOK... IT'S ALL BREAKING DOWN. WHEREVER WE ARE... IT'S COLLAPSING IN ON ITSELF!
MAYBE THEY'VE KILLED HIM...
ALL I'M FEELIN'...IS COLD...
WE'RE DEAD, LOGAN.
NOTHIN' LIKE A LITTLE OPTIMISM...
STOP. DON'T DO THAT.
JEANNIE...
...I CAN FEEL YOU GIVIN' UP. THIS IS OUR BUSINESS. FACIN' DOWN DEATH COMES WITH THE TERRITORY.
SAVE THE SPEECHES.
NO SPEECH. BUT UNTIL WE TAKE OUR LAST BREATH... I'M GONNA KEEP LIVIN'...
...BUT IF THIS IS OUR LAST BREATH... WE AIN'T WASTIN' IT--

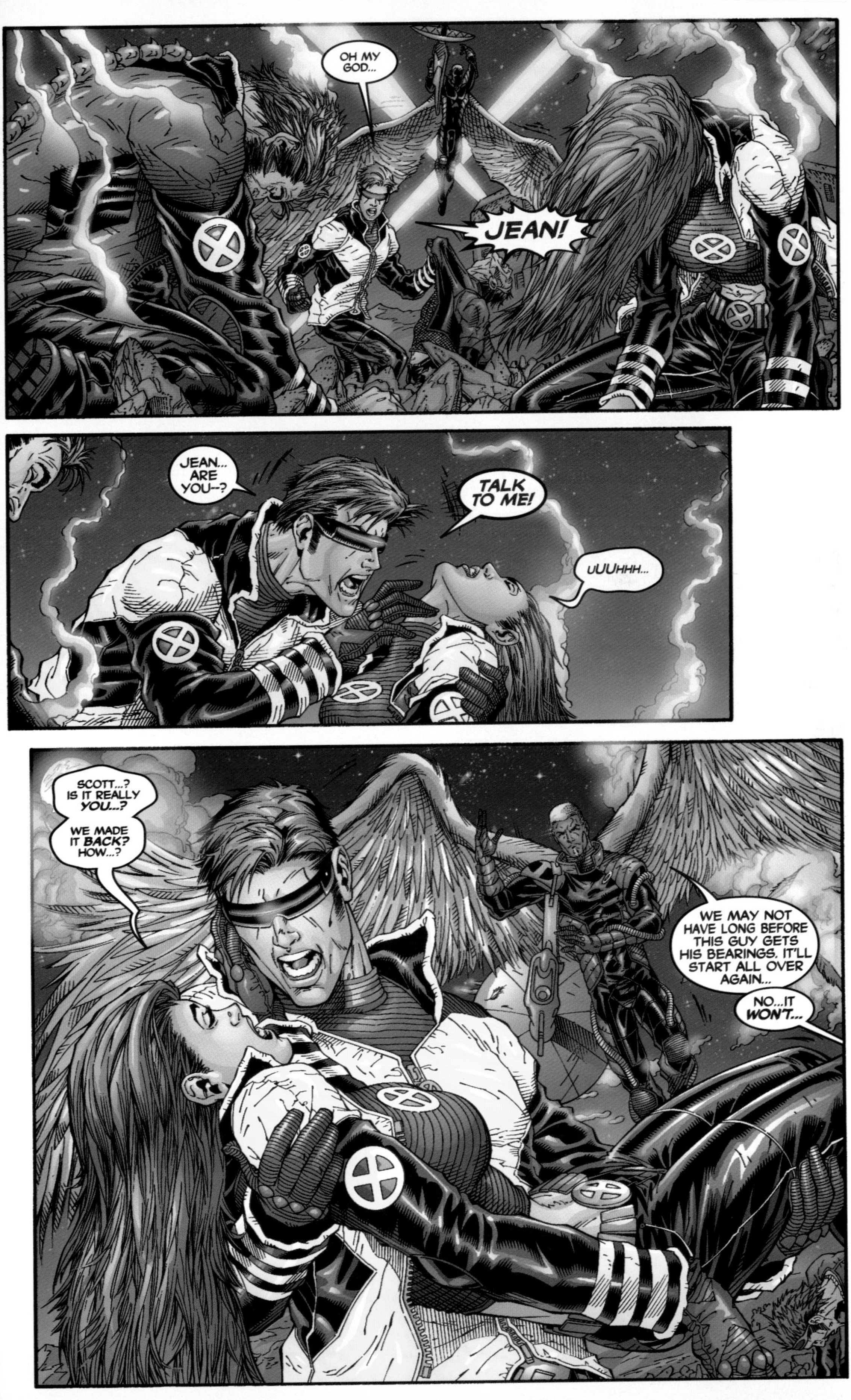
OH MY GOD...
JEAN!
JEAN... ARE YOU--?
TALK TO ME!
UUUHHH...
SCOTT...? IS IT REALLY YOU...?
WE MADE IT BACK? HOW...?
WE MAY NOT HAVE LONG BEFORE THIS GUY GETS HIS BEARINGS. IT'LL START ALL OVER AGAIN...
NO...IT WON'T...

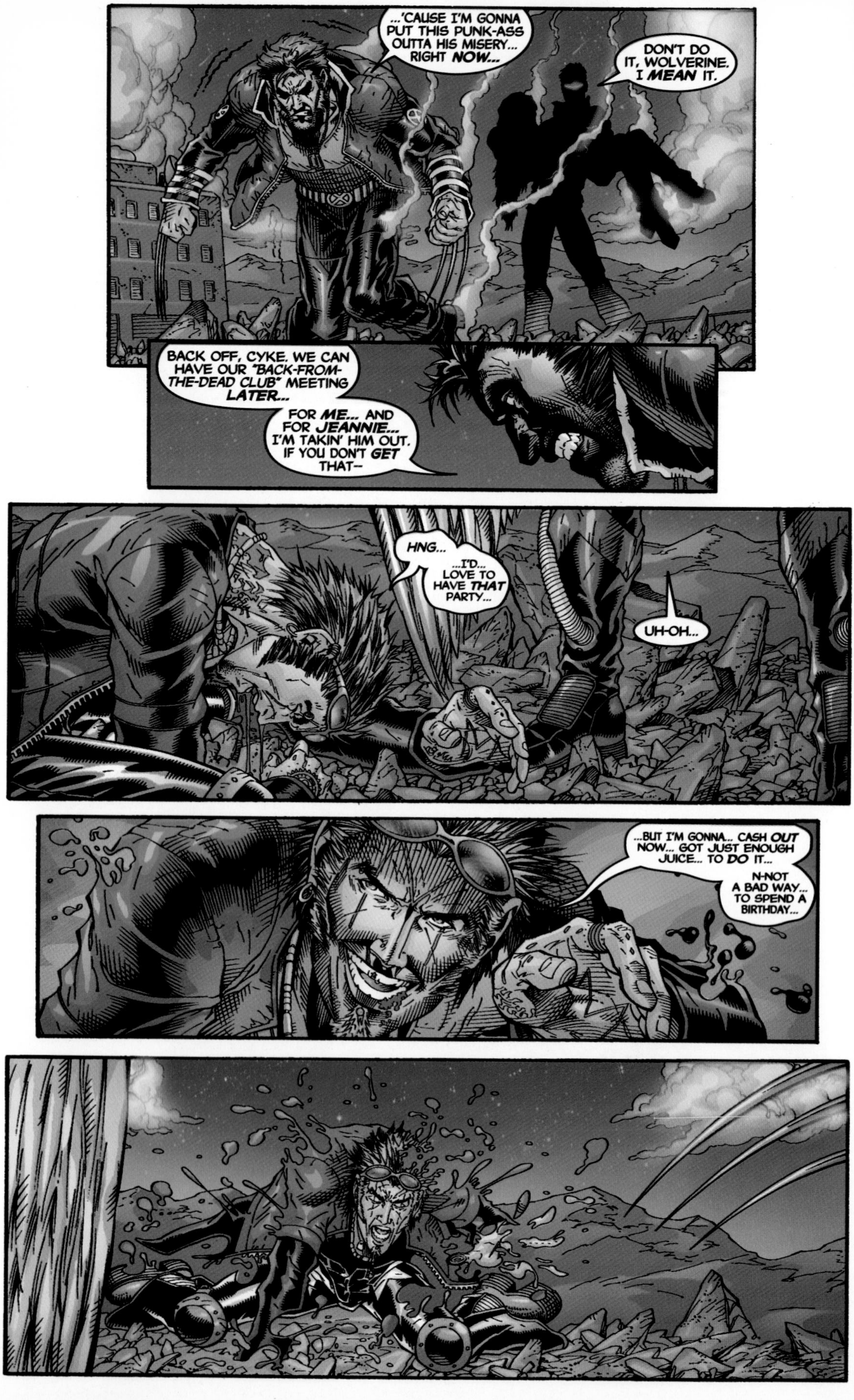

...'CAUSE I'M GONNA PUT THIS PUNK-ASS OUTTA HIS MISERY... RIGHT NOW...
DON'T DO IT, WOLVERINE. I MEAN IT.
BACK OFF, CYKE. WE CAN HAVE OUR "BACK-FROM-THE-DEAD CLUB" MEETING LATER...
FOR ME... AND FOR JEANNIE... I'M TAKIN' HIM OUT. IF YOU DON'T GET THAT--
HNG... ...I'D... LOVE TO HAVE THAT PARTY...
UH-OH...
...BUT I'M GONNA... CASH OUT NOW... GOT JUST ENOUGH JUICE... TO DO IT...
N-NOT A BAD WAY... TO SPEND A BIRTHDAY...

NO--!

KID MUST'VE HAD A *DEATH WISH*...

...WILD-EYED CHAOS-BRINGER OUT TO HAVE A GOOD TIME. LIVE FAST, DIE YOUNG. LEAVE A GOOD-LOOKING CORPSE.

I CAN RELATE.

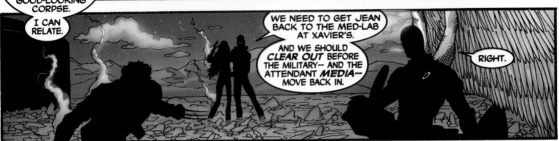

WE NEED TO GET JEAN BACK TO THE MED-LAB AT XAVIER'S.

AND WE SHOULD *CLEAR OUT* BEFORE THE MILITARY-- AND THE ATTENDANT *MEDIA*-- MOVE BACK IN.

RIGHT.

I'LL... BE OKAY. JUST... HARD TO REMEMBER...WHAT *HAPPENED*...

I REMEMBER, JEANNIE. EVERY *BIT* OF IT.

JUST ANOTHER DAY ON THE JOB, EH...?

... RIGHT.

LET'S *MOVE*, PEOPLE. NO ONE EVER CHANGED THE WORLD BY JUST *STANDING AROUND*...

SNNF

USELESS BEAUTY

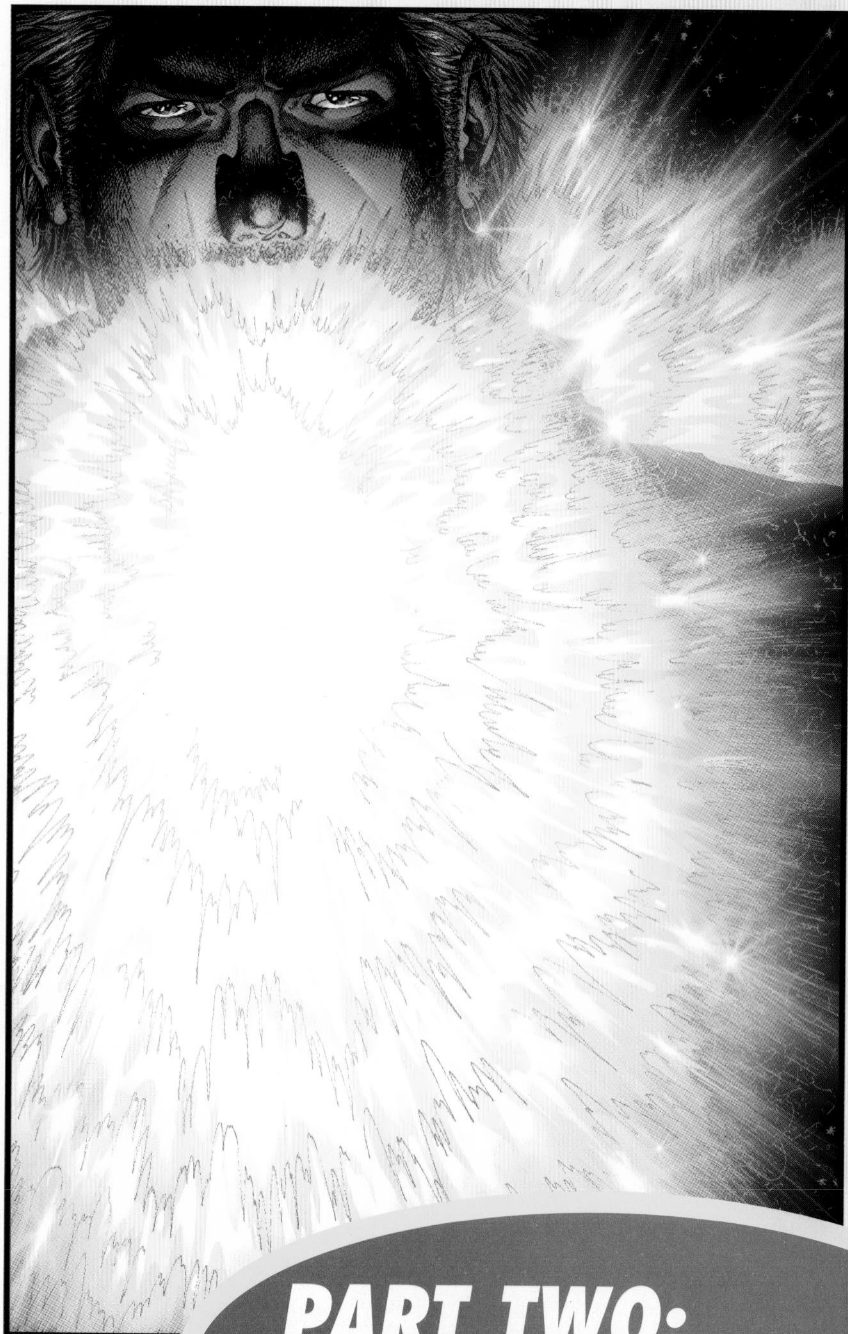

PART TWO: UNCANNY X-MEN #395

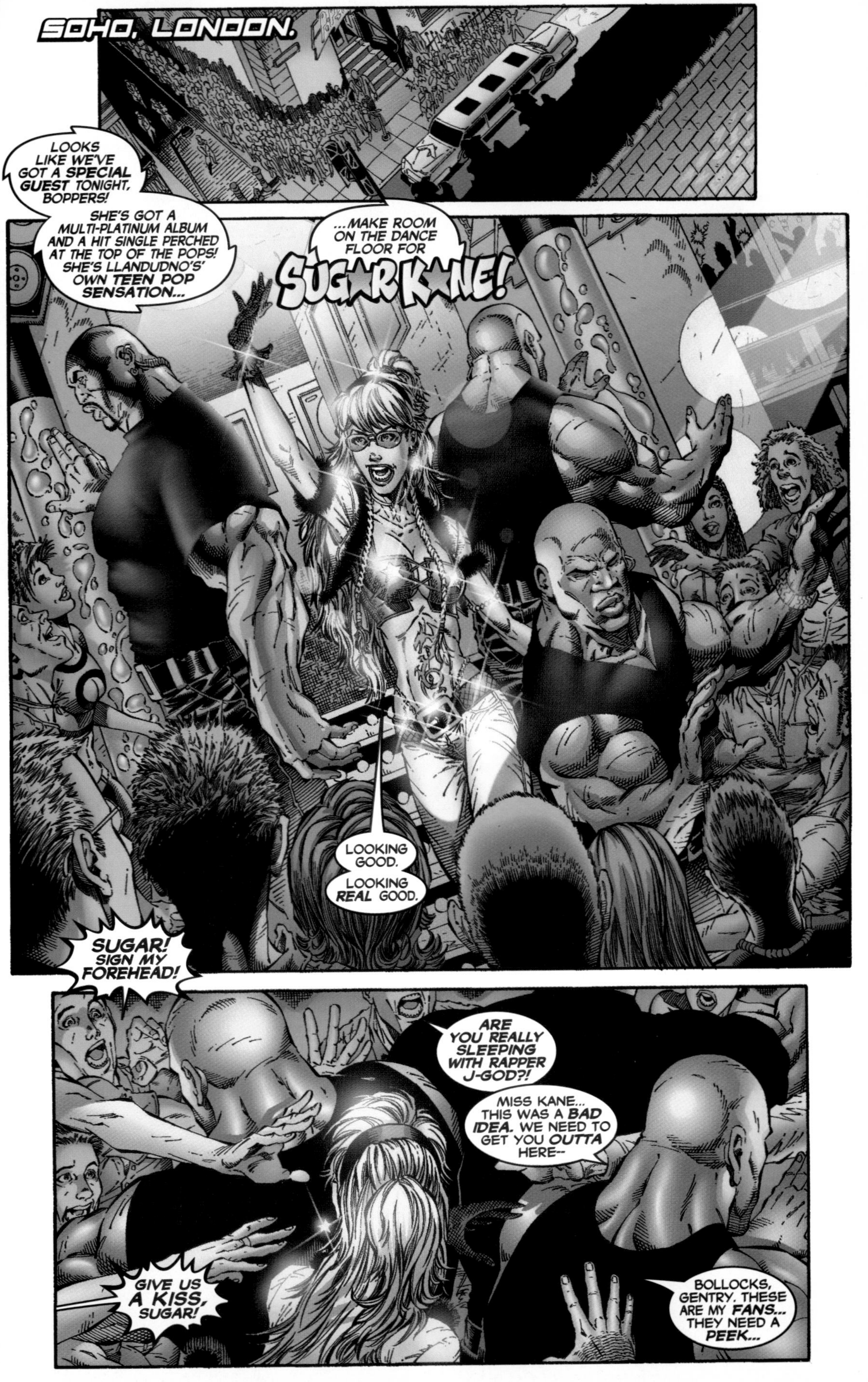
SOHO, LONDON.
LOOKS LIKE WE'VE GOT A SPECIAL GUEST TONIGHT, BOPPERS!
SHE'S GOT A MULTI-PLATINUM ALBUM AND A HIT SINGLE PERCHED AT THE TOP OF THE POPS! SHE'S LLANDUDNO'S' OWN TEEN POP SENSATION...
...MAKE ROOM ON THE DANCE FLOOR FOR
SUGAR KANE!
LOOKING GOOD.
LOOKING REAL GOOD.
SUGAR! SIGN MY FOREHEAD!
ARE YOU REALLY SLEEPING WITH RAPPER J-GOD?!
MISS KANE... THIS WAS A BAD IDEA. WE NEED TO GET YOU OUTTA HERE--
GIVE US A KISS, SUGAR!
BOLLOCKS, GENTRY. THESE ARE MY FANS... THEY NEED A PEEK...

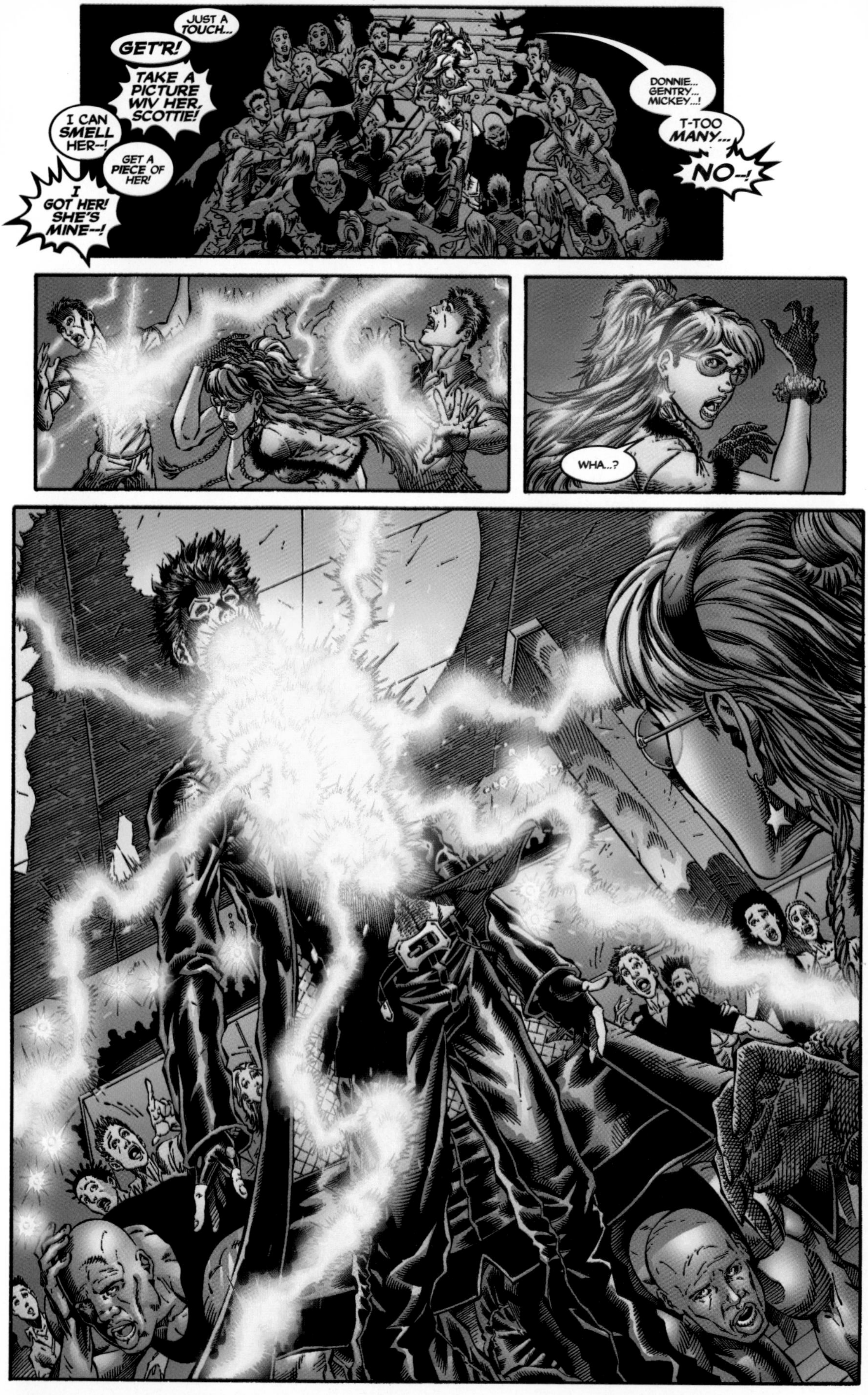
JUST A TOUCH...
GET'R!
TAKE A PICTURE WIV HER, SCOTTIE!
I CAN SMELL HER--!
GET A PIECE OF HER!
I GOT HER! SHE'S MINE--!
DONNIE... GENTRY... MICKEY...!
T-TOO MANY...
NO--!
WHA...?

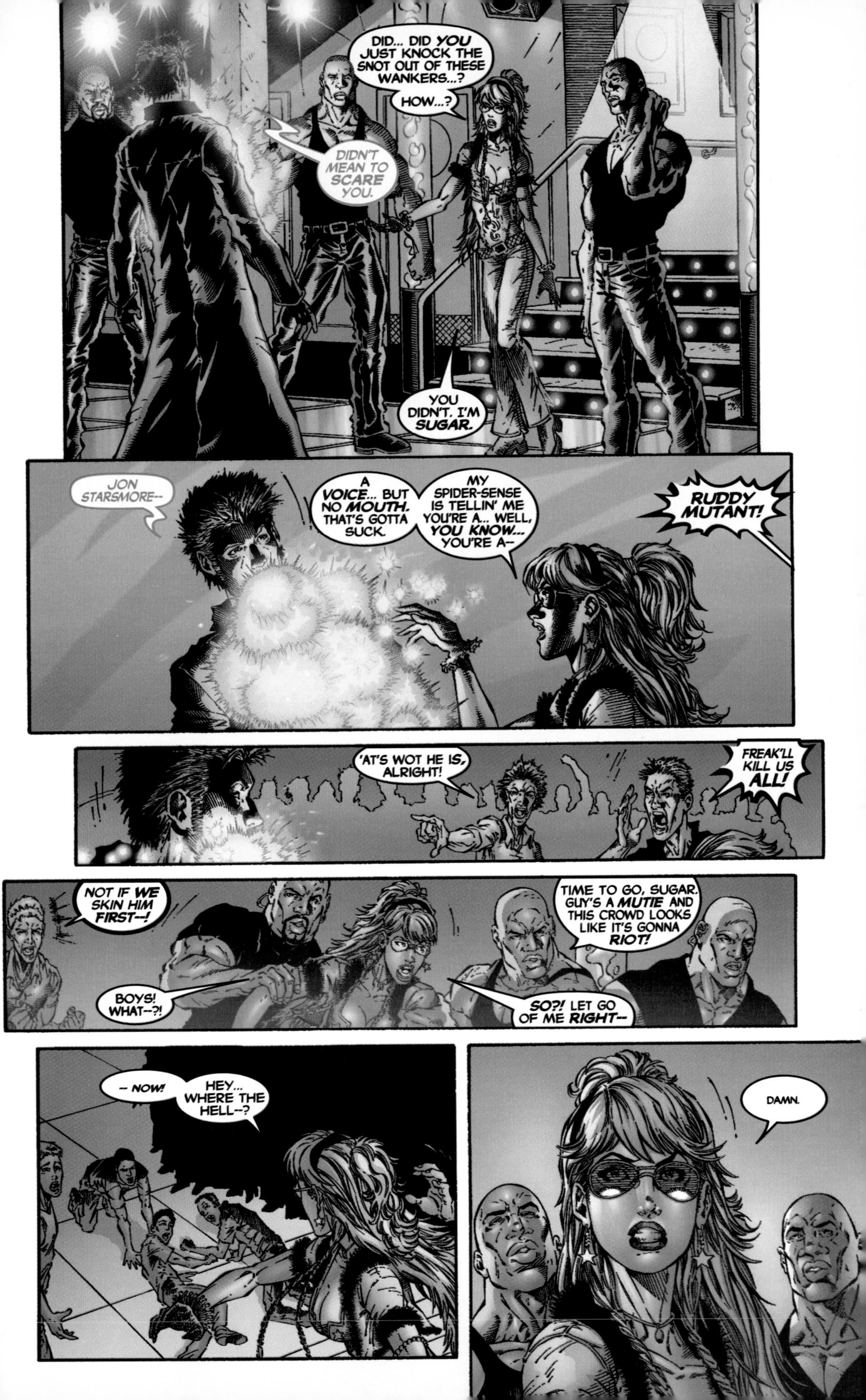
DID... DID YOU JUST KNOCK THE SNOT OUT OF THESE WANKERS...?
HOW...?
DIDN'T MEAN TO SCARE YOU.
YOU DIDN'T. I'M SUGAR.
JON STARSMORE--
A VOICE... BUT NO MOUTH. THAT'S GOTTA SUCK.
MY SPIDER-SENSE IS TELLIN' ME YOU'RE A... WELL, YOU KNOW... YOU'RE A--
RUDDY MUTANT!
'AT'S WOT HE IS, ALRIGHT!
FREAK'LL KILL US ALL!
NOT IF WE SKIN HIM FIRST--!
TIME TO GO, SUGAR. GUY'S A MUTIE AND THIS CROWD LOOKS LIKE IT'S GONNA RIOT!
BOYS! WHAT--?!
SO?! LET GO OF ME RIGHT--
-- NOW!
HEY... WHERE THE HELL--?
DAMN.

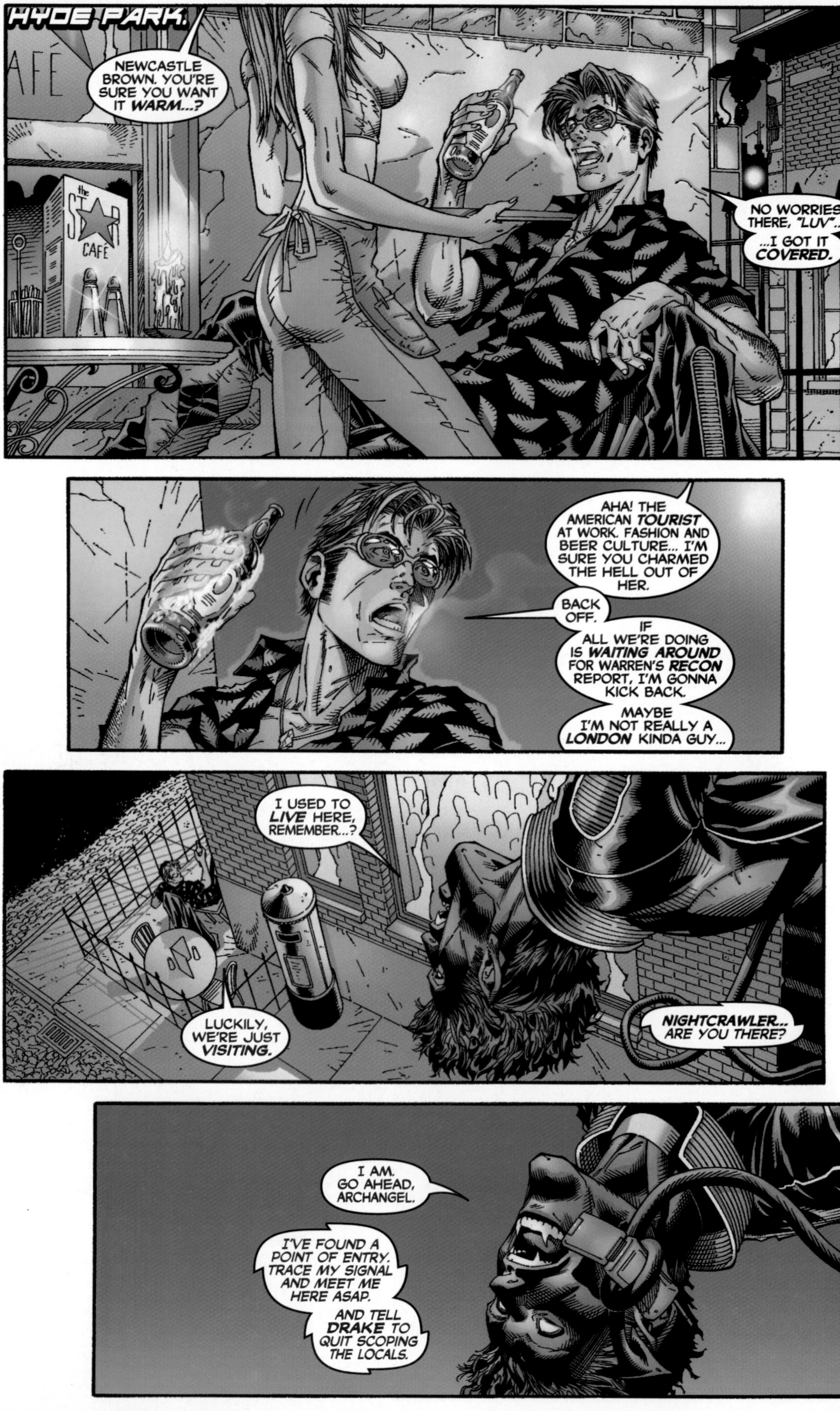
HYDE PARK.
NEWCASTLE BROWN. YOU'RE SURE YOU WANT IT WARM...?
NO WORRIES THERE, "LUV"... ...I GOT IT COVERED.
AHA! THE AMERICAN TOURIST AT WORK. FASHION AND BEER CULTURE... I'M SURE YOU CHARMED THE HELL OUT OF HER.
BACK OFF.
IF ALL WE'RE DOING IS WAITING AROUND FOR WARREN'S RECON REPORT, I'M GONNA KICK BACK.
MAYBE I'M NOT REALLY A LONDON KINDA GUY...
I USED TO LIVE HERE, REMEMBER...?
LUCKILY, WE'RE JUST VISITING.
NIGHTCRAWLER... ARE YOU THERE?
I AM. GO AHEAD, ARCHANGEL.
I'VE FOUND A POINT OF ENTRY. TRACE MY SIGNAL AND MEET ME HERE ASAP.
AND TELL DRAKE TO QUIT SCOPING THE LOCALS.

SO... THIS IS *IT?* WHADDA *STINK*...

WHAT *TOOK* YOU TWO SO LONG?

WHATEVER SPIKE CEREBRA PICKED UP...IT'S *HERE.* MY HANDHELD *CONFIRMS* IT. *MASSIVE* MUTANT READINGS.

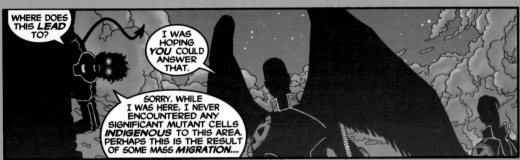

WHERE DOES THIS *LEAD* TO?

I WAS HOPING *YOU* COULD ANSWER THAT.

SORRY. WHILE I WAS HERE, I NEVER ENCOUNTERED ANY SIGNIFICANT MUTANT CELLS *INDIGENOUS* TO THIS AREA. PERHAPS THIS IS THE RESULT OF SOME MASS *MIGRATION*...

DEEP ENOUGH?

Y'KNOW... ONE OF THE WAITRESSES I WAS *HITTING ON* WAS YAMMERING ABOUT SOME KINDA *LEPER COLONY* UNDERNEATH LONDON...

...TYPICAL *URBAN LEGEND* STUFF.

JA, BUT CURIOUS INDEED. THERE'S AN *OPENING* UP AHEAD...

UHHH... I THINK *THIS* IS WHAT YOUR EQUIPMENT WAS READING, WARREN...

MEIN GOTT.

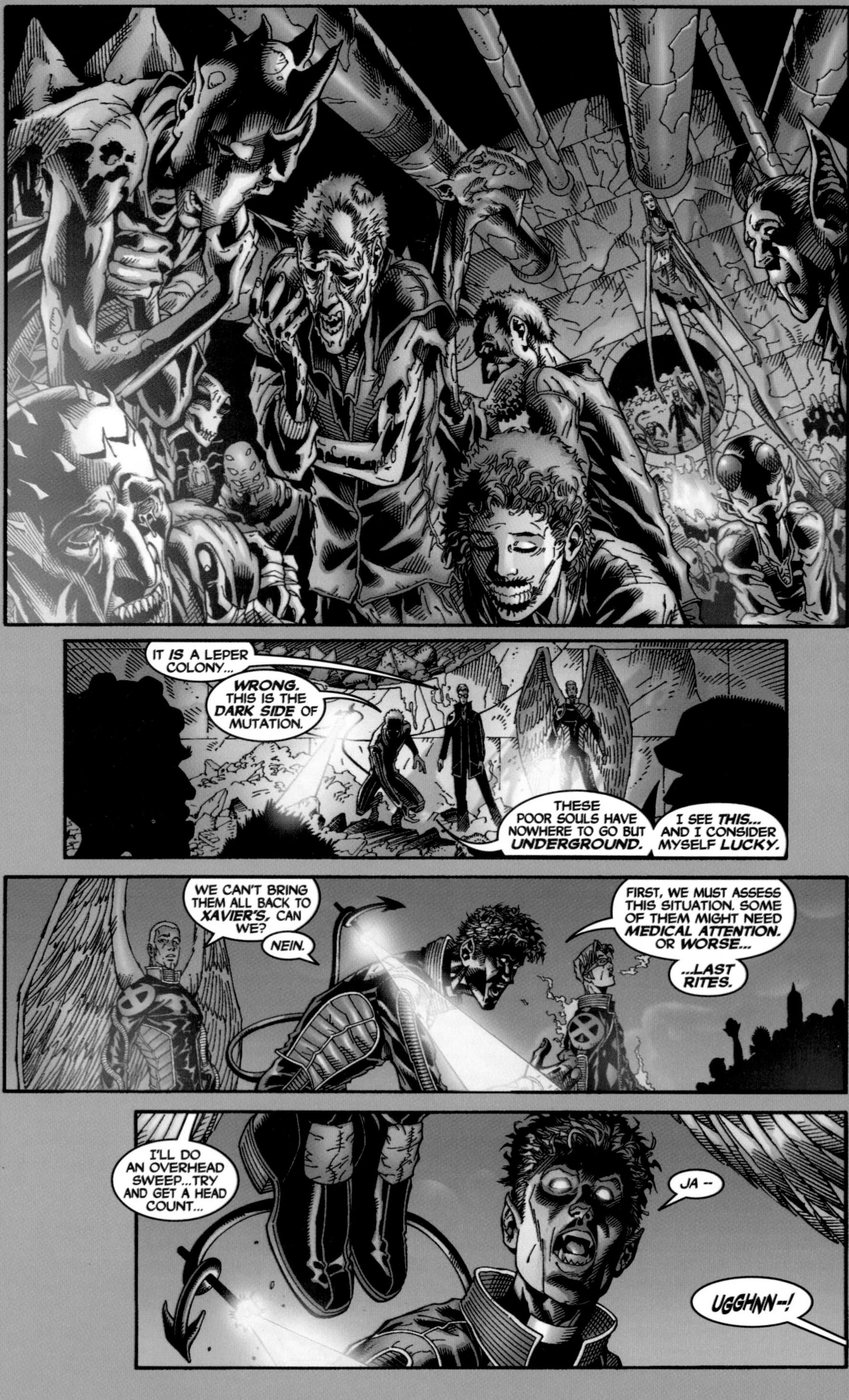
IT IS A LEPER COLONY...
WRONG. THIS IS THE DARK SIDE OF MUTATION.
THESE POOR SOULS HAVE NOWHERE TO GO BUT UNDERGROUND.
I SEE THIS... AND I CONSIDER MYSELF LUCKY.
WE CAN'T BRING THEM ALL BACK TO XAVIER'S, CAN WE?
NEIN.
FIRST, WE MUST ASSESS THIS SITUATION. SOME OF THEM MIGHT NEED MEDICAL ATTENTION. OR WORSE...
...LAST RITES.
I'LL DO AN OVERHEAD SWEEP...TRY AND GET A HEAD COUNT...
JA --
UGGHNN--!

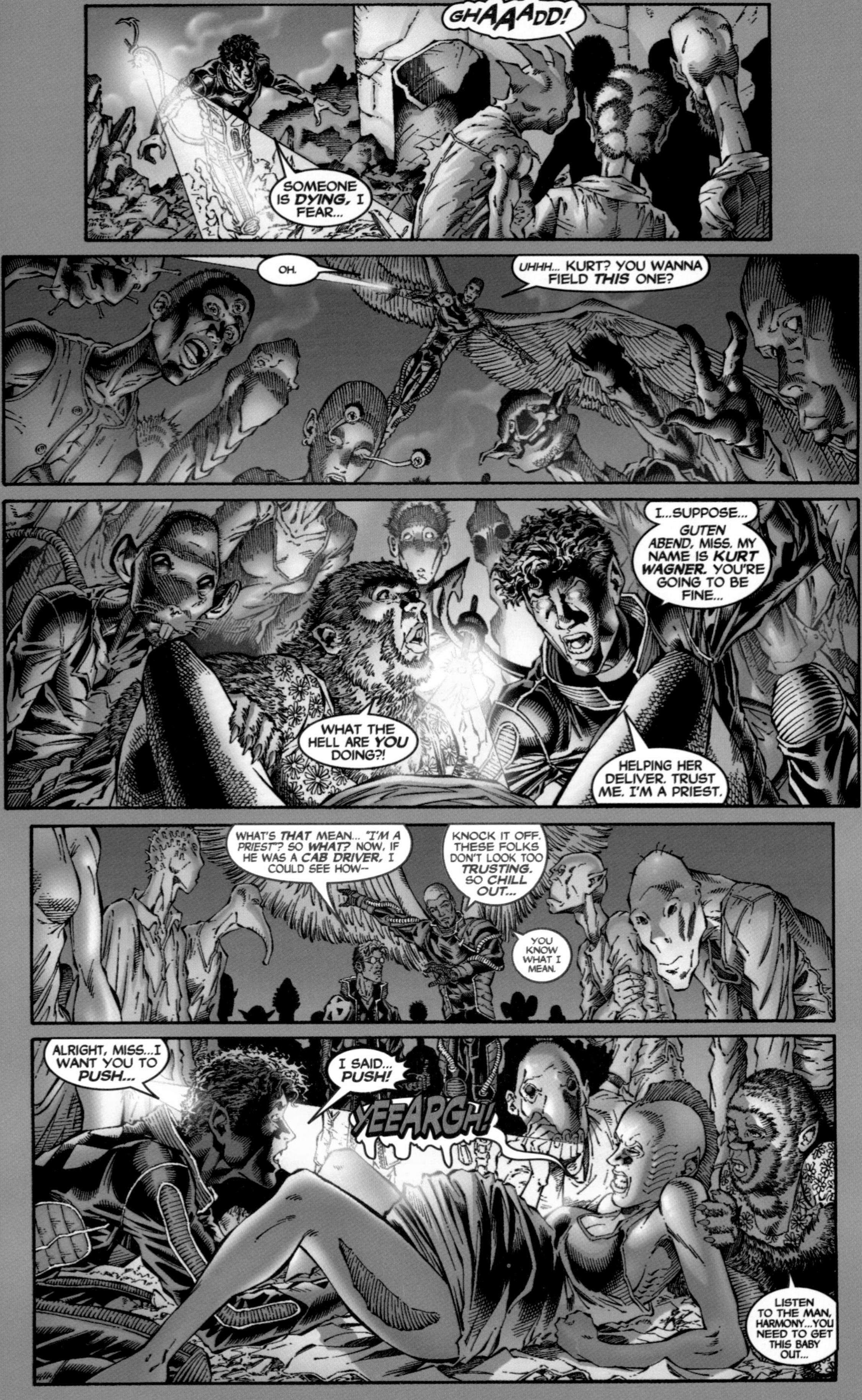
GHAAADD!
SOMEONE IS DYING, I FEAR...
OH.
UHHH... KURT? YOU WANNA FIELD THIS ONE?
I...SUPPOSE... GUTEN ABEND, MISS. MY NAME IS KURT WAGNER. YOU'RE GOING TO BE FINE...
WHAT THE HELL ARE YOU DOING?!
HELPING HER DELIVER. TRUST ME. I'M A PRIEST.
WHAT'S THAT MEAN... "I'M A PRIEST"? SO WHAT? NOW, IF HE WAS A CAB DRIVER, I COULD SEE HOW--
KNOCK IT OFF. THESE FOLKS DON'T LOOK TOO TRUSTING. SO CHILL OUT...
YOU KNOW WHAT I MEAN.
ALRIGHT, MISS...I WANT YOU TO PUSH...
I SAID... PUSH!
YEEARGH!
LISTEN TO THE MAN, HARMONY...YOU NEED TO GET THIS BABY OUT...

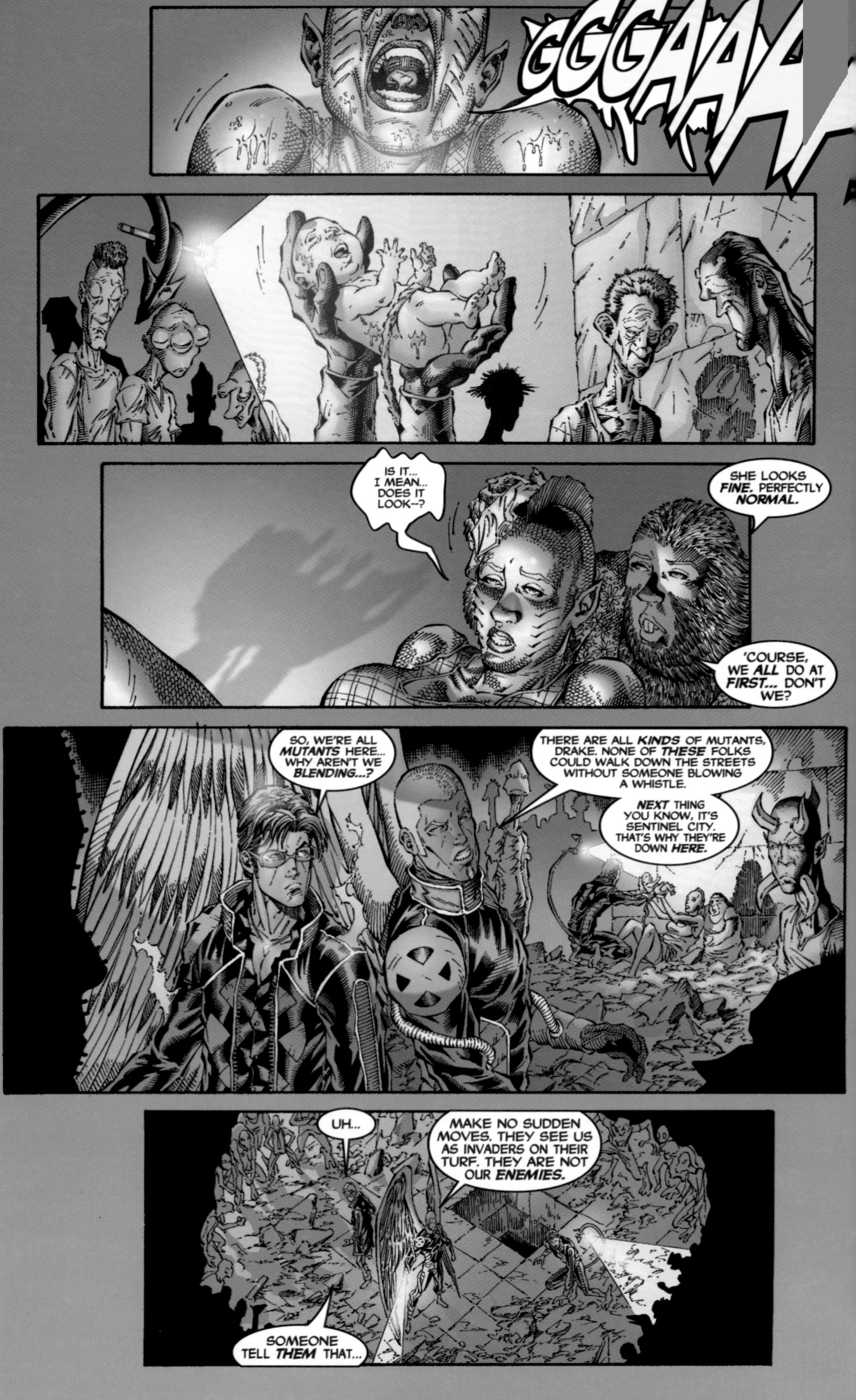

GGGAAA
IS IT... I MEAN... DOES IT LOOK--?
SHE LOOKS FINE. PERFECTLY NORMAL.
'COURSE, WE ALL DO AT FIRST... DON'T WE?
SO, WE'RE ALL MUTANTS HERE... WHY AREN'T WE BLENDING...?
THERE ARE ALL KINDS OF MUTANTS, DRAKE. NONE OF THESE FOLKS COULD WALK DOWN THE STREETS WITHOUT SOMEONE BLOWING A WHISTLE.
NEXT THING YOU KNOW, IT'S SENTINEL CITY. THAT'S WHY THEY'RE DOWN HERE.
UH...
MAKE NO SUDDEN MOVES. THEY SEE US AS INVADERS ON THEIR TURF. THEY ARE NOT OUR ENEMIES.
SOMEONE TELL THEM THAT...

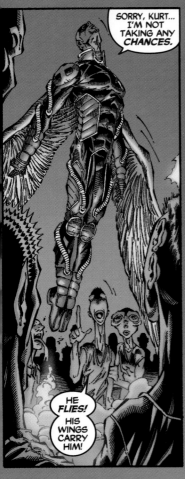

SORRY, KURT... I'M NOT TAKING ANY *CHANCES.*

HE *FLIES!* HIS WINGS CARRY HIM!

GOOD PLAN.

WE MAY COME IN PEACE, BUT LIKE YOU SAID... THERE ARE ALL *KINDS* OF MUTANTS...

ARCHANGEL! ICEMAN! YOU MOVE *TOO SOON!* THIS BEHAVIOR ONLY *PANICS* THEM! WE'RE NOT HERE TO INSTIGATE *CONFLICT--*

STAND ASIDE...

...LET *ME* DEAL WITH THESE INTRUDERS.

WELL DONE! THE *CYCLOPS* IS GONNA *STOMP ASS,* LADS!

GOD BLESS! A GOOD CRACK OF THEIR SPINES AND THEY'RE *DONE FOR!*

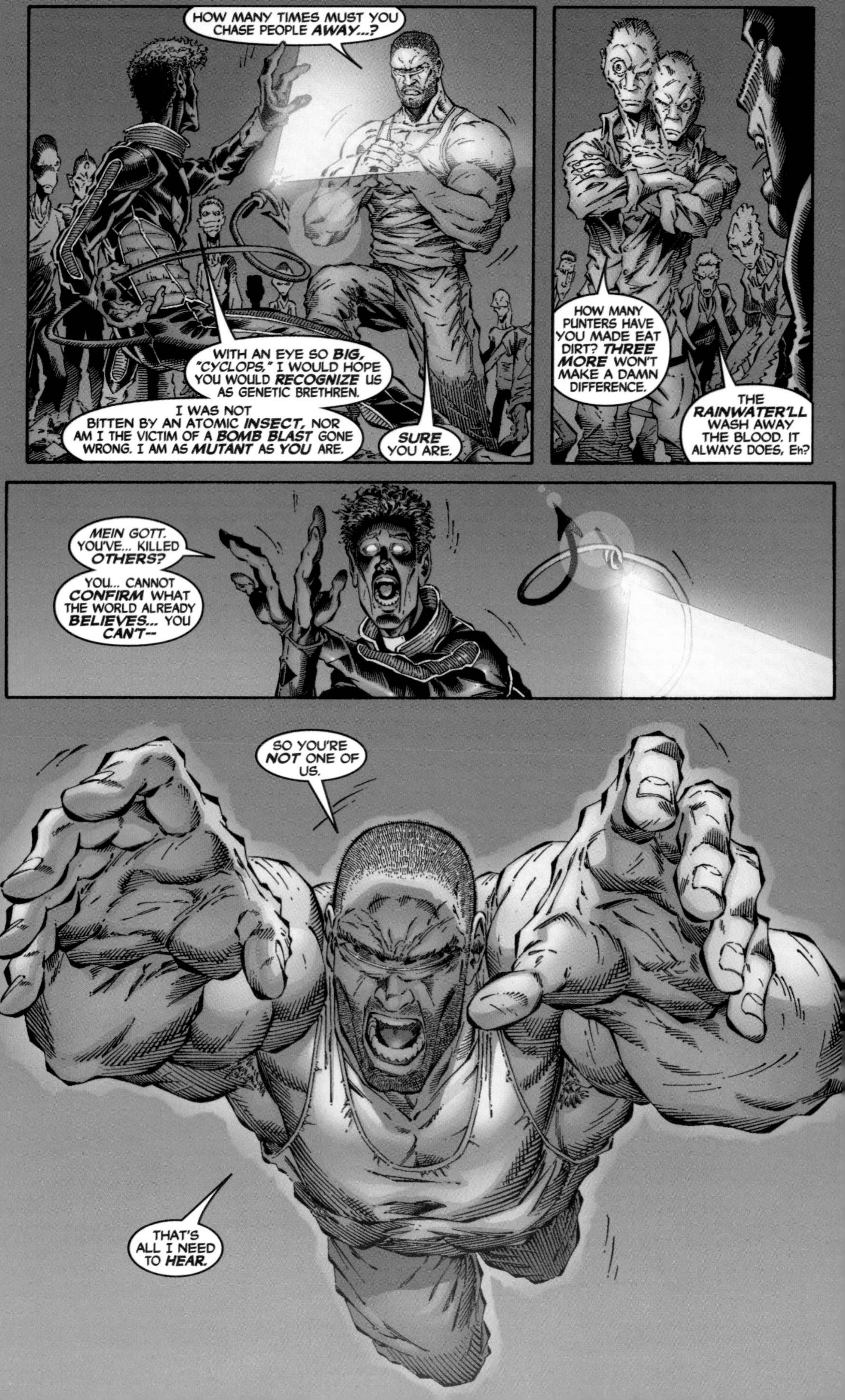
HOW MANY TIMES MUST YOU CHASE PEOPLE AWAY...?
WITH AN EYE SO BIG, "CYCLOPS," I WOULD HOPE YOU WOULD RECOGNIZE US AS GENETIC BRETHREN.
I WAS NOT BITTEN BY AN ATOMIC INSECT, NOR AM I THE VICTIM OF A BOMB BLAST GONE WRONG. I AM AS MUTANT AS YOU ARE.
SURE YOU ARE.
HOW MANY PUNTERS HAVE YOU MADE EAT DIRT? THREE MORE WON'T MAKE A DAMN DIFFERENCE.
THE RAINWATER'LL WASH AWAY THE BLOOD. IT ALWAYS DOES, Eh?
MEIN GOTT. YOU'VE... KILLED OTHERS?
YOU... CANNOT CONFIRM WHAT THE WORLD ALREADY BELIEVES... YOU CAN'T--
SO YOU'RE NOT ONE OF US.
THAT'S ALL I NEED TO HEAR.

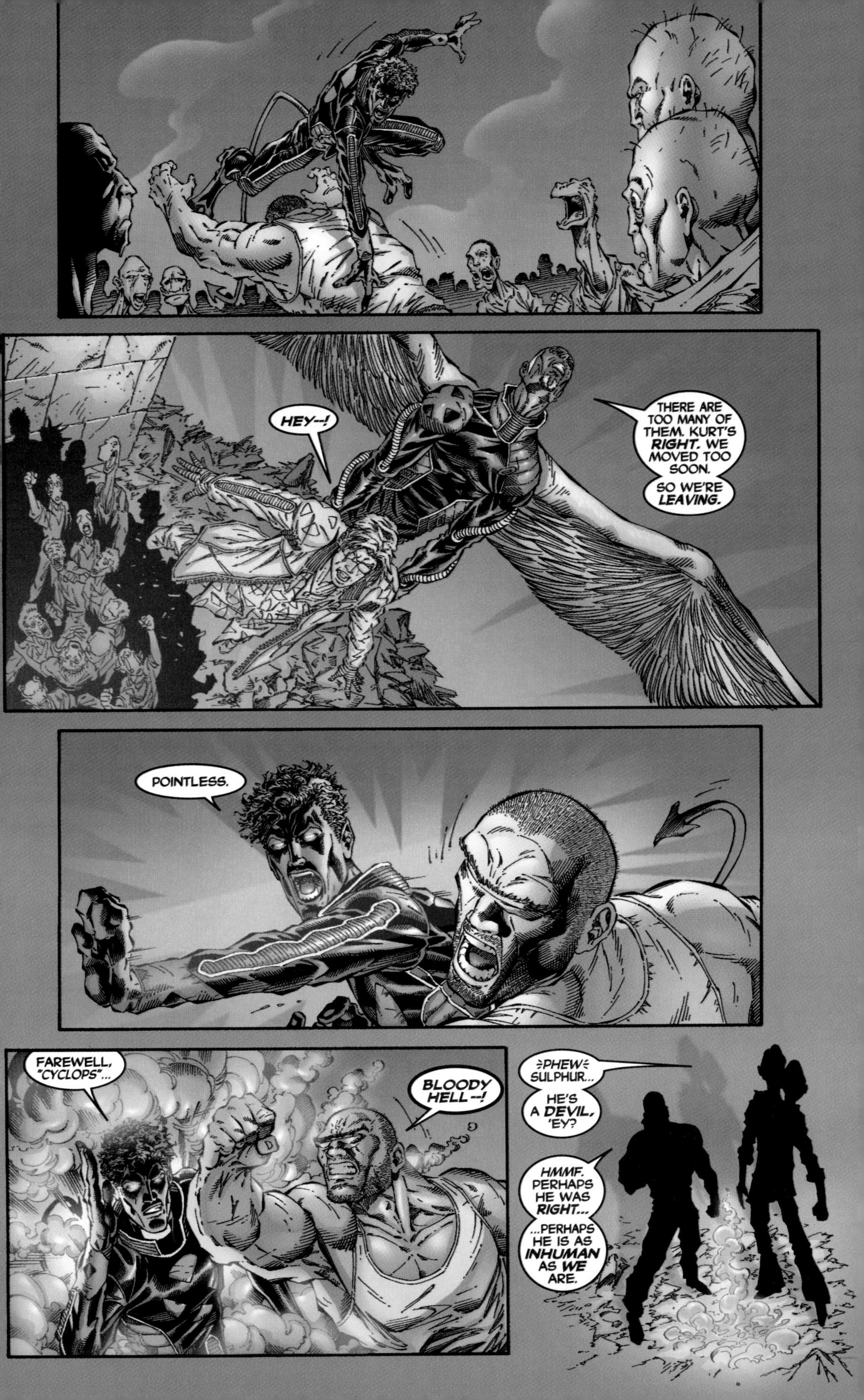
HEY--!
THERE ARE TOO MANY OF THEM. KURT'S RIGHT. WE MOVED TOO SOON.
SO WE'RE LEAVING.
POINTLESS.
FAREWELL, "CYCLOPS"...
BLOODY HELL--!
PHEW SULPHUR...
HE'S A DEVIL, 'EY?
HMMF. PERHAPS HE WAS RIGHT...
...PERHAPS HE IS AS INHUMAN AS WE ARE.

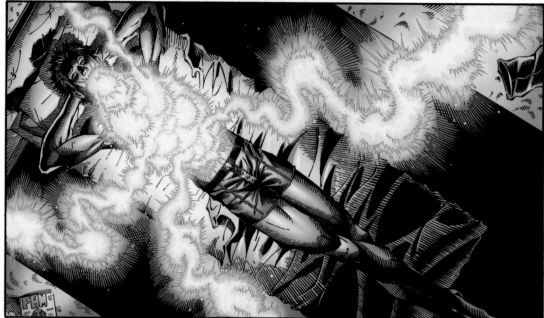

KNOCK KNOCK

GORDON BENNETT!

STARSMORE? YOU *IN* THERE?

MAYBE.

WHO'RE *YOU*? THIS HOTEL DOESN'T HAVE BELLMEN...

GEEZ --!

C'MON, KID... WE GOT *MISS KANE* WAITING IN THE LIMO DOWNSTAIRS. SHE WANTS TO *TALK* TO YOU...

Y-YEAH... LET'S *GO*...

IS THIS A JOKE...?

LOOK, JUST STAY OUTTA *MY* HEAD, IF YA PLEASE. SAVE IT FOR MISS KANE.

HERE HE IS. NOW, JUST SAY THE *WORD*, AND WE'LL TOSS HIM IN THE SKIP OUT BACK.

DONNIE... WE'LL HAVE NONE OF *THAT*.

SO, *JON*... WHAT'RE YOU DOING SQUATTING IN *THIS* DOSSHOUSE? YOU'VE GOT MORE STYLE THAN *THAT*, HAVEN'T YOU...?

ROOM RATE'S WITHIN MY *PRICE RANGE*... TILL I FIND A FLAT ON ME *OWN*.

SO, WHAT'S THIS ALL ABOUT? WHAT DO YOU WANT WITH THE LIKES OF *ME*? YOU FANCY *SLUMMIN'* IT WITH A FREAK FOR A NIGHT--?

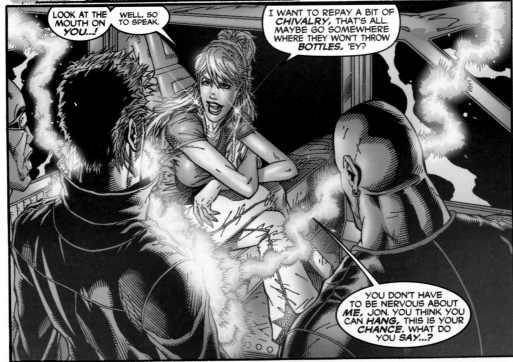

LOOK AT THE MOUTH ON *YOU...*!

WELL, SO TO SPEAK.

I WANT TO REPAY A BIT OF *CHIVALRY*, THAT'S ALL. MAYBE GO SOMEWHERE WHERE THEY WON'T THROW *BOTTLES*, 'EY?

YOU DON'T HAVE TO BE NERVOUS ABOUT *ME*, JON. YOU THINK YOU CAN *HANG*, THIS IS YOUR *CHANCE*. WHAT DO YOU *SAY...*?

HOW'S THE CONNECTION? ARE YOU *RECEIVING* ME ALL RIGHT...?

LOUD AND CLEAR, PAL. GO AHEAD.

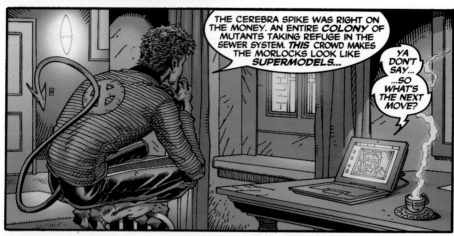

THE CEREBRA SPIKE WAS RIGHT ON THE MONEY. AN ENTIRE *COLONY* OF MUTANTS TAKING REFUGE IN THE SEWER SYSTEM. *THIS* CROWD MAKES THE MORLOCKS LOOK LIKE *SUPERMODELS*...

YA DON'T SAY... ...SO WHAT'S THE NEXT MOVE?

WELL, WE ATTEMPTED THE *MISSIONARY* TACTIC, BUT THESE POOR SOULS ARE QUITE *DEFENSIVE*.

BUT, THE FACT IS... THEY NEED OUR HELP. THE WAY THEY'RE *LIVING*... IS NO LIFE AT ALL.

I WOULDN'T UNDERESTIMATE THEIR *SURVIVAL SKILLS*, IF I WERE YOU. MAYBE IT'S ENOUGH OFFERIN' UP AN *ALTERNATIVE*. MAYBE HELP 'EM GET OUT OF THE CITY...

A GOOD THOUGHT, *MEIN FREUND*. THERE ARE SO *MANY* OF THEM... THEY WILL NOT REMAIN *UNDISCOVERED* FOR LONG...

SO... WHAT ABOUT *STARSMORE*...?

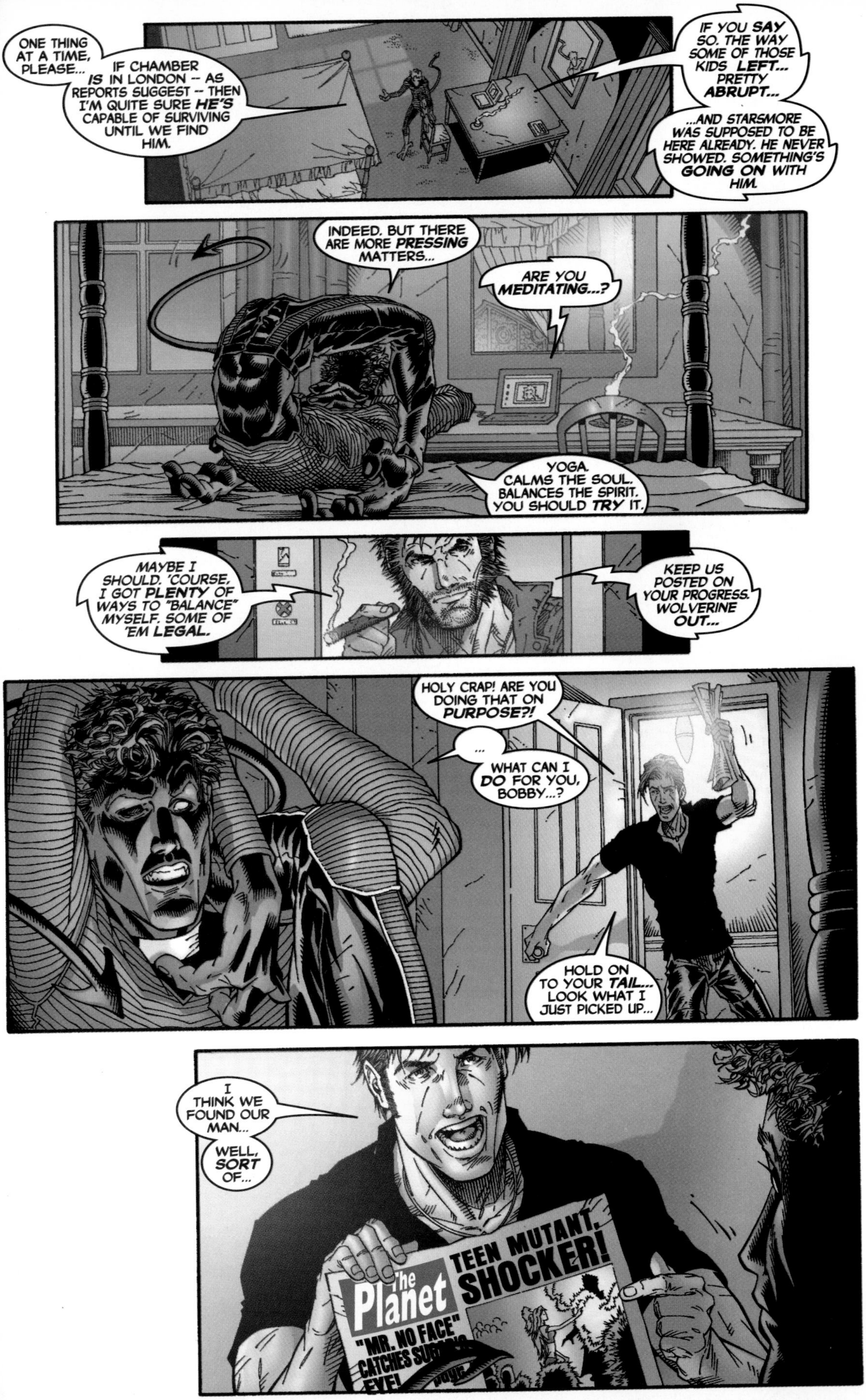

ONE THING AT A TIME, PLEASE... IF CHAMBER IS IN LONDON -- AS REPORTS SUGGEST -- THEN I'M QUITE SURE HE'S CAPABLE OF SURVIVING UNTIL WE FIND HIM.
IF YOU SAY SO. THE WAY SOME OF THOSE KIDS LEFT... PRETTY ABRUPT...
...AND STARSMORE WAS SUPPOSED TO BE HERE ALREADY. HE NEVER SHOWED. SOMETHING'S GOING ON WITH HIM.
INDEED. BUT THERE ARE MORE PRESSING MATTERS...
ARE YOU MEDITATING...?
YOGA. CALMS THE SOUL. BALANCES THE SPIRIT. YOU SHOULD TRY IT.
MAYBE I SHOULD. 'COURSE, I GOT PLENTY OF WAYS TO "BALANCE" MYSELF. SOME OF 'EM LEGAL.
KEEP US POSTED ON YOUR PROGRESS. WOLVERINE OUT...
HOLY CRAP! ARE YOU DOING THAT ON PURPOSE?!
...
WHAT CAN I DO FOR YOU, BOBBY...?
HOLD ON TO YOUR TAIL... LOOK WHAT I JUST PICKED UP...
I THINK WE FOUND OUR MAN...
WELL, SORT OF...
The Planet
TEEN MUTANT, SHOCKER!
"MR. NO FACE"

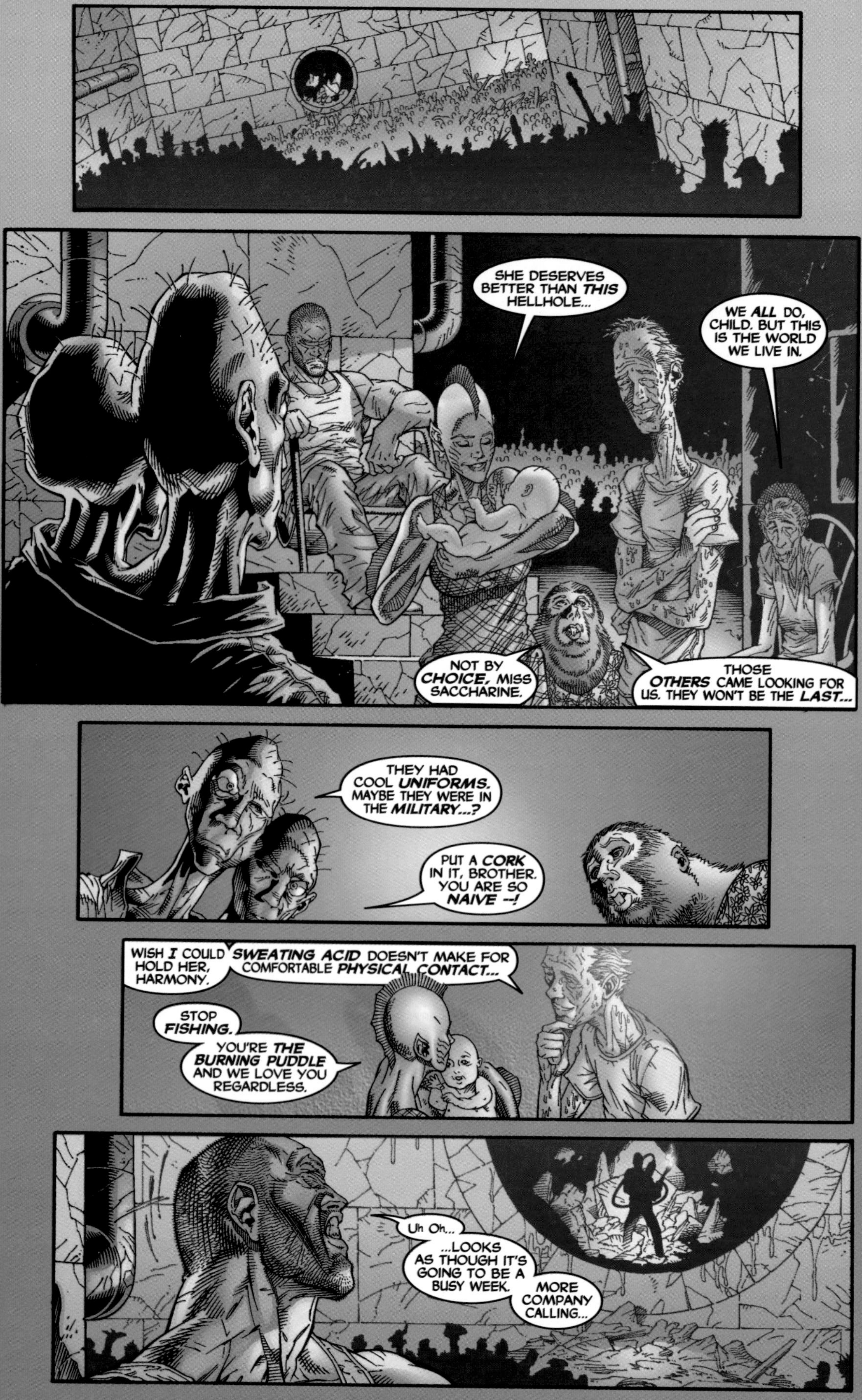

SHE DESERVES BETTER THAN THIS HELLHOLE...
WE ALL DO, CHILD. BUT THIS IS THE WORLD WE LIVE IN.
NOT BY CHOICE, MISS SACCHARINE.
THOSE OTHERS CAME LOOKING FOR US. THEY WON'T BE THE LAST...
THEY HAD COOL UNIFORMS. MAYBE THEY WERE IN THE MILITARY...?
PUT A CORK IN IT, BROTHER. YOU ARE SO NAIVE --!
WISH I COULD HOLD HER, HARMONY.
SWEATING ACID DOESN'T MAKE FOR COMFORTABLE PHYSICAL CONTACT...
STOP FISHING.
YOU'RE THE BURNING PUDDLE AND WE LOVE YOU REGARDLESS.
Uh Oh...
...LOOKS AS THOUGH IT'S GOING TO BE A BUSY WEEK.
MORE COMPANY CALLING...

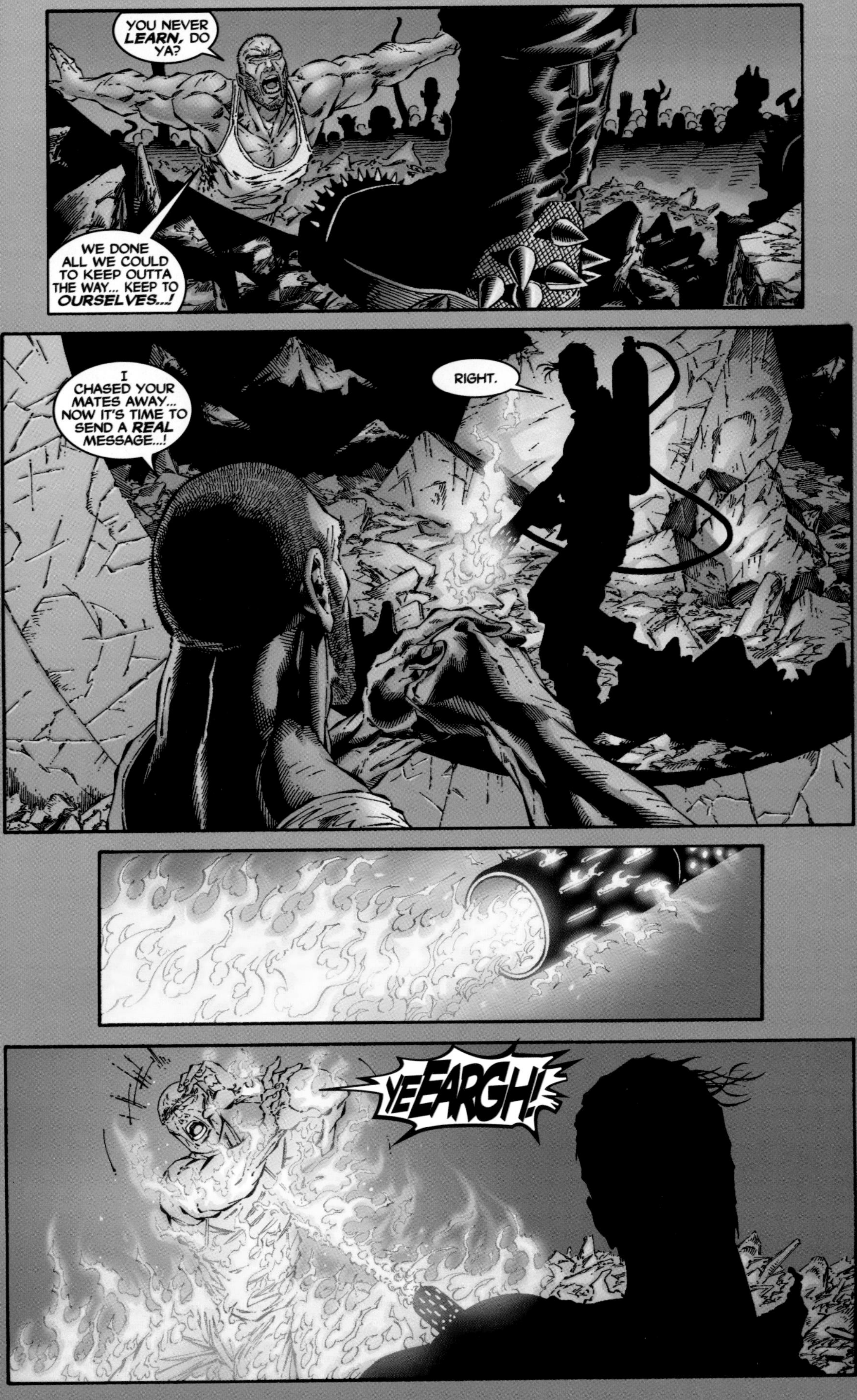
YOU NEVER LEARN, DO YA?
WE DONE ALL WE COULD TO KEEP OUTTA THE WAY... KEEP TO OURSELVES...!
I CHASED YOUR MATES AWAY... NOW IT'S TIME TO SEND A REAL MESSAGE...!
RIGHT.
YEEARGH!

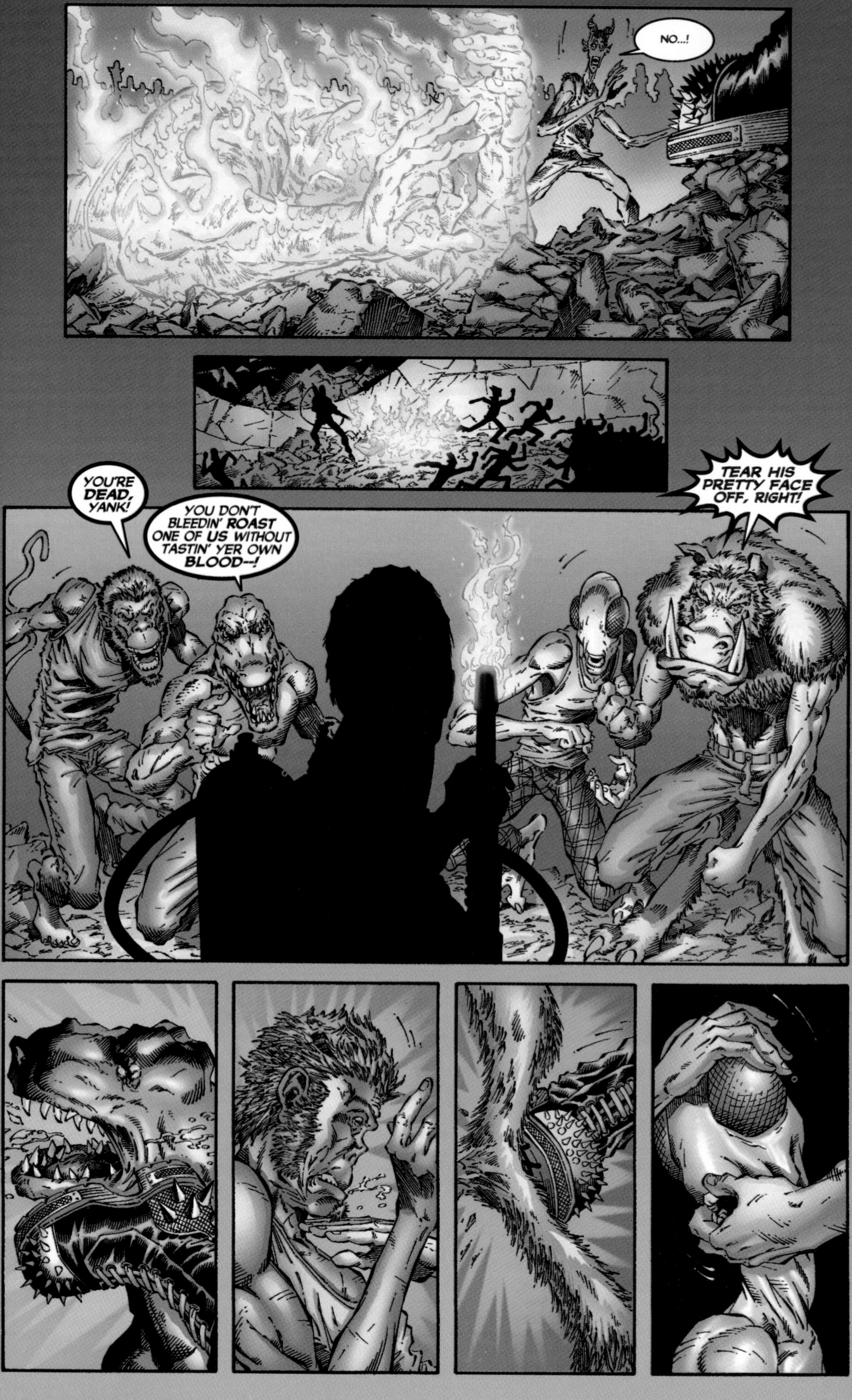
NO...!
YOU'RE DEAD, YANK!
YOU DON'T BLEEDIN' ROAST ONE OF US WITHOUT TASTIN' YER OWN BLOOD--!
TEAR HIS PRETTY FACE OFF, RIGHT!

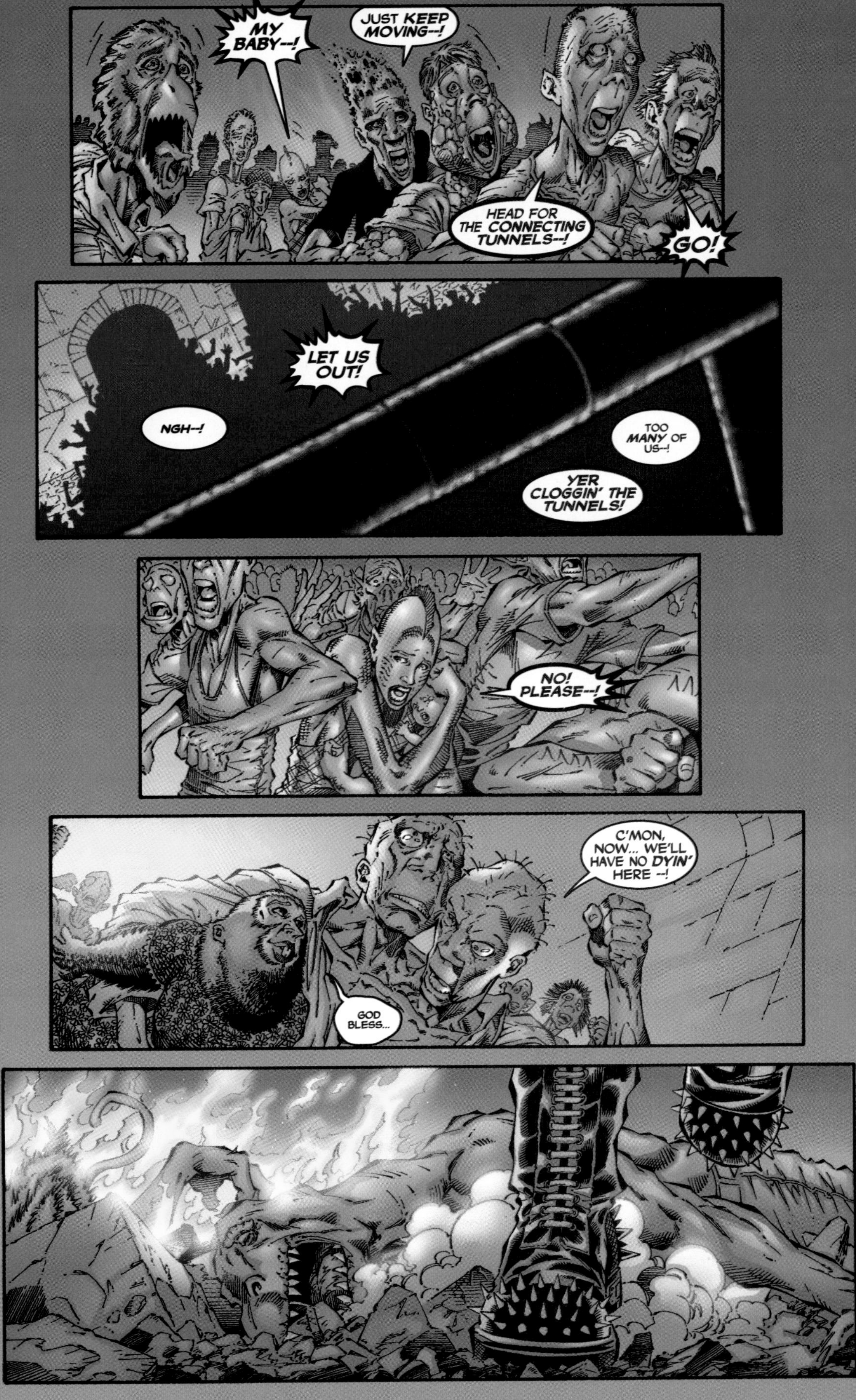
MY BABY--!
JUST KEEP MOVING--!
HEAD FOR THE CONNECTING TUNNELS--!
GO!
LET US OUT!
NGH--!
TOO MANY OF US--!
YER CLOGGIN' THE TUNNELS!
NO! PLEASE--!
C'MON, NOW... WE'LL HAVE NO DYIN' HERE --!
GOD BLESS...

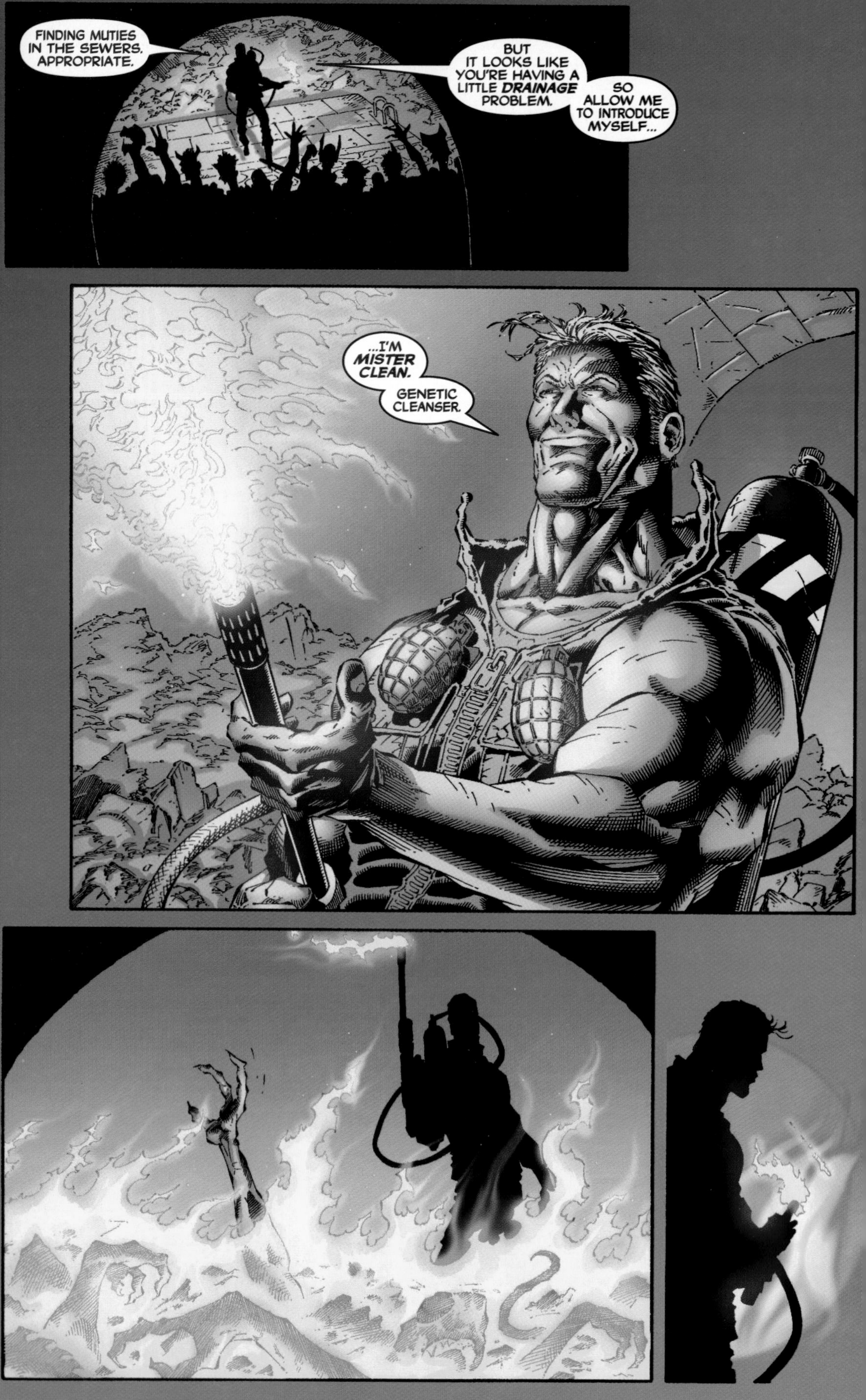
FINDING MUTIES IN THE SEWERS. APPROPRIATE.
BUT IT LOOKS LIKE YOU'RE HAVING A LITTLE DRAINAGE PROBLEM.
SO ALLOW ME TO INTRODUCE MYSELF...
...I'M MISTER CLEAN.
GENETIC CLEANSER.

Art By Barry Windsor-Smith

BEASTS ROAM THE STREETS OF LONDON!

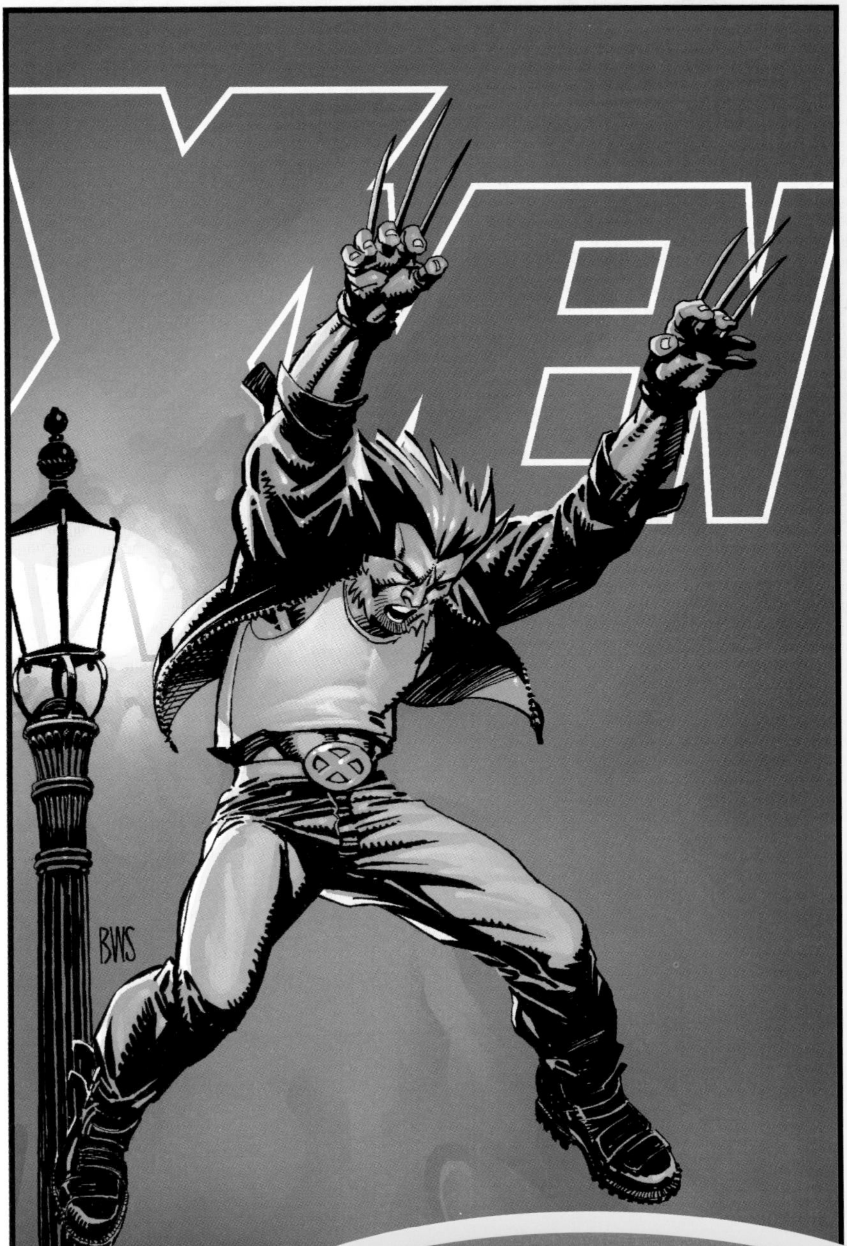

X-MEN
BWS

Variant Cover:
UNCANNY X-MEN #395

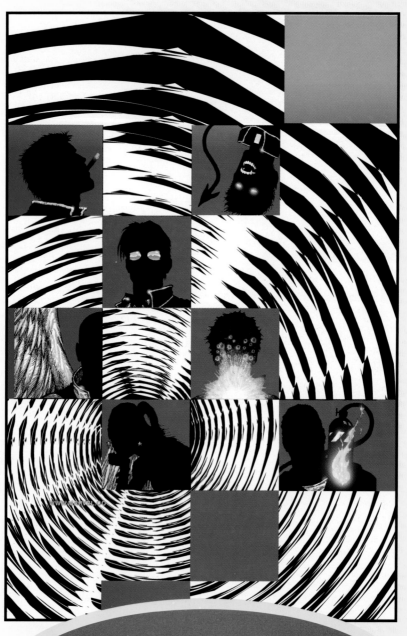

PART THREE:
UNCANNY X-MEN #396

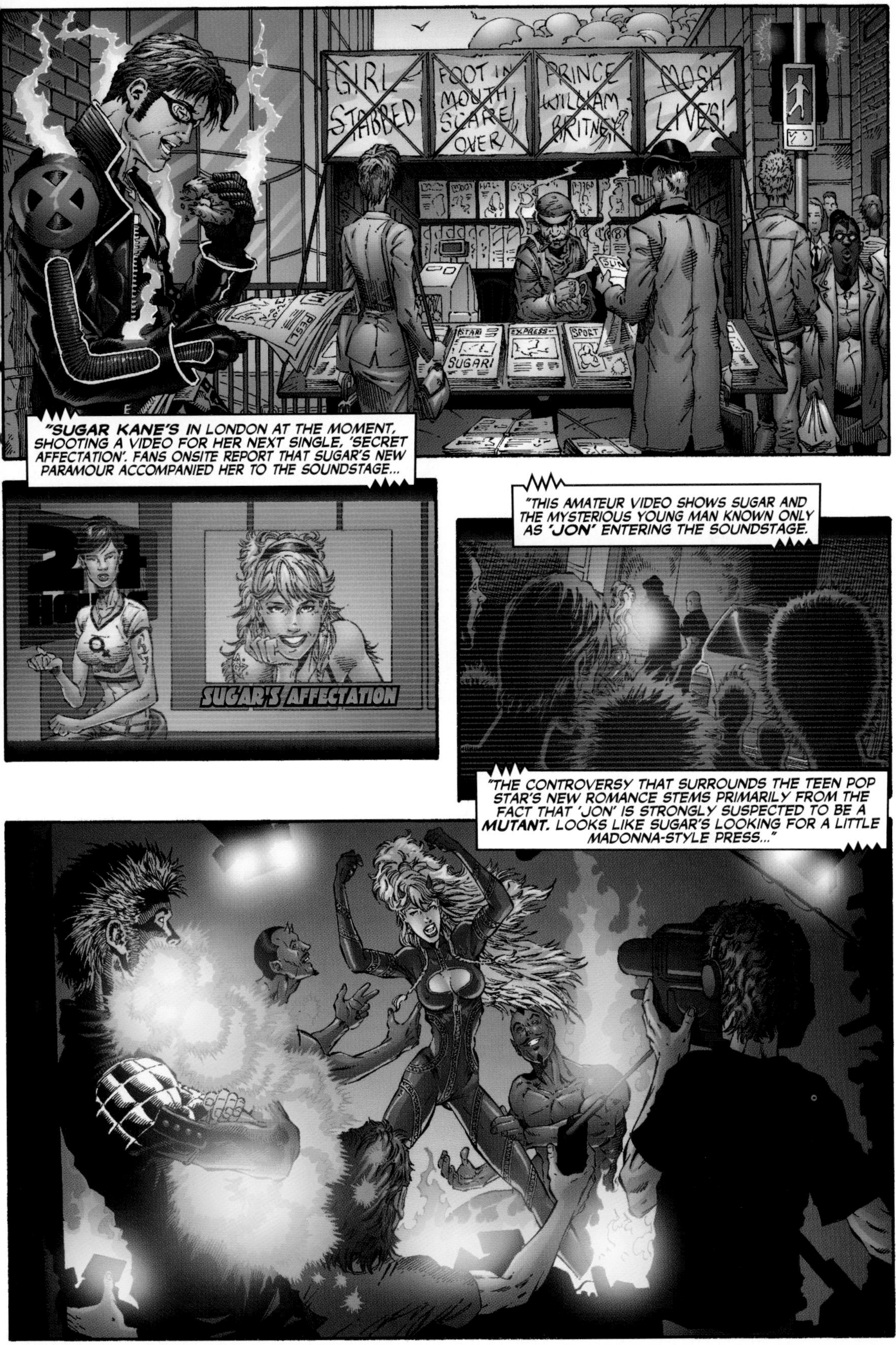
GIRL STABBED
FOOT IN MOUTH SCARE OVER
PRINCE WILLIAM BRITNEY?
MOSH LIVES!
STAR SUGAR!
EXPRESS
SPORT
"SUGAR KANE'S IN LONDON AT THE MOMENT, SHOOTING A VIDEO FOR HER NEXT SINGLE, 'SECRET AFFECTATION'. FANS ONSITE REPORT THAT SUGAR'S NEW PARAMOUR ACCOMPANIED HER TO THE SOUNDSTAGE...
SUGAR'S AFFECTATION
"THIS AMATEUR VIDEO SHOWS SUGAR AND THE MYSTERIOUS YOUNG MAN KNOWN ONLY AS 'JON' ENTERING THE SOUNDSTAGE.
"THE CONTROVERSY THAT SURROUNDS THE TEEN POP STAR'S NEW ROMANCE STEMS PRIMARILY FROM THE FACT THAT 'JON' IS STRONGLY SUSPECTED TO BE A MUTANT. LOOKS LIKE SUGAR'S LOOKING FOR A LITTLE MADONNA-STYLE PRESS..."

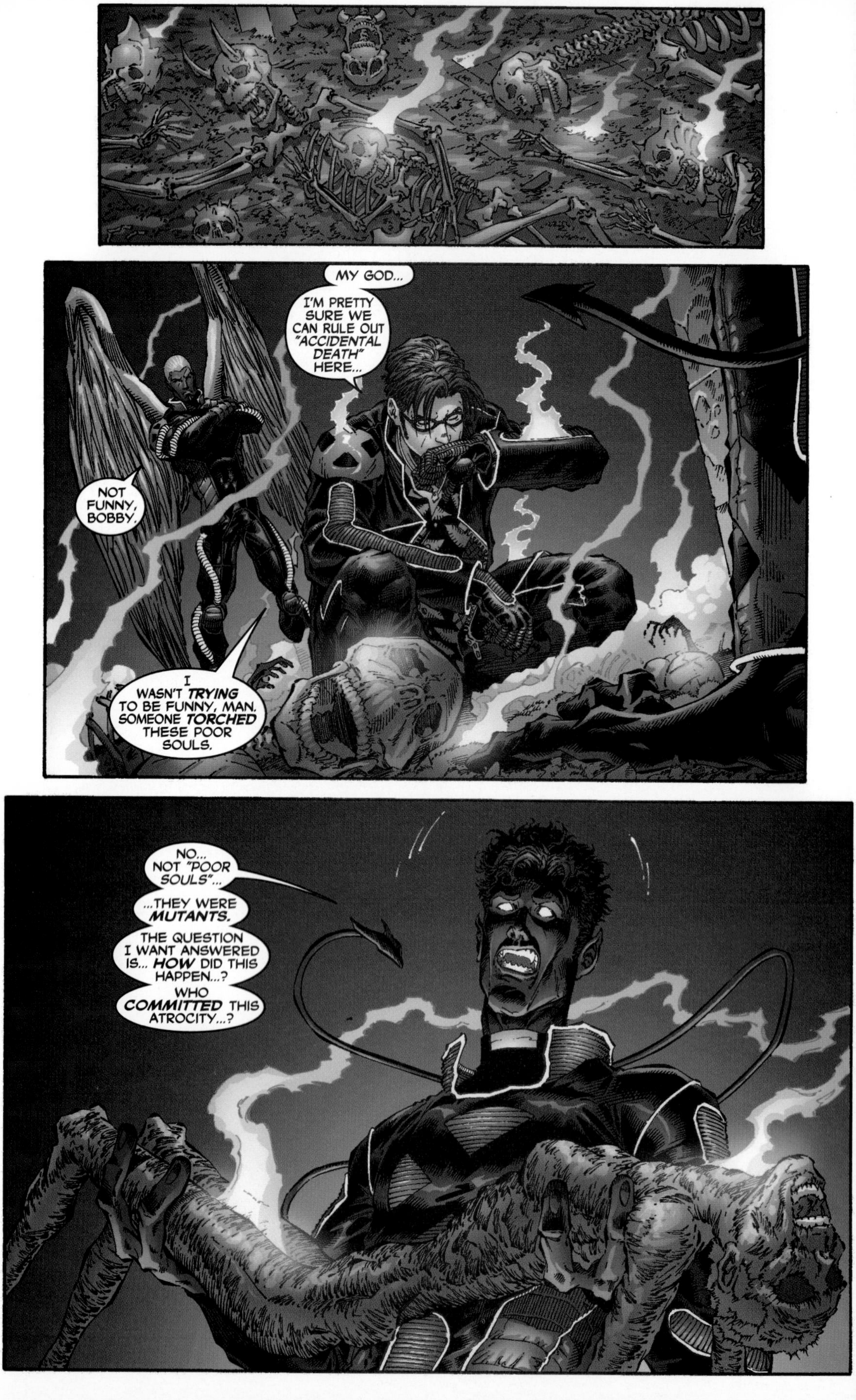
MY GOD...
I'M PRETTY SURE WE CAN RULE OUT "ACCIDENTAL DEATH" HERE...
NOT FUNNY, BOBBY.
I WASN'T TRYING TO BE FUNNY, MAN. SOMEONE TORCHED THESE POOR SOULS.
NO... NOT "POOR SOULS"...
...THEY WERE MUTANTS.
THE QUESTION I WANT ANSWERED IS... HOW DID THIS HAPPEN...?
WHO COMMITTED THIS ATROCITY...?

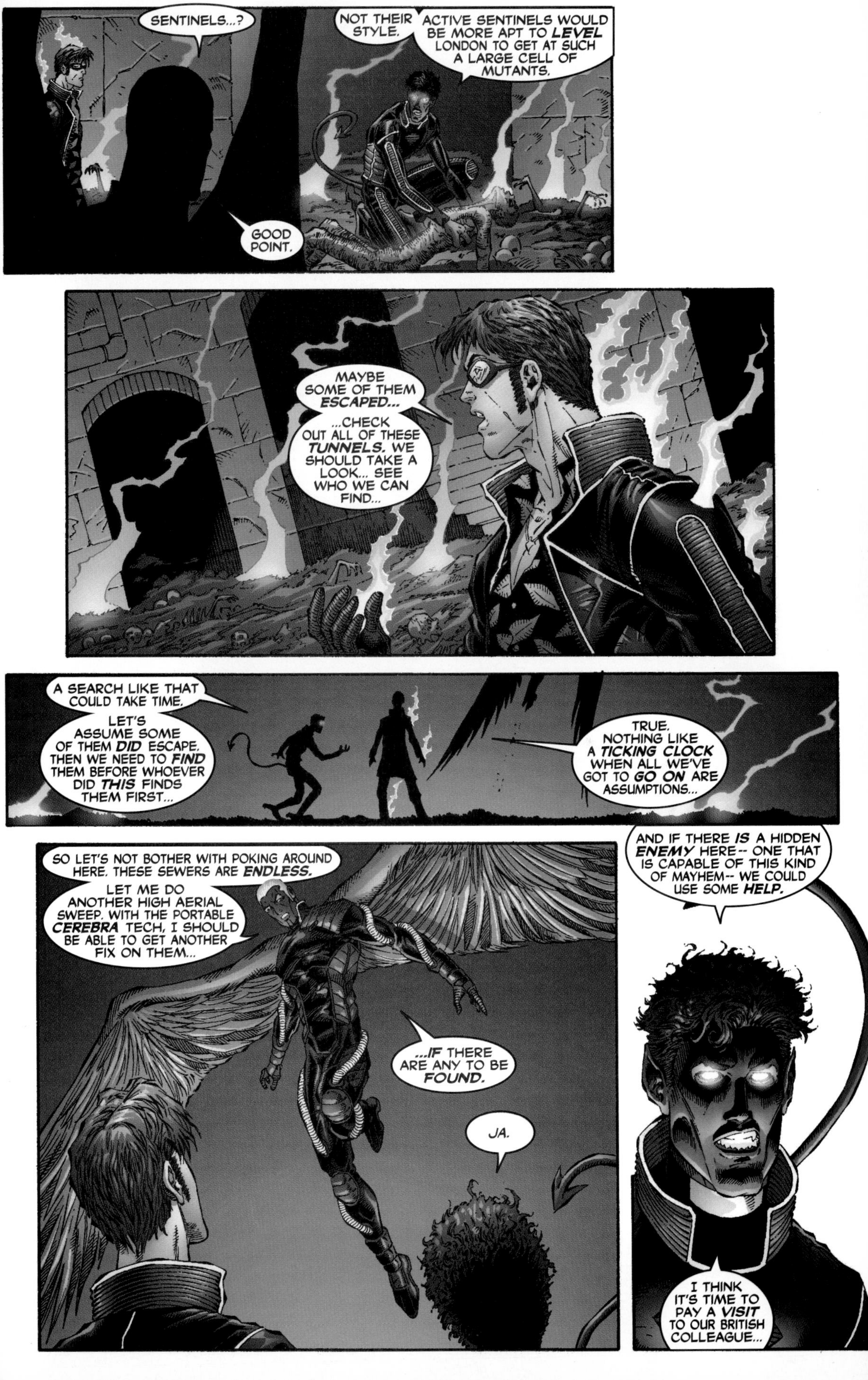
SENTINELS...?
NOT THEIR STYLE.
ACTIVE SENTINELS WOULD BE MORE APT TO LEVEL LONDON TO GET AT SUCH A LARGE CELL OF MUTANTS.
GOOD POINT.
MAYBE SOME OF THEM ESCAPED...
...CHECK OUT ALL OF THESE TUNNELS. WE SHOULD TAKE A LOOK... SEE WHO WE CAN FIND...
A SEARCH LIKE THAT COULD TAKE TIME.
LET'S ASSUME SOME OF THEM DID ESCAPE. THEN WE NEED TO FIND THEM BEFORE WHOEVER DID THIS FINDS THEM FIRST...
TRUE. NOTHING LIKE A TICKING CLOCK WHEN ALL WE'VE GOT TO GO ON ARE ASSUMPTIONS...
SO LET'S NOT BOTHER WITH POKING AROUND HERE. THESE SEWERS ARE ENDLESS.
LET ME DO ANOTHER HIGH AERIAL SWEEP. WITH THE PORTABLE CEREBRA TECH, I SHOULD BE ABLE TO GET ANOTHER FIX ON THEM...
...IF THERE ARE ANY TO BE FOUND.
JA.
AND IF THERE IS A HIDDEN ENEMY HERE-- ONE THAT IS CAPABLE OF THIS KIND OF MAYHEM-- WE COULD USE SOME HELP.
I THINK IT'S TIME TO PAY A VISIT TO OUR BRITISH COLLEAGUE...

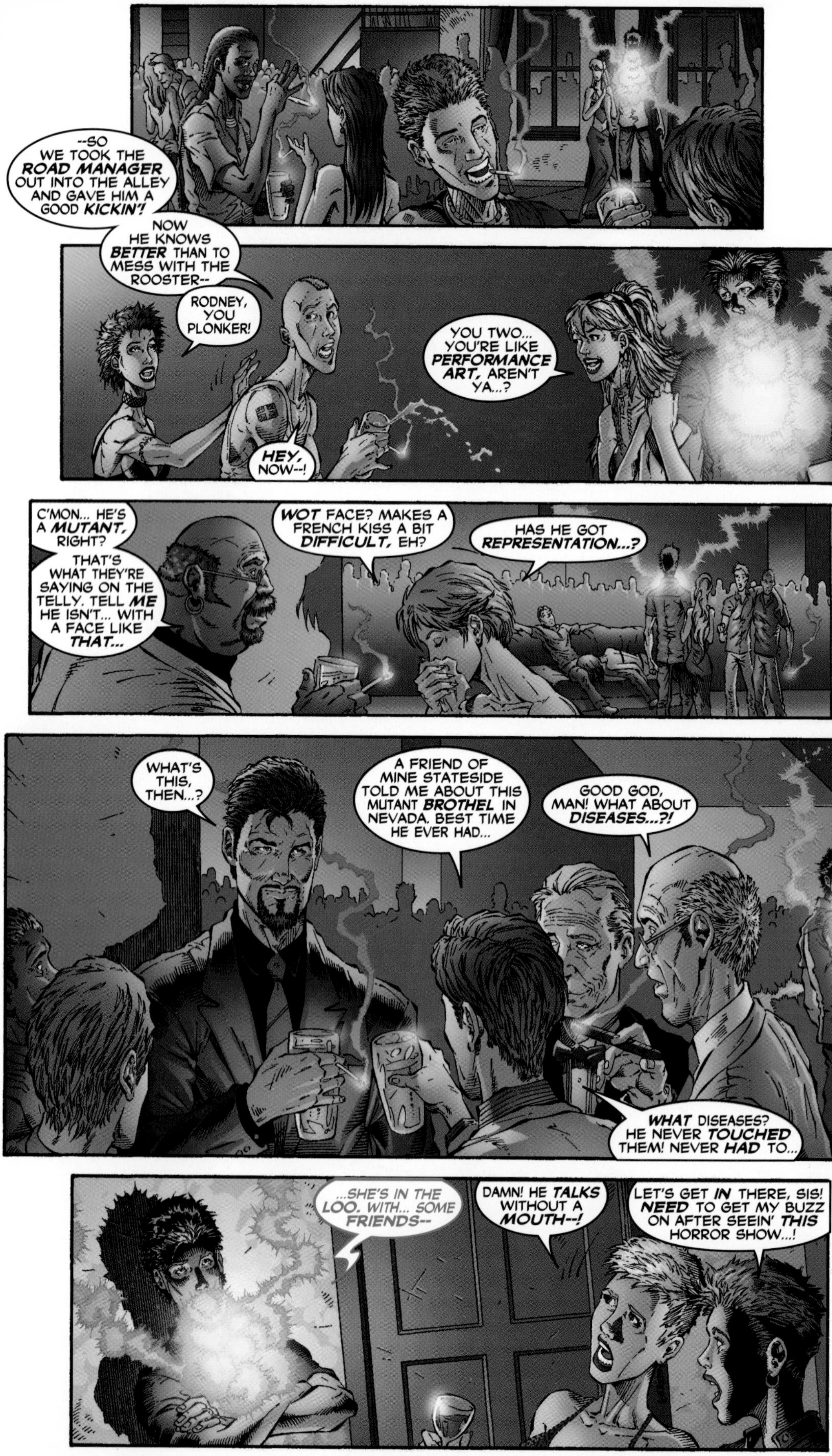
--SO WE TOOK THE ROAD MANAGER OUT INTO THE ALLEY AND GAVE HIM A GOOD KICKIN'!
NOW HE KNOWS BETTER THAN TO MESS WITH THE ROOSTER--
RODNEY, YOU PLONKER!
YOU TWO... YOU'RE LIKE PERFORMANCE ART, AREN'T YA...?
HEY, NOW--!
C'MON... HE'S A MUTANT, RIGHT?
THAT'S WHAT THEY'RE SAYING ON THE TELLY. TELL ME HE ISN'T... WITH A FACE LIKE THAT...
WOT FACE? MAKES A FRENCH KISS A BIT DIFFICULT, EH?
HAS HE GOT REPRESENTATION...?
WHAT'S THIS, THEN...?
A FRIEND OF MINE STATESIDE TOLD ME ABOUT THIS MUTANT BROTHEL IN NEVADA. BEST TIME HE EVER HAD...
GOOD GOD, MAN! WHAT ABOUT DISEASES...?!
WHAT DISEASES? HE NEVER TOUCHED THEM! NEVER HAD TO...
...SHE'S IN THE LOO. WITH... SOME FRIENDS--
DAMN! HE TALKS WITHOUT A MOUTH--!
LET'S GET IN THERE, SIS! NEED TO GET MY BUZZ ON AFTER SEEIN' THIS HORROR SHOW...!

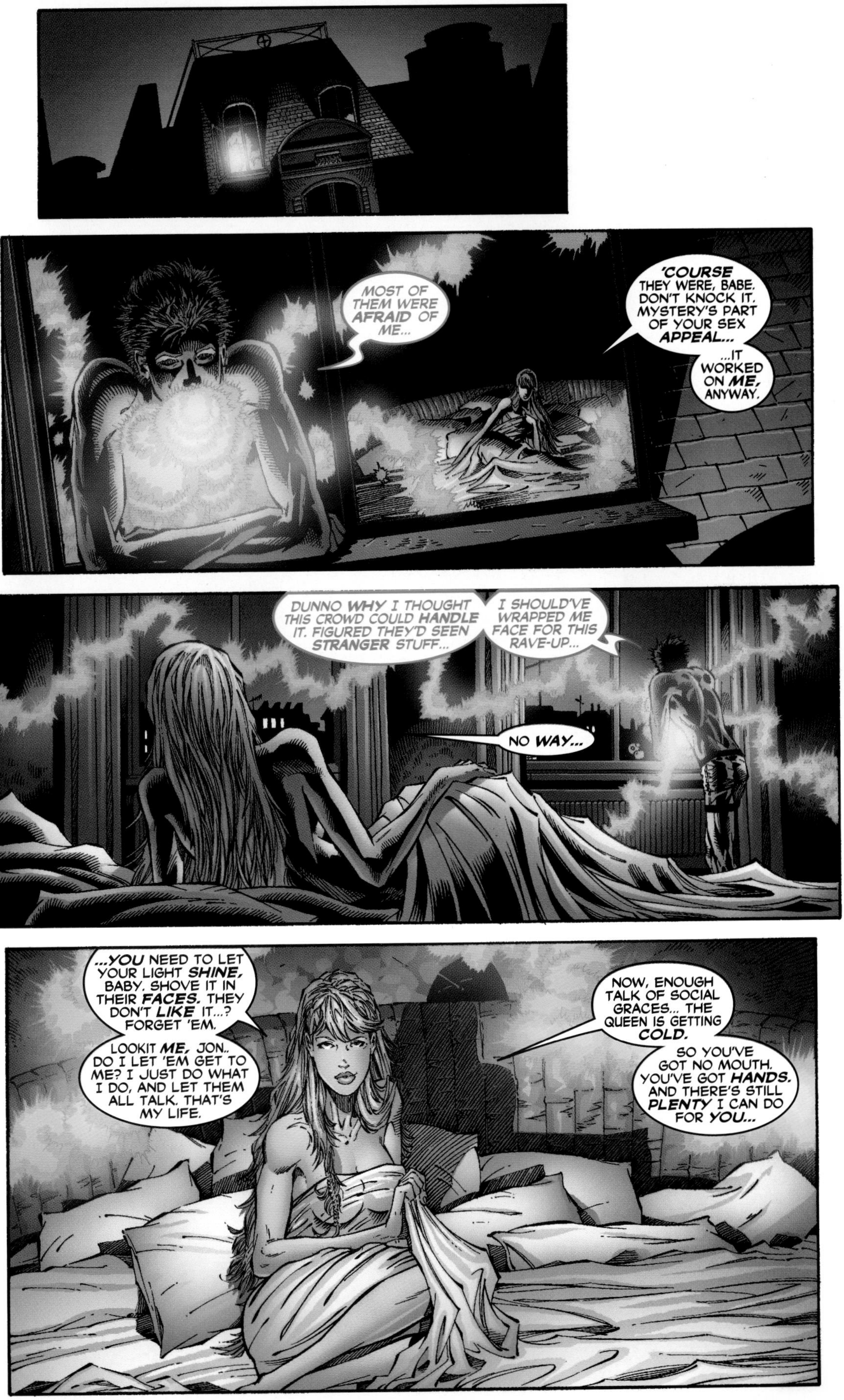
MOST OF THEM WERE AFRAID OF ME...
'COURSE THEY WERE, BABE. DON'T KNOCK IT. MYSTERY'S PART OF YOUR SEX APPEAL...
...IT WORKED ON ME, ANYWAY.
DUNNO WHY I THOUGHT THIS CROWD COULD HANDLE IT. FIGURED THEY'D SEEN STRANGER STUFF...
I SHOULD'VE WRAPPED ME FACE FOR THIS RAVE-UP...
NO WAY...
...YOU NEED TO LET YOUR LIGHT SHINE, BABY. SHOVE IT IN THEIR FACES. THEY DON'T LIKE IT...? FORGET 'EM.
LOOKIT ME, JON.. DO I LET 'EM GET TO ME? I JUST DO WHAT I DO, AND LET THEM ALL TALK. THAT'S MY LIFE.
NOW, ENOUGH TALK OF SOCIAL GRACES... THE QUEEN IS GETTING COLD.
SO YOU'VE GOT NO MOUTH. YOU'VE GOT HANDS. AND THERE'S STILL PLENTY I CAN DO FOR YOU...

NOK
NOK
NOK

"..."

NOK·NOK!

YEAH... I *HEARD* YOU!

DON'T YOU PEOPLE HAVE A *KEY* OF YOUR OWN--?!

?!

NICE DIGS, STARSMORE. WHERE GOETH THE *ROCK,* SO SHALL FOLLOW THE *ROLL...*

CAN I HAVE AN *AUTOGRAPH?*

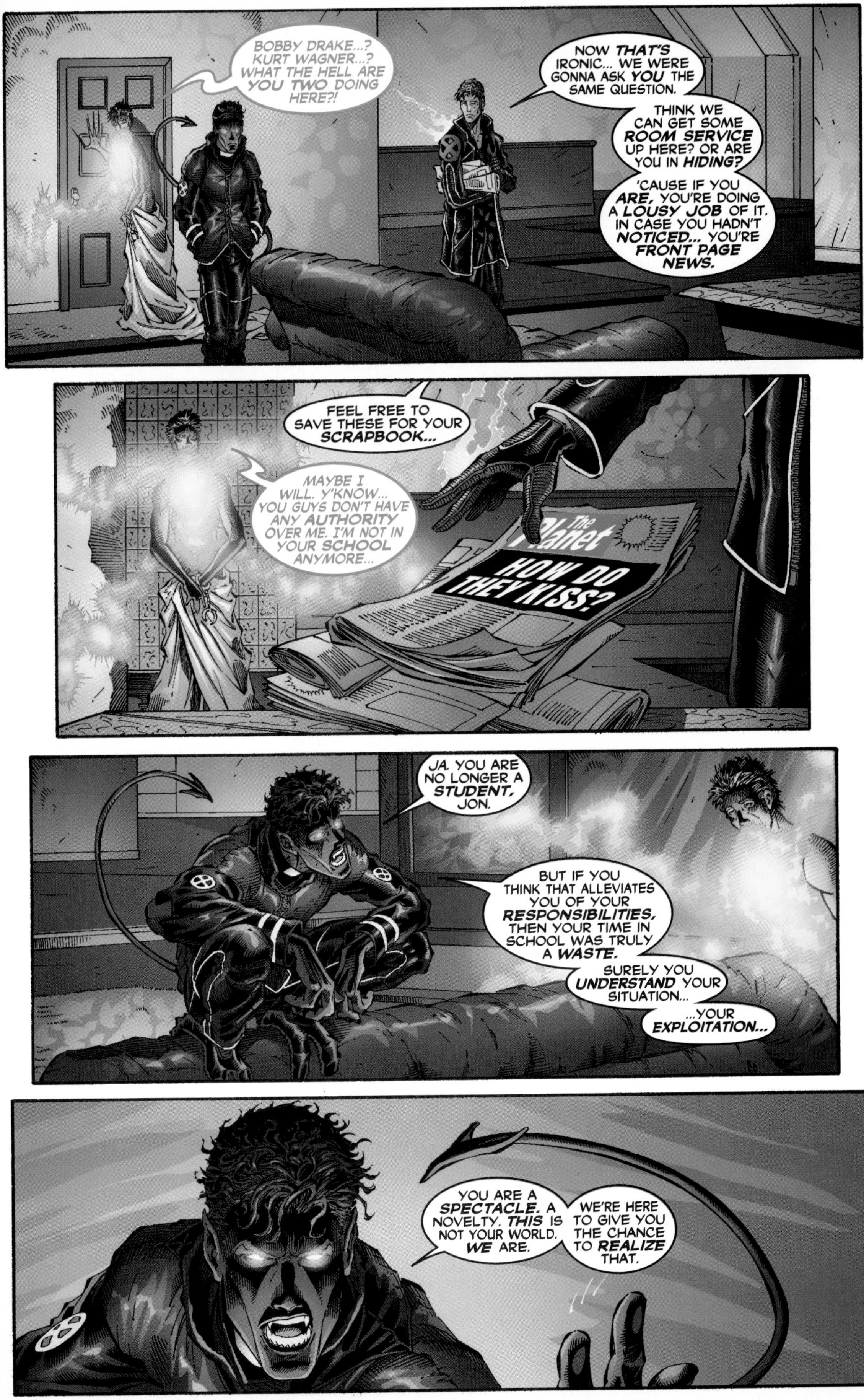

BOBBY DRAKE...? KURT WAGNER...? WHAT THE HELL ARE YOU TWO DOING HERE?!
NOW THAT'S IRONIC... WE WERE GONNA ASK YOU THE SAME QUESTION.
THINK WE CAN GET SOME ROOM SERVICE UP HERE? OR ARE YOU IN HIDING?
'CAUSE IF YOU ARE, YOU'RE DOING A LOUSY JOB OF IT. IN CASE YOU HADN'T NOTICED... YOU'RE FRONT PAGE NEWS.
FEEL FREE TO SAVE THESE FOR YOUR SCRAPBOOK...
MAYBE I WILL. Y'KNOW... YOU GUYS DON'T HAVE ANY AUTHORITY OVER ME. I'M NOT IN YOUR SCHOOL ANYMORE...
The Planet
HOW DO THEY KISS?
JA. YOU ARE NO LONGER A STUDENT, JON.
BUT IF YOU THINK THAT ALLEVIATES YOU OF YOUR RESPONSIBILITIES, THEN YOUR TIME IN SCHOOL WAS TRULY A WASTE.
SURELY YOU UNDERSTAND YOUR SITUATION...
...YOUR EXPLOITATION...
YOU ARE A SPECTACLE. A NOVELTY. THIS IS NOT YOUR WORLD. WE ARE.
WE'RE HERE TO GIVE YOU THE CHANCE TO REALIZE THAT.

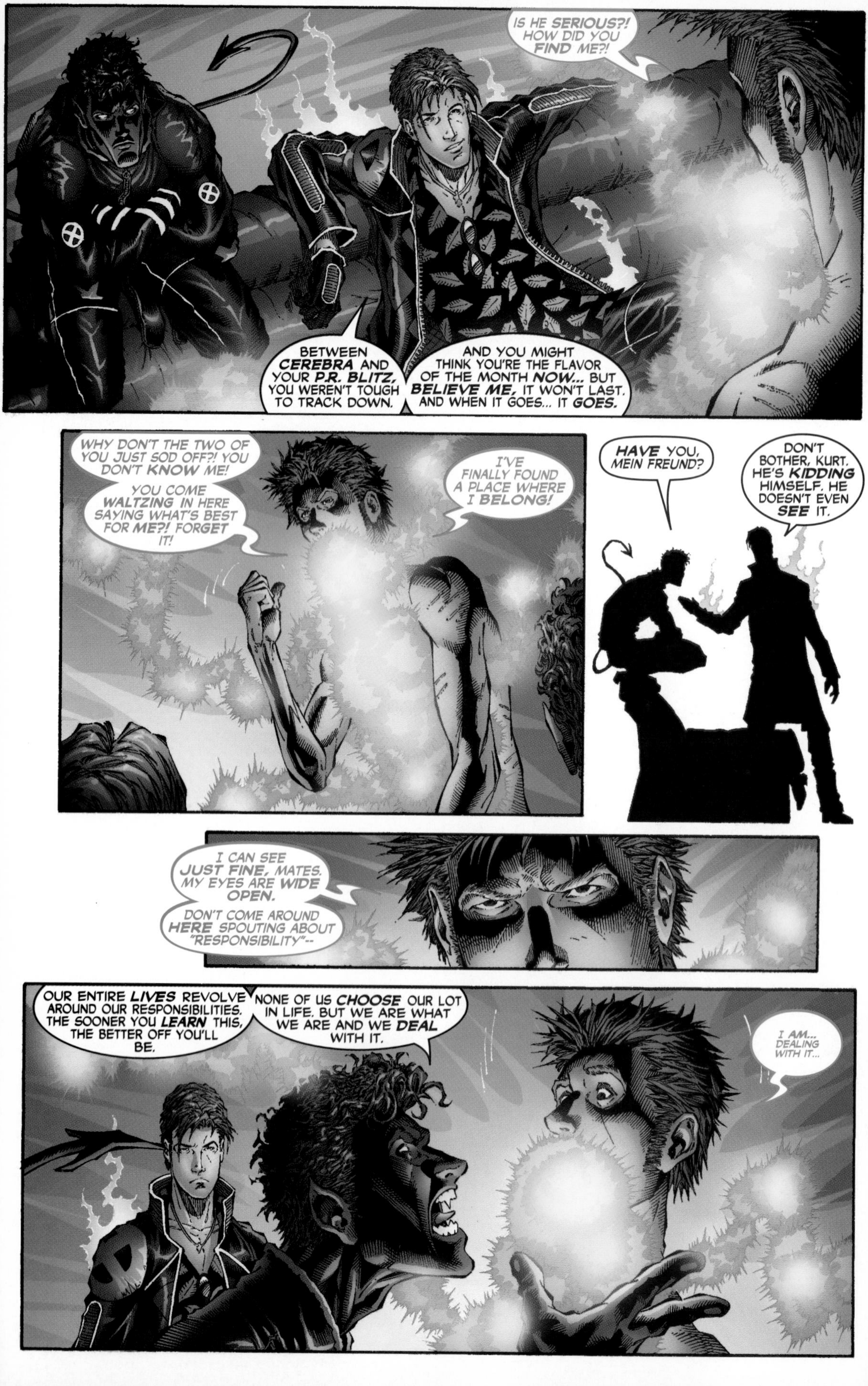
IS HE SERIOUS?! HOW DID YOU FIND ME?!
BETWEEN CEREBRA AND YOUR P.R. BLITZ, YOU WEREN'T TOUGH TO TRACK DOWN.
AND YOU MIGHT THINK YOU'RE THE FLAVOR OF THE MONTH NOW... BUT BELIEVE ME, IT WON'T LAST. AND WHEN IT GOES... IT GOES.
WHY DON'T THE TWO OF YOU JUST SOD OFF?! YOU DON'T KNOW ME!
YOU COME WALTZING IN HERE SAYING WHAT'S BEST FOR ME?! FORGET IT!
I'VE FINALLY FOUND A PLACE WHERE I BELONG!
HAVE YOU, MEIN FREUND?
DON'T BOTHER, KURT. HE'S KIDDING HIMSELF. HE DOESN'T EVEN SEE IT.
I CAN SEE JUST FINE, MATES. MY EYES ARE WIDE OPEN.
DON'T COME AROUND HERE SPOUTING ABOUT "RESPONSIBILITY"--
OUR ENTIRE LIVES REVOLVE AROUND OUR RESPONSIBILITIES. THE SOONER YOU LEARN THIS, THE BETTER OFF YOU'LL BE.
NONE OF US CHOOSE OUR LOT IN LIFE. BUT WE ARE WHAT WE ARE AND WE DEAL WITH IT.
I AM... DEALING WITH IT...

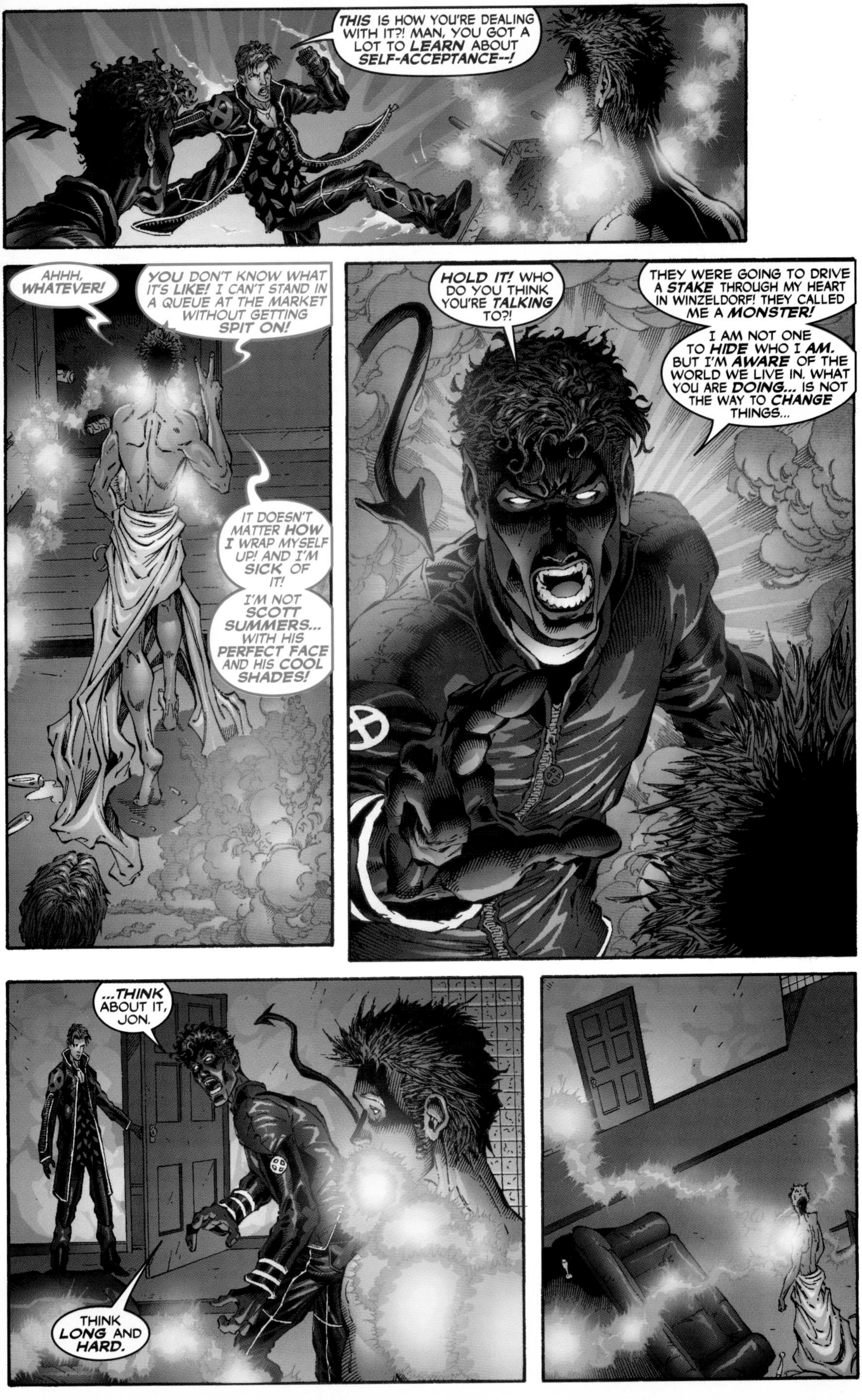

THIS IS HOW YOU'RE DEALING WITH IT?! MAN, YOU GOT A LOT TO LEARN ABOUT SELF-ACCEPTANCE--!
AHHH, WHATEVER!
YOU DON'T KNOW WHAT IT'S LIKE! I CAN'T STAND IN A QUEUE AT THE MARKET WITHOUT GETTING SPIT ON!
IT DOESN'T MATTER HOW I WRAP MYSELF UP! AND I'M SICK OF IT!
I'M NOT SCOTT SUMMERS... WITH HIS PERFECT FACE AND HIS COOL SHADES!
HOLD IT! WHO DO YOU THINK YOU'RE TALKING TO?!
THEY WERE GOING TO DRIVE A STAKE THROUGH MY HEART IN WINZELDORF! THEY CALLED ME A MONSTER!
I AM NOT ONE TO HIDE WHO I AM. BUT I'M AWARE OF THE WORLD WE LIVE IN. WHAT YOU ARE DOING... IS NOT THE WAY TO CHANGE THINGS...
...THINK ABOUT IT, JON.
THINK LONG AND HARD.

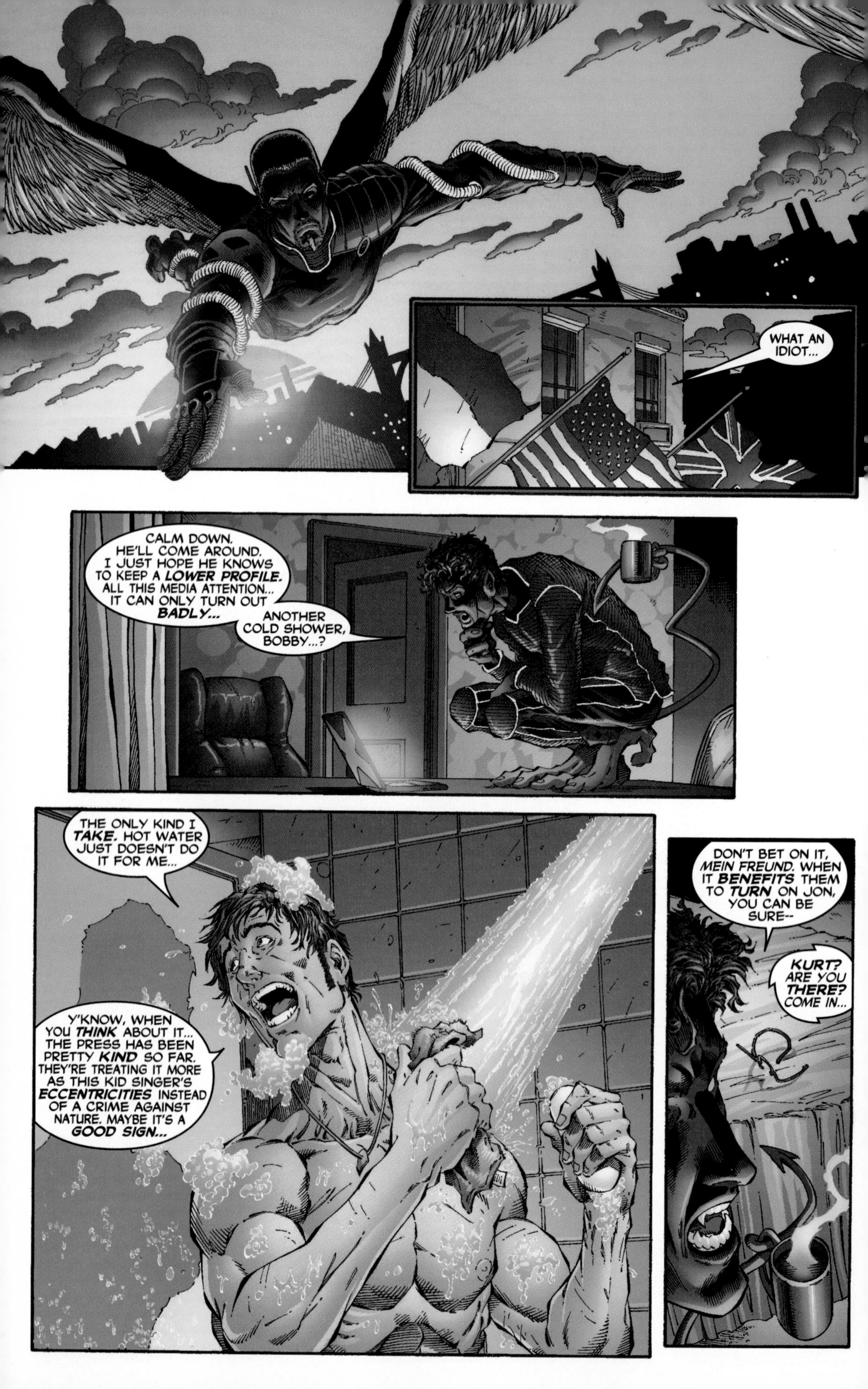
WHAT AN IDIOT...
CALM DOWN. HE'LL COME AROUND. I JUST HOPE HE KNOWS TO KEEP A LOWER PROFILE. ALL THIS MEDIA ATTENTION... IT CAN ONLY TURN OUT BADLY...
ANOTHER COLD SHOWER, BOBBY...?
THE ONLY KIND I TAKE. HOT WATER JUST DOESN'T DO IT FOR ME...
Y'KNOW, WHEN YOU THINK ABOUT IT... THE PRESS HAS BEEN PRETTY KIND SO FAR. THEY'RE TREATING IT MORE AS THIS KID SINGER'S ECCENTRICITIES INSTEAD OF A CRIME AGAINST NATURE. MAYBE IT'S A GOOD SIGN...
DON'T BET ON IT, MEIN FREUND. WHEN IT BENEFITS THEM TO TURN ON JON, YOU CAN BE SURE--
KURT? ARE YOU THERE? COME IN...

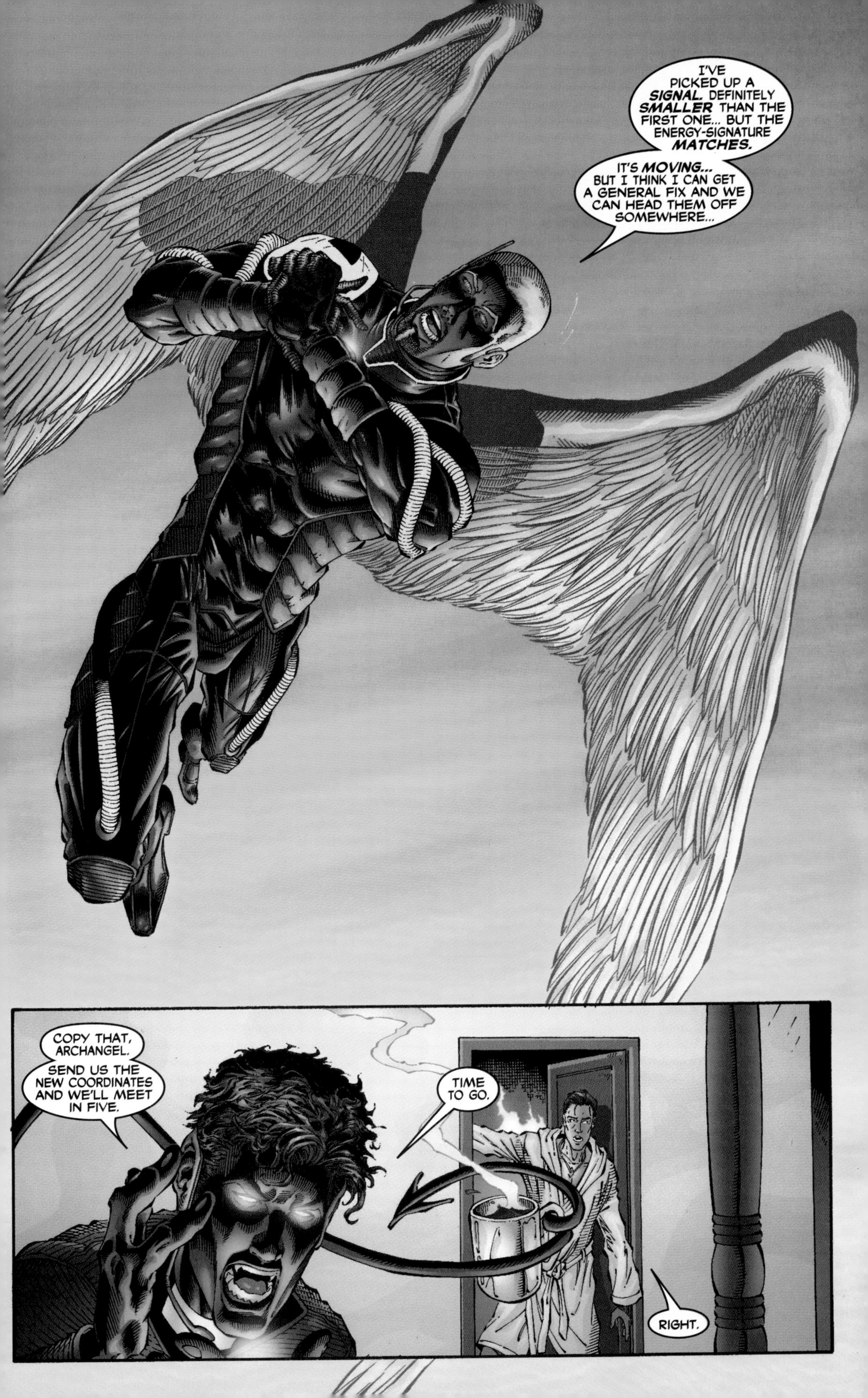
I'VE PICKED UP A SIGNAL. DEFINITELY SMALLER THAN THE FIRST ONE... BUT THE ENERGY-SIGNATURE MATCHES.
IT'S MOVING... BUT I THINK I CAN GET A GENERAL FIX AND WE CAN HEAD THEM OFF SOMEWHERE...
COPY THAT, ARCHANGEL.
SEND US THE NEW COORDINATES AND WE'LL MEET IN FIVE.
TIME TO GO.
RIGHT.

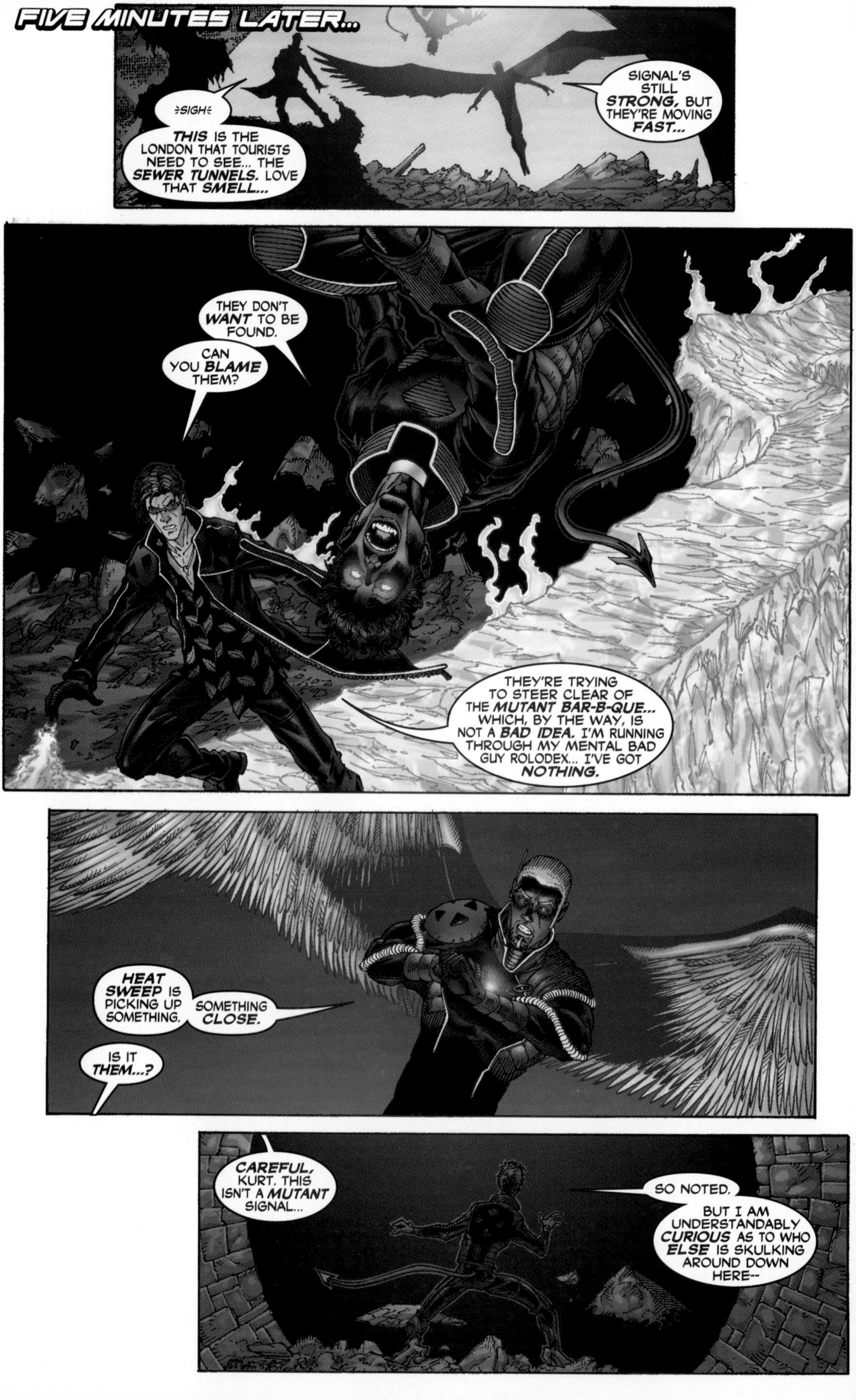

FIVE MINUTES LATER...
≥SIGH≤
THIS IS THE LONDON THAT TOURISTS NEED TO SEE... THE SEWER TUNNELS. LOVE THAT SMELL...
SIGNAL'S STILL STRONG, BUT THEY'RE MOVING FAST...
THEY DON'T WANT TO BE FOUND.
CAN YOU BLAME THEM?
THEY'RE TRYING TO STEER CLEAR OF THE MUTANT BAR-B-QUE... WHICH, BY THE WAY, IS NOT A BAD IDEA. I'M RUNNING THROUGH MY MENTAL BAD GUY ROLODEX... I'VE GOT NOTHING.
HEAT SWEEP IS PICKING UP SOMETHING.
SOMETHING CLOSE.
IS IT THEM...?
CAREFUL, KURT. THIS ISN'T A MUTANT SIGNAL...
SO NOTED.
BUT I AM UNDERSTANDABLY CURIOUS AS TO WHO ELSE IS SKULKING AROUND DOWN HERE--

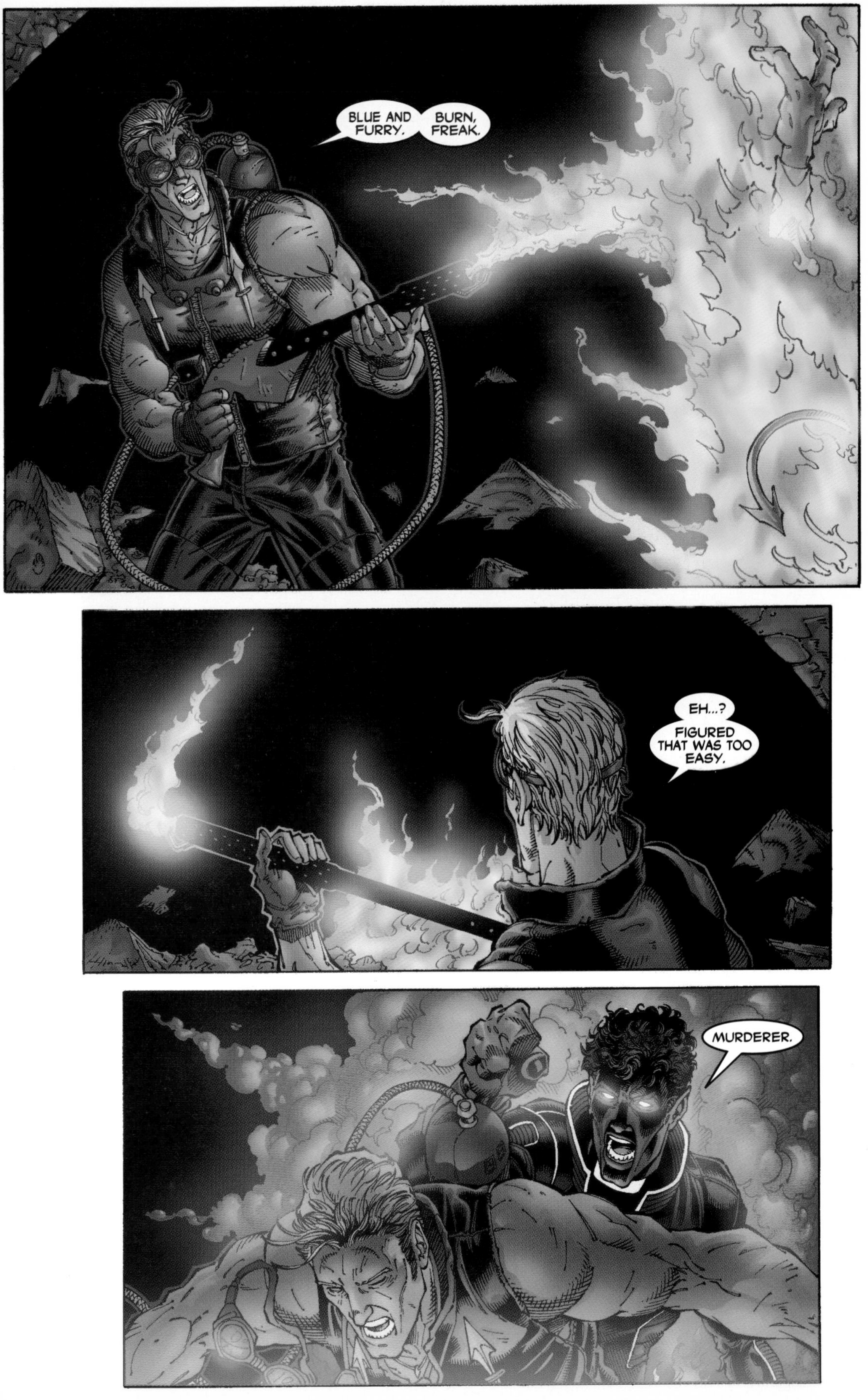
BLUE AND FURRY.
BURN, FREAK.
EH...?
FIGURED THAT WAS TOO EASY.
MURDERER.

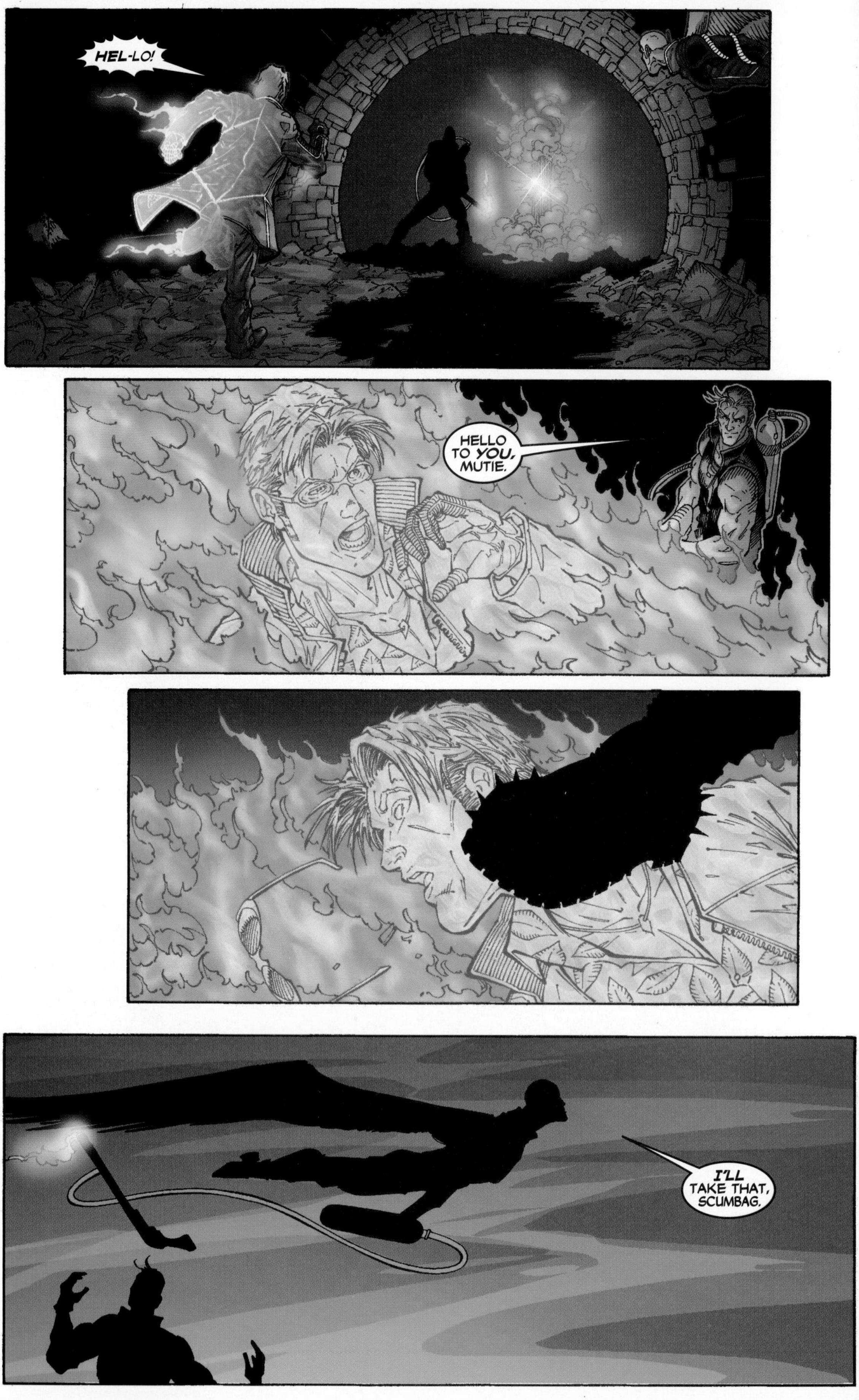
HEL-LO!
HELLO TO YOU, MUTIE.
I'LL TAKE THAT, SCUMBAG.

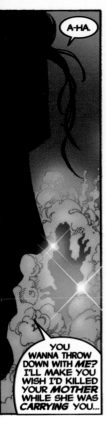

A-HA.

YOU WANNA THROW DOWN WITH *ME?* I'LL MAKE YOU WISH I'D KILLED YOUR *MOTHER* WHILE SHE WAS *CARRYING* YOU...

PERHAPS.

PERHAPS *NOT.*

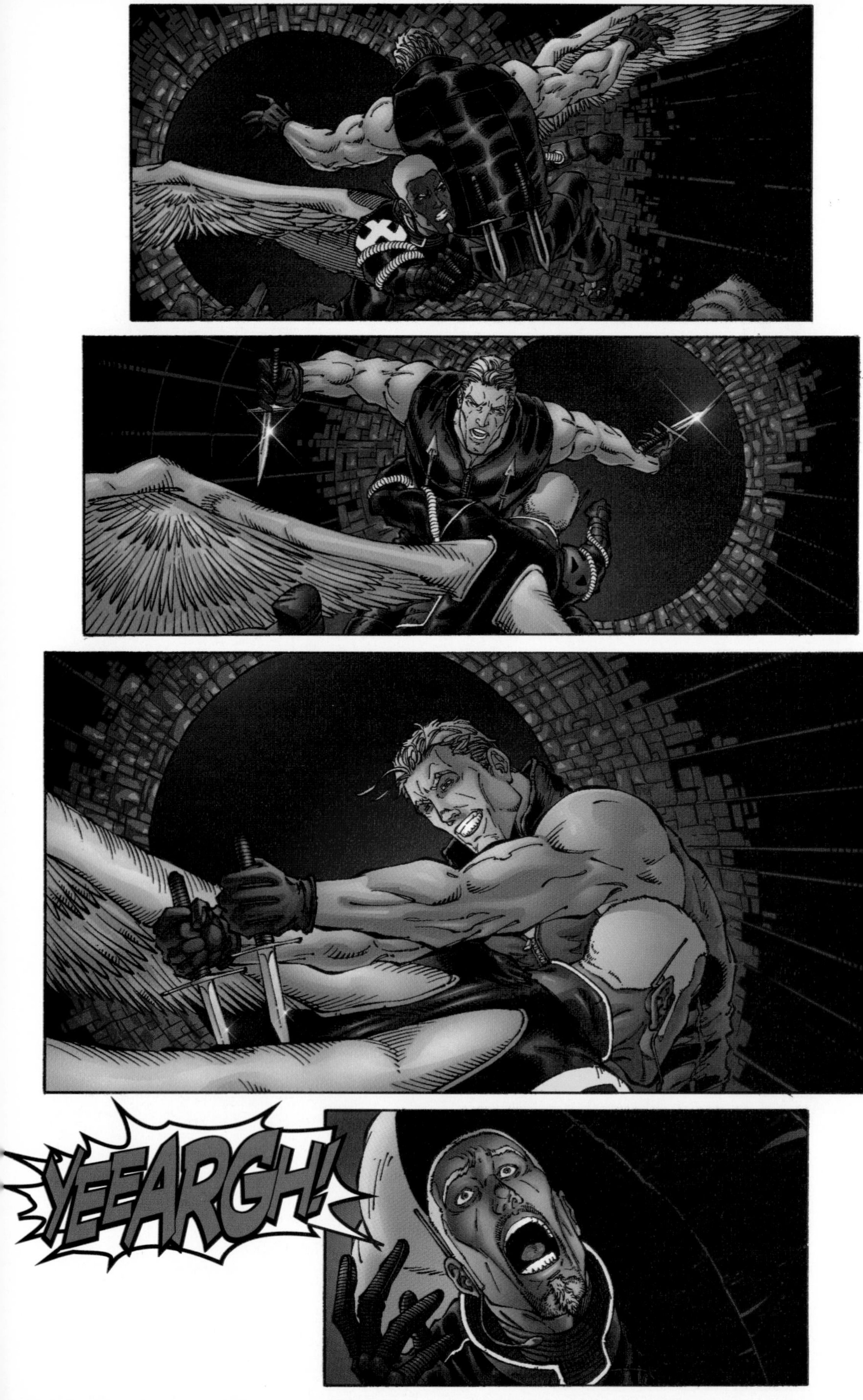
YEEARGH!

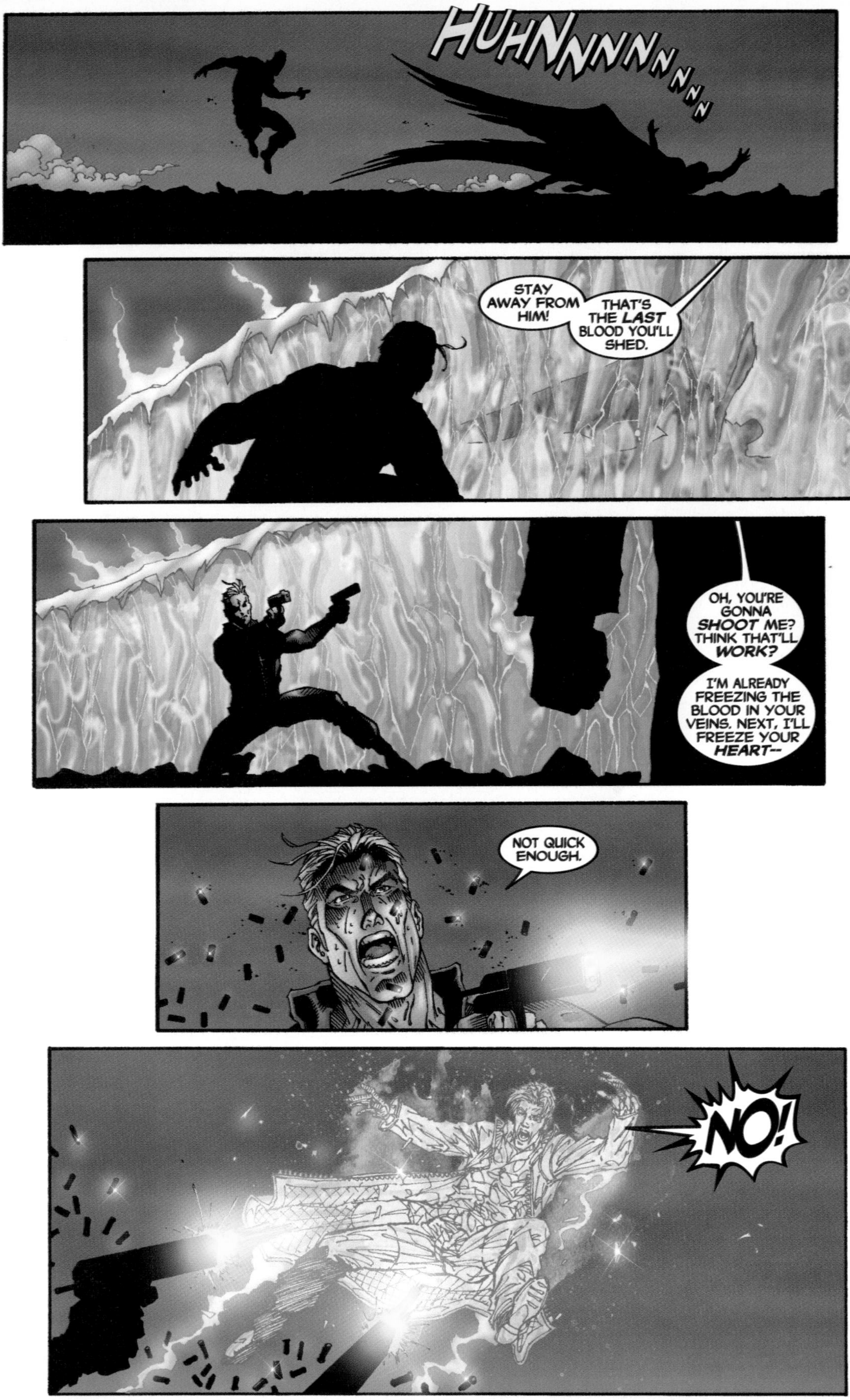
HUHNNNNNNNN
STAY AWAY FROM HIM!
THAT'S THE LAST BLOOD YOU'LL SHED.
OH, YOU'RE GONNA SHOOT ME? THINK THAT'LL WORK?
I'M ALREADY FREEZING THE BLOOD IN YOUR VEINS. NEXT, I'LL FREEZE YOUR HEART--
NOT QUICK ENOUGH.
NO!

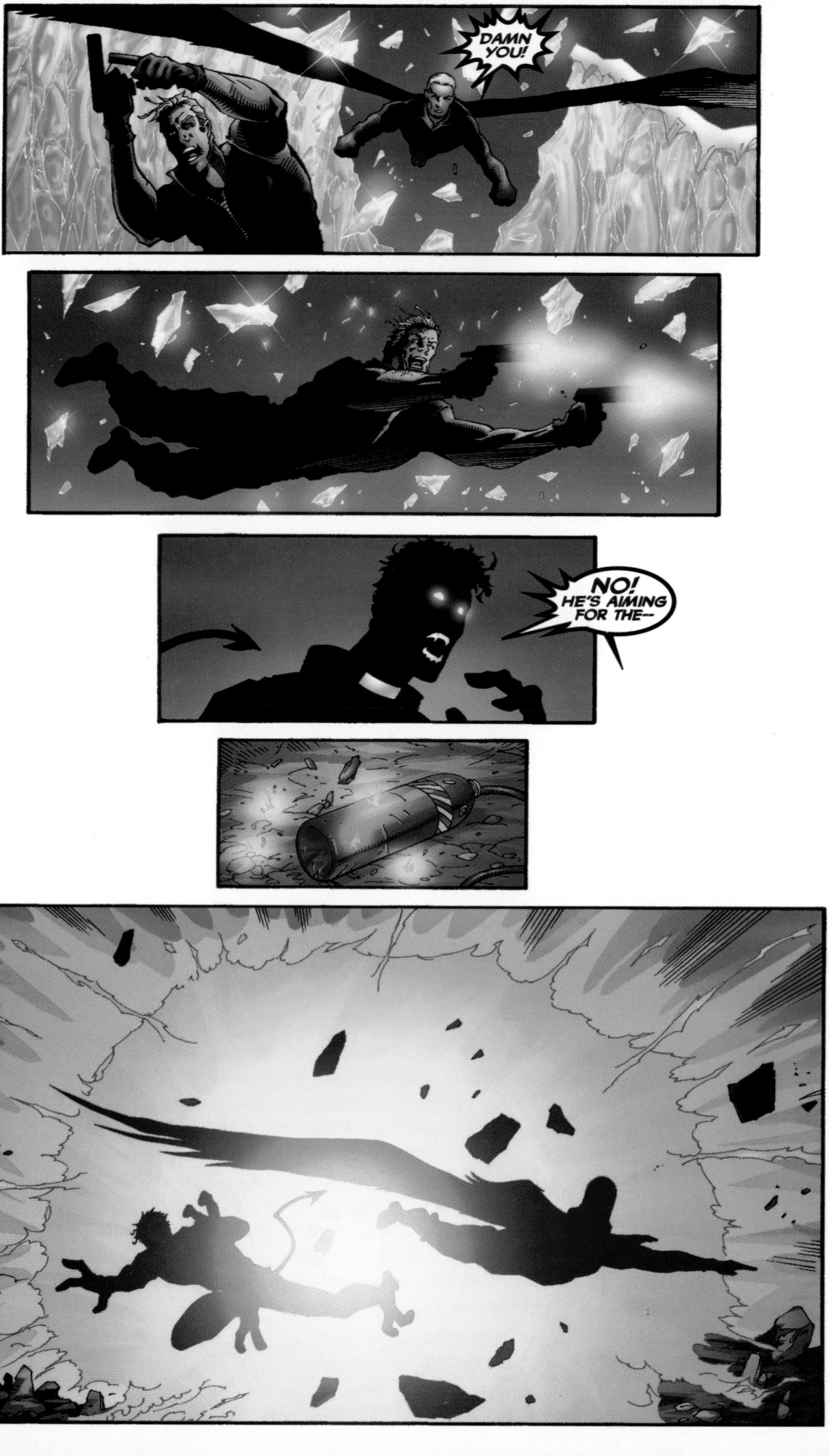
DAMN YOU!
NO! HE'S AIMING FOR THE--

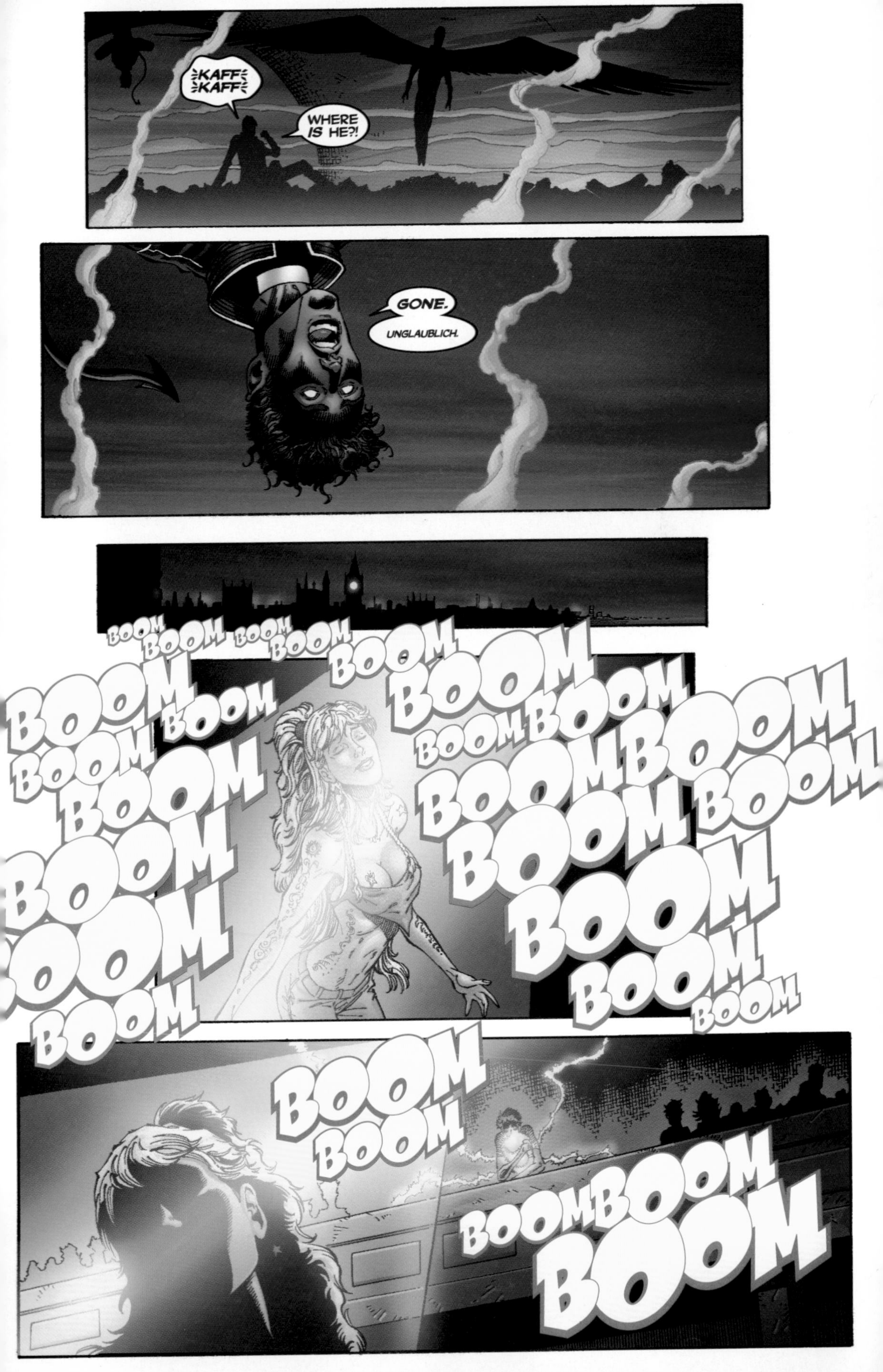
KAFF KAFF
WHERE IS HE?!
GONE.
UNGLAUBLICH.
BOOM BOOM BOOM BOOM
BOOM
BOOM
BOOM
BOOM BOOM
BOOM
BOOM
BOOM
BOOM
BOOM
BOOMBOOM
BOOMBOOM
BOOM BOOM BOOM
BOOM
BOOM
BOOM
BOOM
BOOM
BOOMBOOM
BOOM

HEY, SUGAR... ...WHAT ARE WE DOING HERE?

YOU MEAN, OTHER THAN DANCING THE NIGHT AWAY?

SOME PEOPLE LOOK AT ME LIKE I'M SCUM, OTHERS ARE CONGRATULATING ME.

AND THEY REALLY LOVE YOU.

OF COURSE THEY DO, JON. I'VE BEEN MARKETED THAT WAY.

I'M A FAD. I KNOW THAT. I'VE BEEN SCULPTED TO PLEASE THE RIGHT DEMO AND IT'S MADE US ALL STINKIN' RICH... 'CAUSE THIS FAD IS WHAT'S IN.

IT'S NOT LIKE KIDS HAVE A CHOICE ANYMORE. SIX TRANSNATIONAL CORPORATIONS RUN EVERYTHING NOW. I'M JUST PART OF THE SYSTEM.

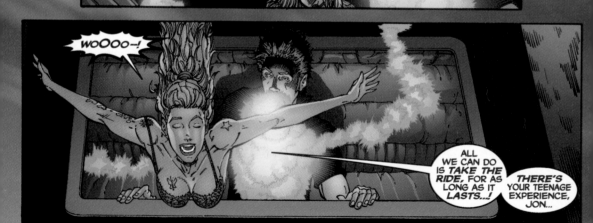

WOOOO~!

ALL WE CAN DO IS TAKE THE RIDE, FOR AS LONG AS IT LASTS...!

THERE'S YOUR TEENAGE EXPERIENCE, JON...

...KINDA PUTS THAT MUTANT THING INTO PERSPECTIVE, EH?

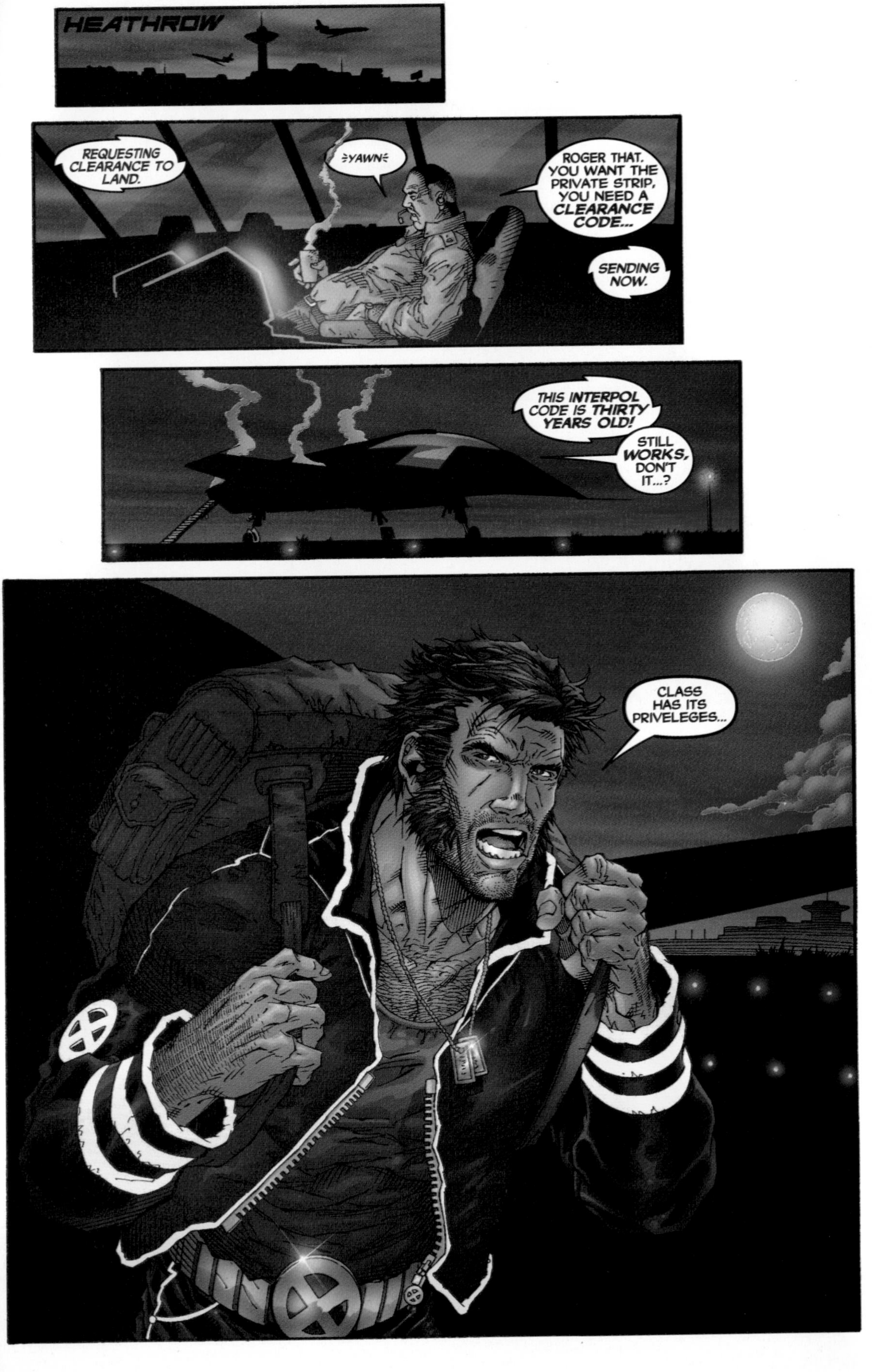
HEATHROW
REQUESTING CLEARANCE TO LAND.
≥YAWN≤
ROGER THAT. YOU WANT THE PRIVATE STRIP, YOU NEED A CLEARANCE CODE...
SENDING NOW.
THIS INTERPOL CODE IS THIRTY YEARS OLD!
STILL WORKS, DON'T IT...?
CLASS HAS ITS PRIVELEGES...

A COMPLETE UNKNOWN

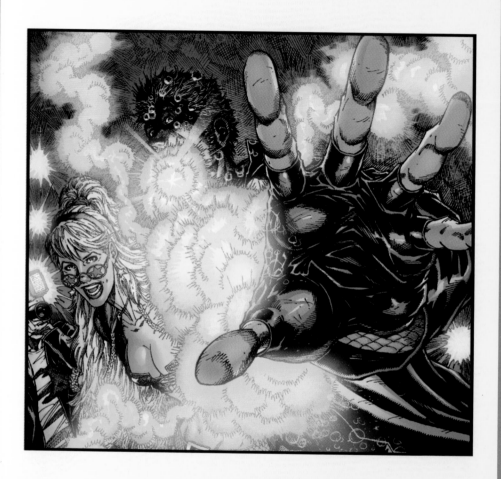

PART FOUR: UNCANNY X-MEN #397

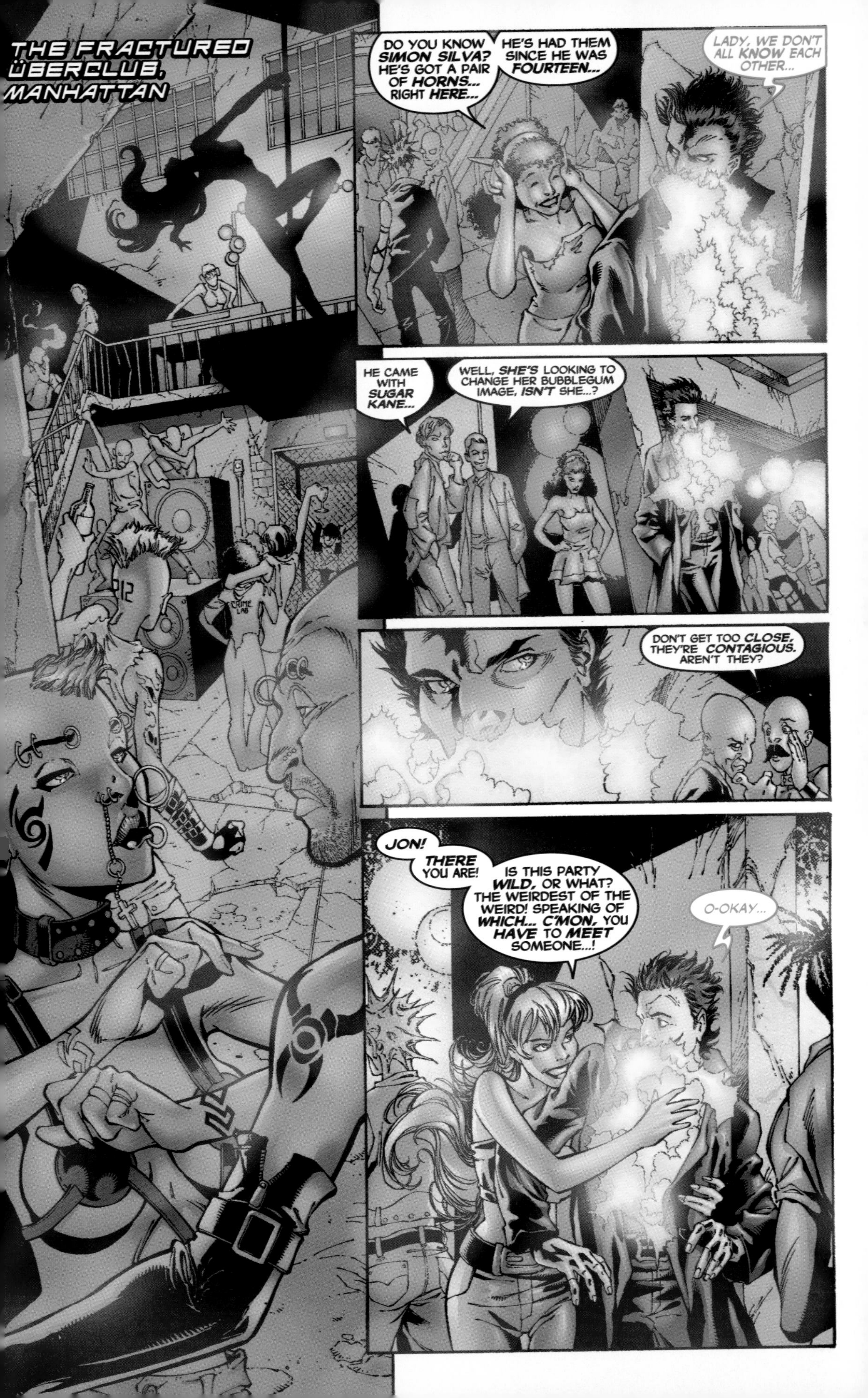
THE FRACTURED ÜBERCLUB, MANHATTAN
DO YOU KNOW SIMON SILVA? HE'S GOT A PAIR OF HORNS... RIGHT HERE...
HE'S HAD THEM SINCE HE WAS FOURTEEN...
LADY, WE DON'T ALL KNOW EACH OTHER...
HE CAME WITH SUGAR KANE...
WELL, SHE'S LOOKING TO CHANGE HER BUBBLEGUM IMAGE, ISN'T SHE...?
DON'T GET TOO CLOSE, THEY'RE CONTAGIOUS. AREN'T THEY?
JON!
THERE YOU ARE!
IS THIS PARTY WILD, OR WHAT? THE WEIRDEST OF THE WEIRD! SPEAKING OF WHICH... C'MON, YOU HAVE TO MEET SOMEONE...!
O-OKAY...

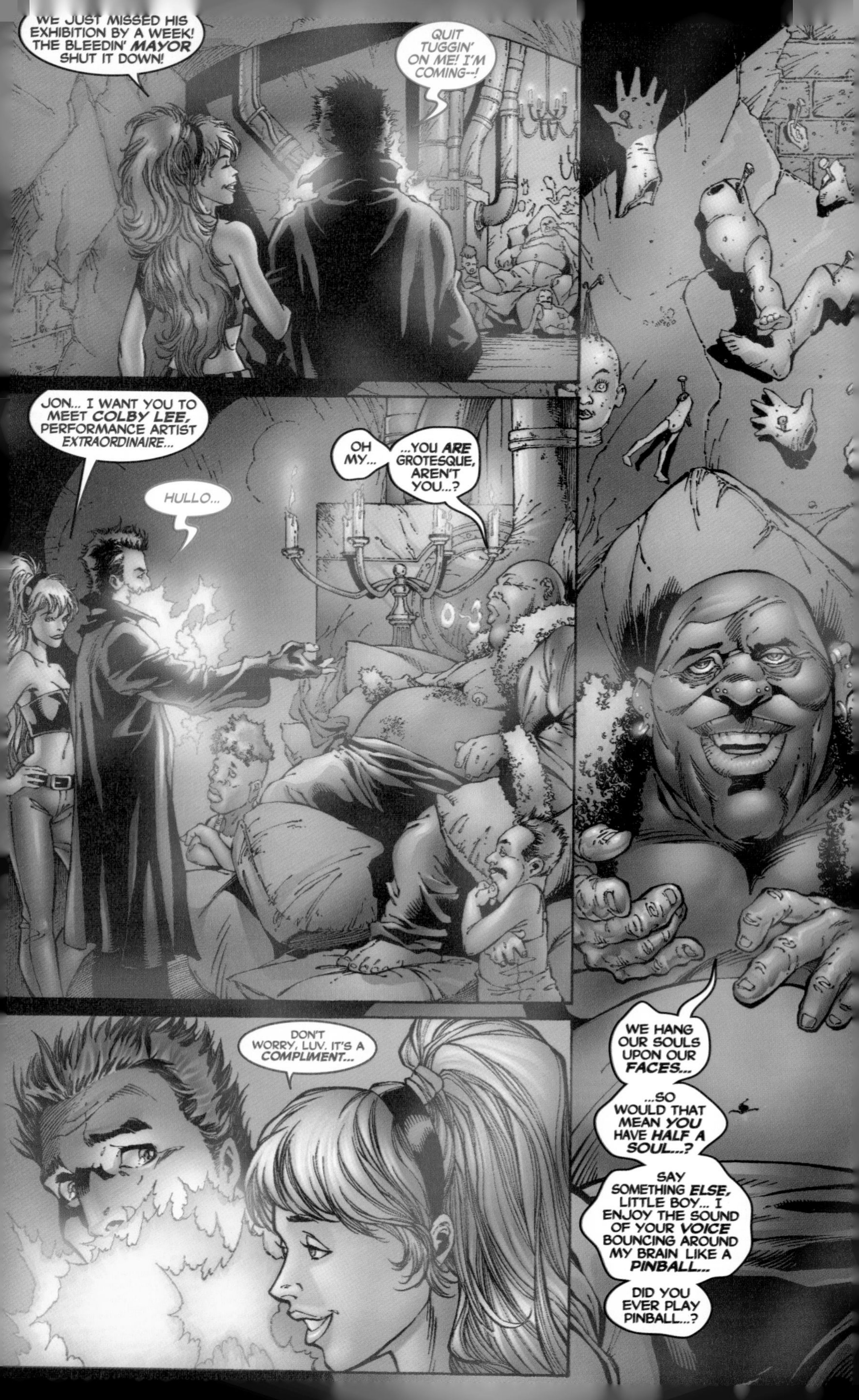
WE JUST MISSED HIS EXHIBITION BY A WEEK! THE BLEEDIN' MAYOR SHUT IT DOWN!
QUIT TUGGIN' ON ME! I'M COMING--!
JON... I WANT YOU TO MEET COLBY LEE, PERFORMANCE ARTIST EXTRAORDINAIRE...
HULLO...
OH MY...
...YOU ARE GROTESQUE, AREN'T YOU...?
DON'T WORRY, LUV. IT'S A COMPLIMENT...
WE HANG OUR SOULS UPON OUR FACES...
...SO WOULD THAT MEAN YOU HAVE HALF A SOUL...?
SAY SOMETHING ELSE, LITTLE BOY... I ENJOY THE SOUND OF YOUR VOICE BOUNCING AROUND MY BRAIN LIKE A PINBALL...
DID YOU EVER PLAY PINBALL...?

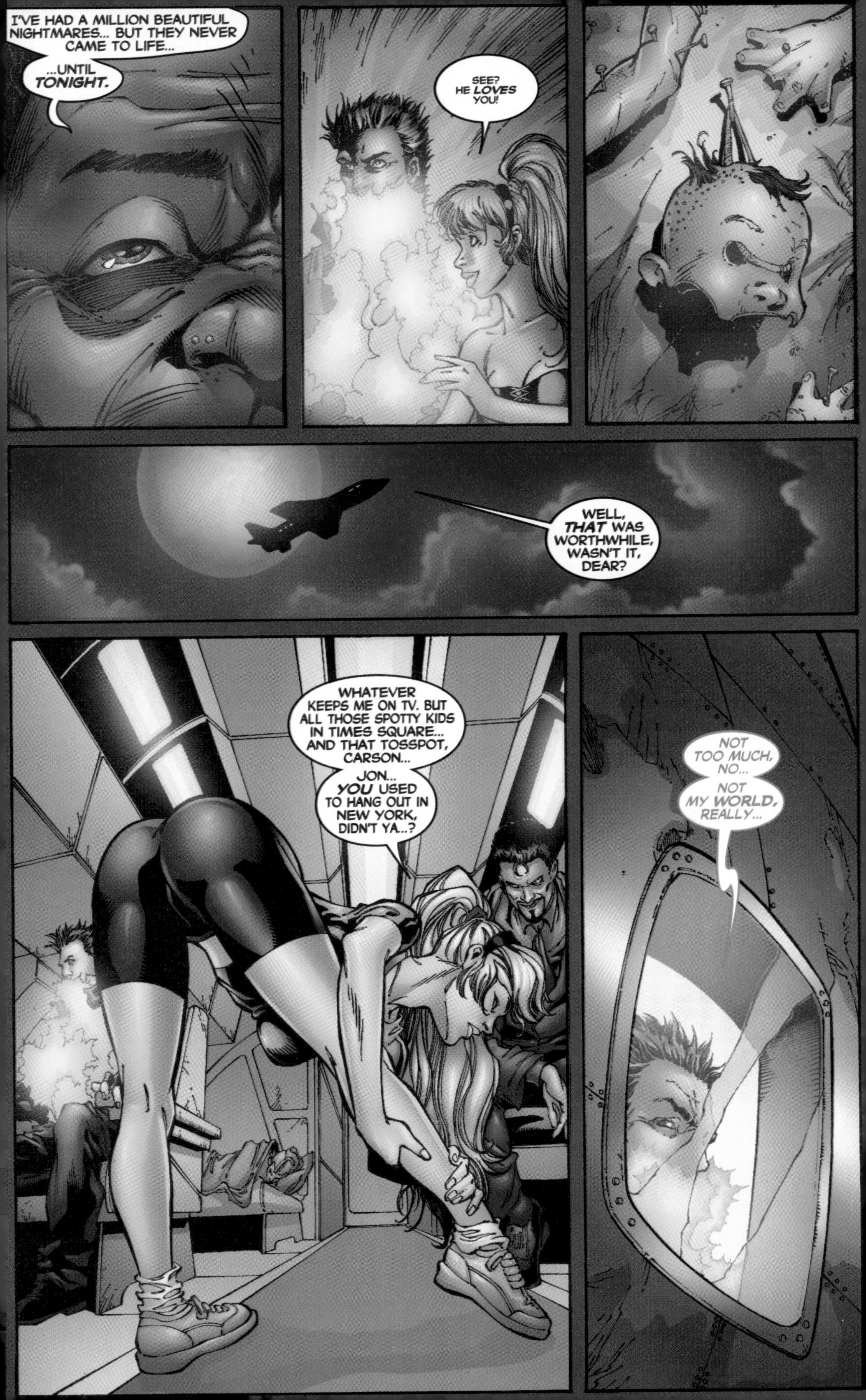

I'VE HAD A MILLION BEAUTIFUL NIGHTMARES... BUT THEY NEVER CAME TO LIFE...
...UNTIL TONIGHT.
SEE? HE LOVES YOU!
WELL, THAT WAS WORTHWHILE, WASN'T IT, DEAR?
WHATEVER KEEPS ME ON TV. BUT ALL THOSE SPOTTY KIDS IN TIMES SQUARE... AND THAT TOSSPOT, CARSON...
JON... YOU USED TO HANG OUT IN NEW YORK, DIDN'T YA...?
NOT TOO MUCH, NO...
NOT MY WORLD, REALLY...

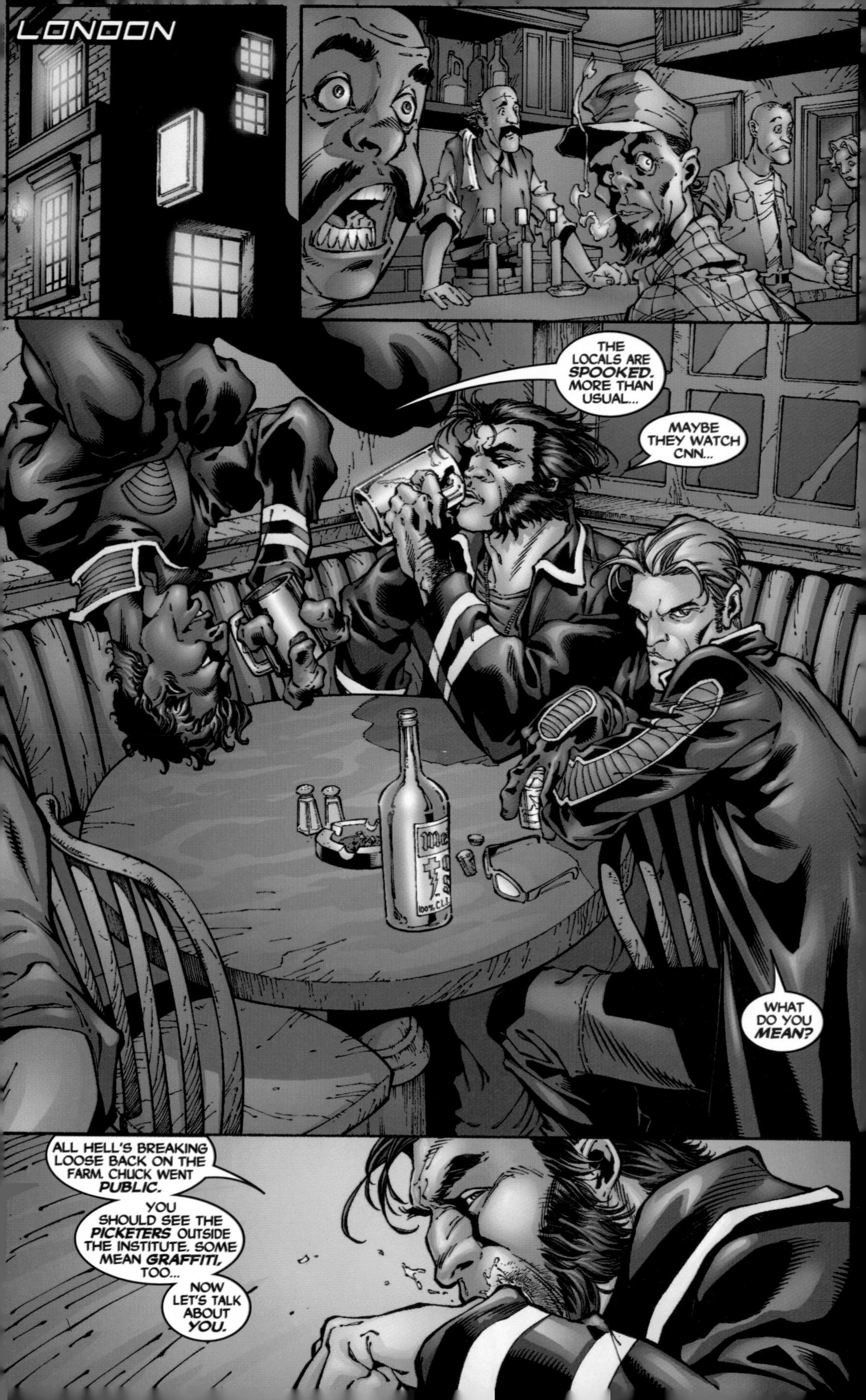
LONDON
THE LOCALS ARE SPOOKED. MORE THAN USUAL...
MAYBE THEY WATCH CNN...
WHAT DO YOU MEAN?
ALL HELL'S BREAKING LOOSE BACK ON THE FARM. CHUCK WENT PUBLIC.
YOU SHOULD SEE THE PICKETERS OUTSIDE THE INSTITUTE. SOME MEAN GRAFFITI, TOO...
NOW LET'S TALK ABOUT YOU.

ONE SECOND, *MEIN FREUND.* ALLOW ME TO CHECK IN...

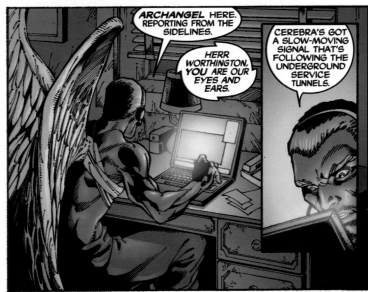

ARCHANGEL HERE. REPORTING FROM THE SIDELINES.

HERR WORTHINGTON, *YOU* ARE OUR EYES AND EARS.

CEREBRA'S GOT A SLOW-MOVING SIGNAL THAT'S FOLLOWING THE UNDERGROUND SERVICE TUNNELS.

THAT'S ALL I NEED TO KNOW, BLONDIE. NOW LOG OFF AND MEET US AT THE NEAREST TRAIN PLATFORM AT DAWN.

THOUGHT YOU'D NEVER ASK.

HE NEEDS TO RECOVER, LOGAN--

HE'S FINE. WE'RE GOIN' LONG AND STRONG.

TELL ME ABOUT *STARSMORE...*

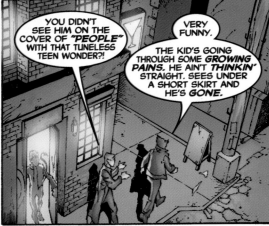

YOU DIDN'T SEE HIM ON THE COVER OF *"PEOPLE"* WITH THAT TUNELESS TEEN WONDER?!

VERY FUNNY.

THE KID'S GOING THROUGH SOME *GROWING PAINS.* HE AIN'T *THINKIN'* STRAIGHT. SEES UNDER A SHORT SKIRT AND HE'S *GONE.*

HE NEEDS SOME GUIDANCE...

...AND I'VE ALREADY GOT HIS *SCENT.*

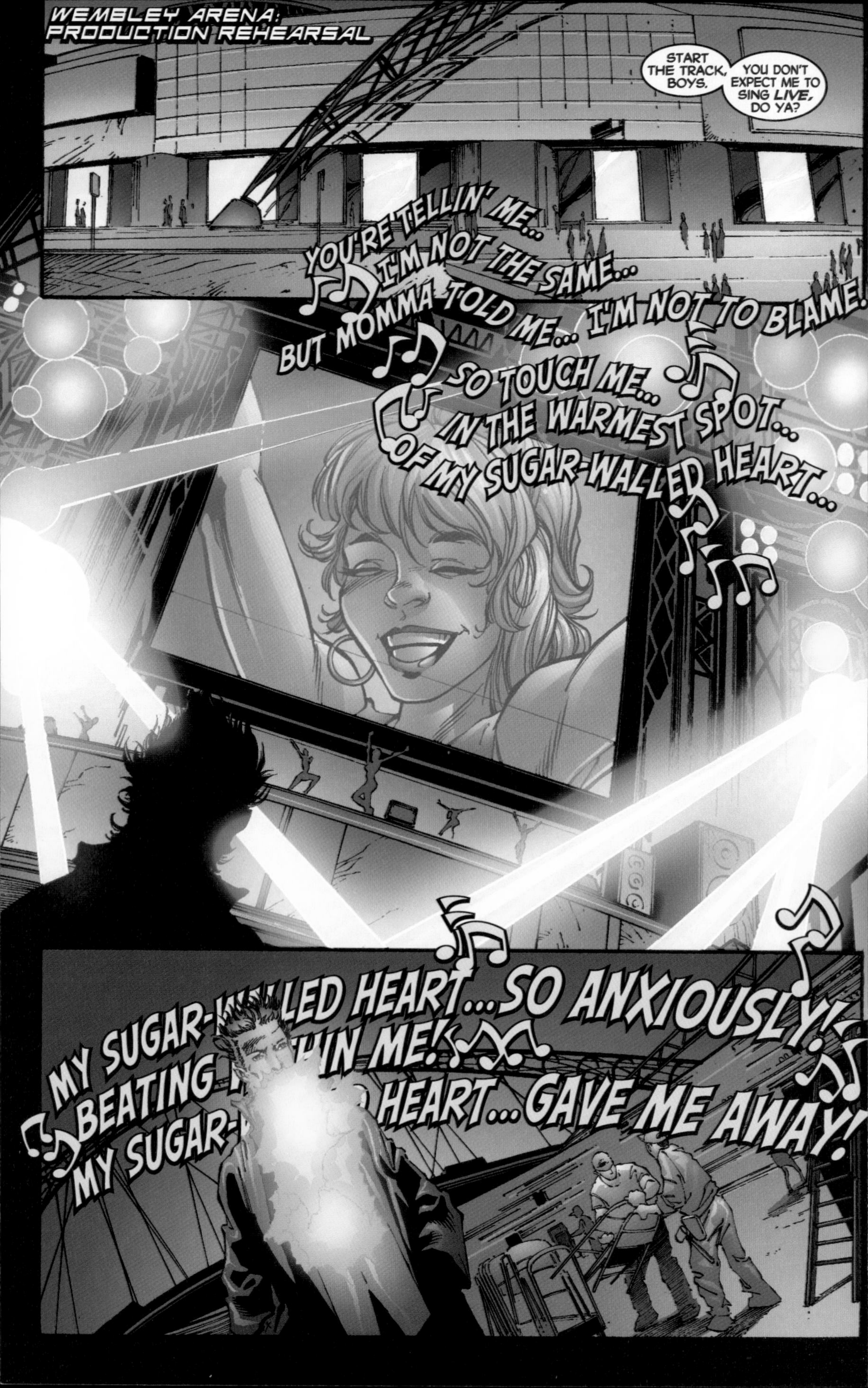
WEMBLEY ARENA: PRODUCTION REHEARSAL
START THE TRACK, BOYS.
YOU DON'T EXPECT ME TO SING LIVE, DO YA?
YOU'RE TELLIN' ME... I'M NOT THE SAME...
BUT MOMMA TOLD ME... I'M NOT TO BLAME!
SO TOUCH ME... IN THE WARMEST SPOT... OF MY SUGAR-WALLED HEART...
LED HEART...SO ANXIOUSLY!
BEATING
IN ME!
MY SUGAR-
HEART...GAVE ME AWAY!

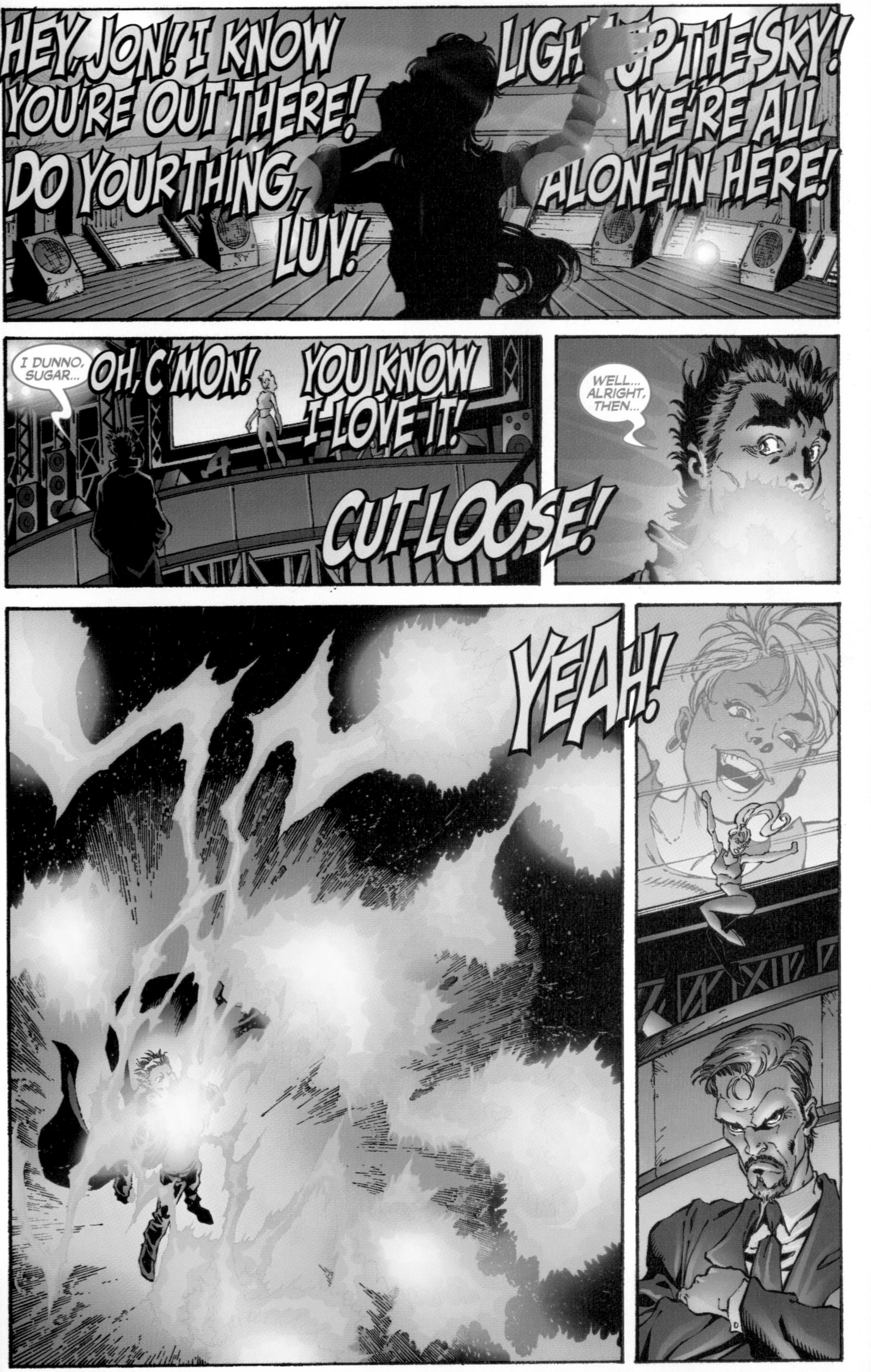
HEY, JON! I KNOW YOU'RE OUT THERE!
DO YOUR THING, LUV!
LIGH UP THE SKY!
WE'RE ALL ALONE IN HERE!
I DUNNO, SUGAR...
OH, C'MON!
YOU KNOW I LOVE IT!
WELL... ALRIGHT, THEN...
CUT LOOSE!
YEAH!

ENJOYING THE RIDE, JON?

EXCUSE ME...?

I CAN *SMELL* YOU ACROSS THE BLEEDIN' *ARENA.* LIKE *TIRES* BURNING...

YOU THINK YOU'RE GETTING A *PIECE* OF ALL THIS...?

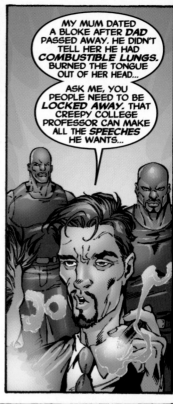

MY MUM DATED A BLOKE AFTER *DAD* PASSED AWAY. HE DIDN'T TELL HER HE HAD *COMBUSTIBLE LUNGS.* BURNED THE TONGUE OUT OF HER HEAD...

ASK ME, YOU PEOPLE NEED TO BE *LOCKED AWAY.* THAT CREEPY COLLEGE PROFESSOR CAN MAKE ALL THE *SPEECHES* HE WANTS...

SUGAR LIKES YOU. SHE'S IN THE *MINORITY* AROUND HERE.

ONLY ONE THING WORSE THAN A *SYCOPHANT...* AND THAT'S A *MUTIE.*

SIM, I--

WE'VE HANDLED SYCOPHANTS BEFORE, HAVEN'T WE, BOYS?

YES, SIR.

WATCH YOUR BACK, KID. PRETTY SOON, IT WON'T *MATTER* WHETHER SUGAR LIKES YOU OR *NOT...*

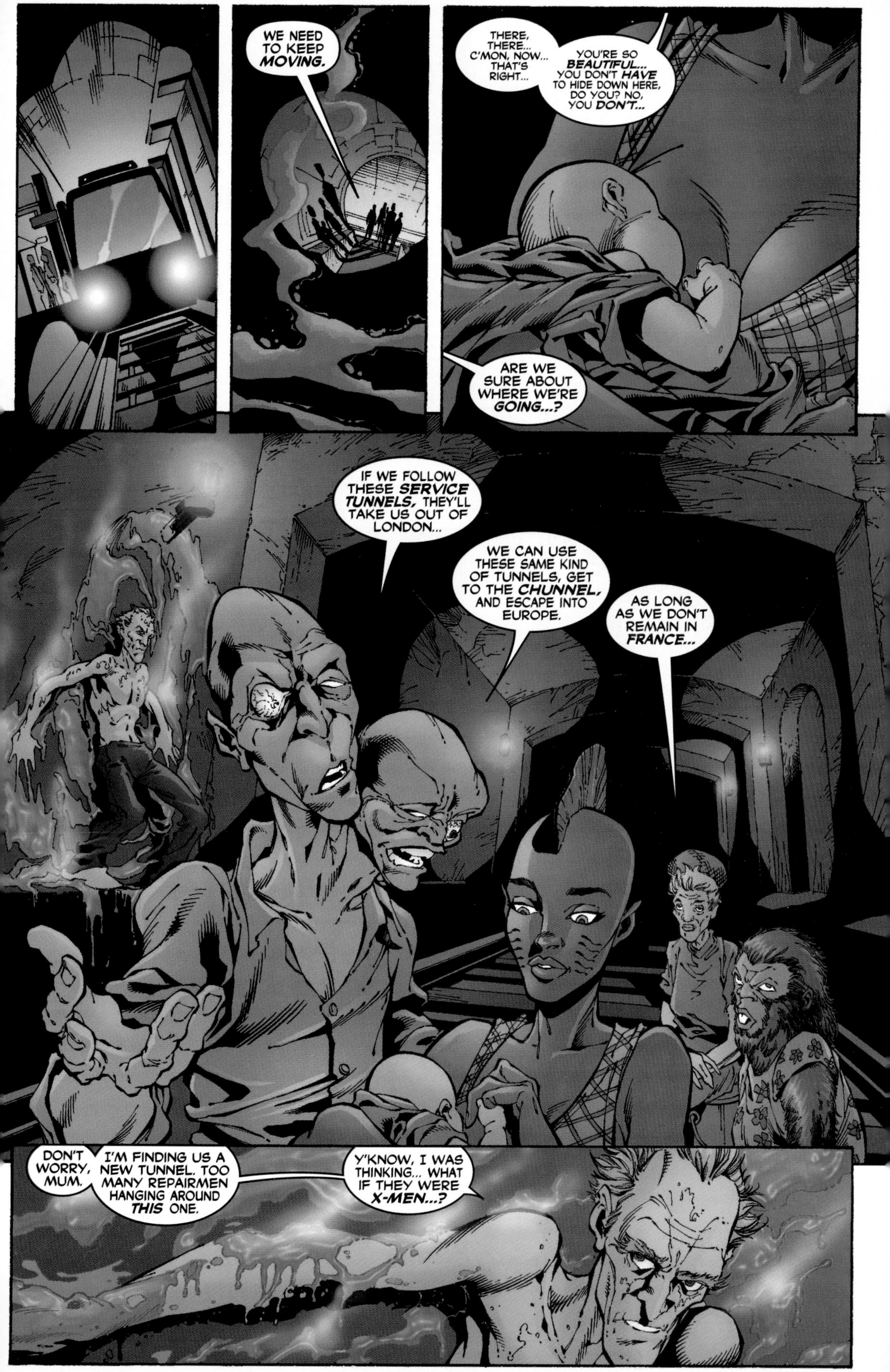
WE NEED TO KEEP *MOVING.*
THERE, THERE... C'MON, NOW... THAT'S RIGHT...
YOU'RE SO *BEAUTIFUL...* YOU DON'T *HAVE* TO HIDE DOWN HERE, DO YOU? NO, YOU *DON'T...*
ARE WE SURE ABOUT WHERE WE'RE *GOING...?*
IF WE FOLLOW THESE *SERVICE TUNNELS,* THEY'LL TAKE US OUT OF LONDON...
WE CAN USE THESE SAME KIND OF TUNNELS, GET TO THE *CHUNNEL,* AND ESCAPE INTO EUROPE.
AS LONG AS WE DON'T REMAIN IN *FRANCE...*
DON'T WORRY, MUM.
I'M FINDING US A NEW TUNNEL. TOO MANY REPAIRMEN HANGING AROUND *THIS* ONE.
Y'KNOW, I WAS THINKING... WHAT IF THEY WERE *X-MEN...?*

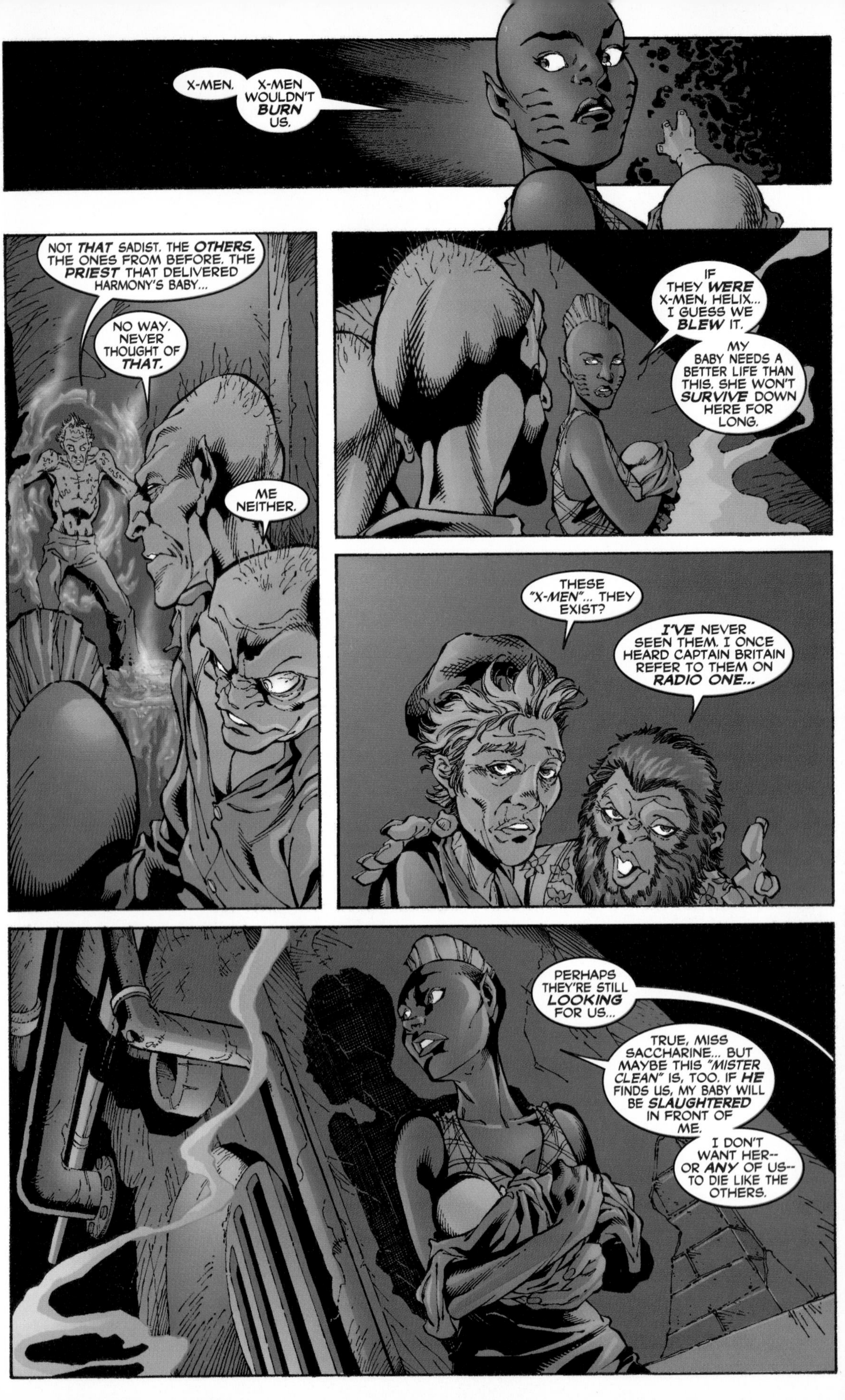
X-MEN.
X-MEN WOULDN'T *BURN* US.
NOT *THAT* SADIST. THE *OTHERS.* THE ONES FROM BEFORE. THE *PRIEST* THAT DELIVERED HARMONY'S BABY...
NO WAY. NEVER THOUGHT OF *THAT.*
ME NEITHER.
IF THEY *WERE* X-MEN, HELIX... I GUESS WE *BLEW* IT.
MY BABY NEEDS A BETTER LIFE THAN THIS. SHE WON'T *SURVIVE* DOWN HERE FOR LONG.
THESE *"X-MEN"*... THEY EXIST?
I'VE NEVER SEEN THEM. I ONCE HEARD CAPTAIN BRITAIN REFER TO THEM ON *RADIO ONE...*
PERHAPS THEY'RE STILL *LOOKING* FOR US...
TRUE, MISS SACCHARINE... BUT MAYBE THIS *"MISTER CLEAN"* IS, TOO. IF *HE* FINDS US, MY BABY WILL BE *SLAUGHTERED* IN FRONT OF ME.
I DON'T WANT HER-- OR *ANY* OF US-- TO DIE LIKE THE OTHERS.

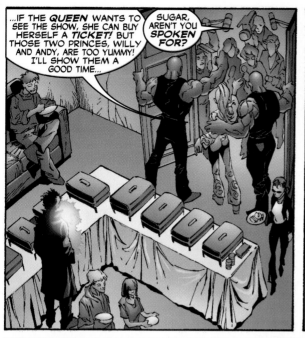

...IF THE *QUEEN* WANTS TO SEE THE SHOW, SHE CAN BUY HERSELF A *TICKET!* BUT THOSE TWO PRINCES, WILLY AND ANDY, ARE TOO YUMMY! I'LL SHOW THEM A GOOD TIME...

SUGAR, AREN'T YOU *SPOKEN FOR?*

WELL, YOU KNOW ME... I'M A GAL WHO KEEPS HER OPTIONS *OPEN...*

BUT YOU WANNA SAY HELLO TO MY LATEST FLAME...?

HE'S GOT STYLISH *GENES*, THAT'S FOR SURE--

LET'S GIVE THE KID A *REST*, SHALL WE, GENTS? SHE'S GOTTA REST THAT *MOUTH* OF HERS...

VERY FUNNY, SIM, MY *MANAGER*, LADIES AND GENTLEMEN...

LET'S SLIDE OUTTA HERE, KITTYCAT.

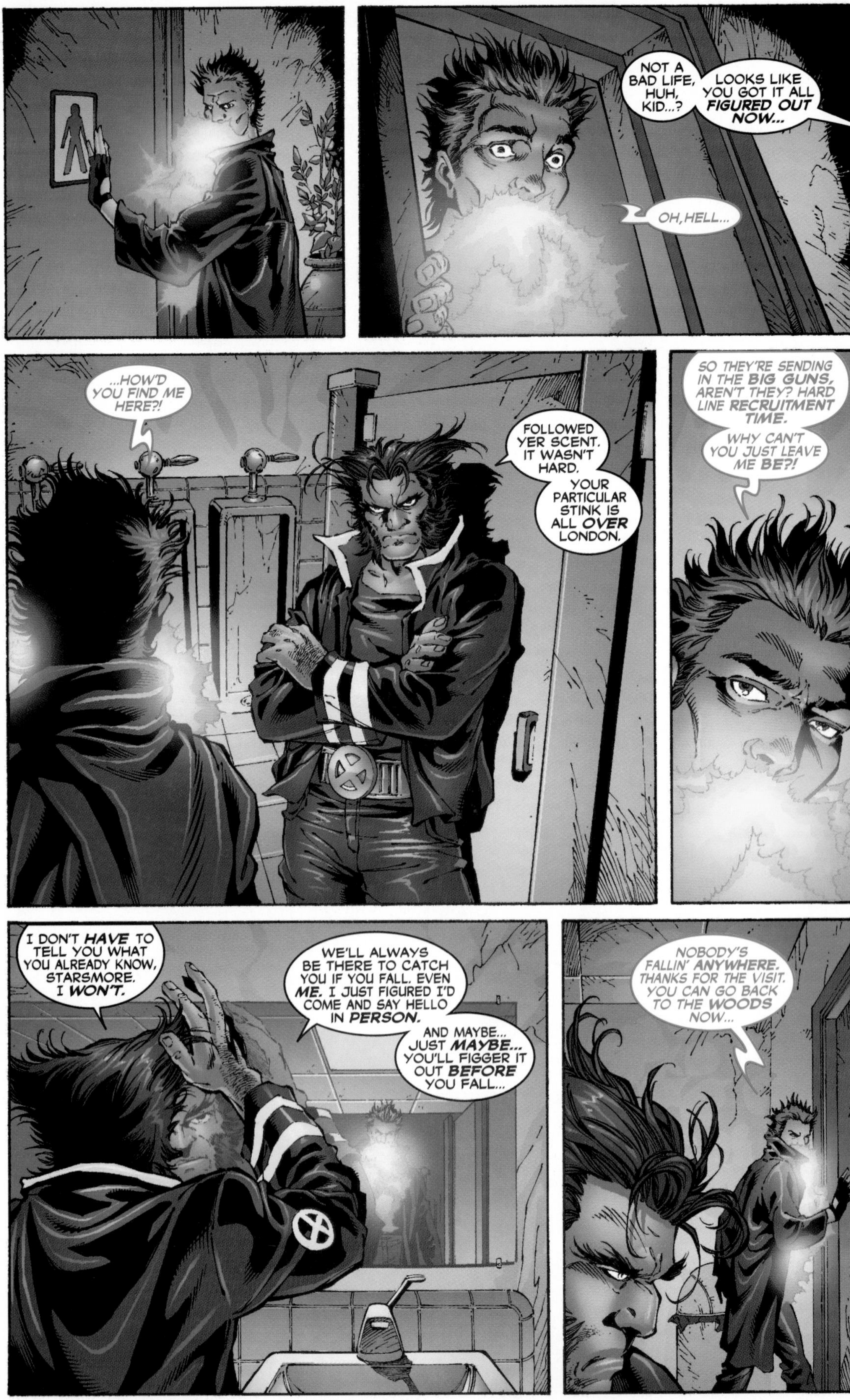
NOT A BAD LIFE, HUH, KID...?
LOOKS LIKE YOU GOT IT ALL FIGURED OUT NOW...
OH, HELL...
...HOW'D YOU FIND ME HERE?!
FOLLOWED YER SCENT. IT WASN'T HARD.
YOUR PARTICULAR STINK IS ALL OVER LONDON.
SO THEY'RE SENDING IN THE BIG GUNS, AREN'T THEY? HARD LINE RECRUITMENT TIME.
WHY CAN'T YOU JUST LEAVE ME BE?!
I DON'T HAVE TO TELL YOU WHAT YOU ALREADY KNOW, STARSMORE. I WON'T.
WE'LL ALWAYS BE THERE TO CATCH YOU IF YOU FALL. EVEN ME. I JUST FIGURED I'D COME AND SAY HELLO IN PERSON.
AND MAYBE... JUST MAYBE... YOU'LL FIGGER IT OUT BEFORE YOU FALL...
NOBODY'S FALLIN' ANYWHERE. THANKS FOR THE VISIT. YOU CAN GO BACK TO THE WOODS NOW...

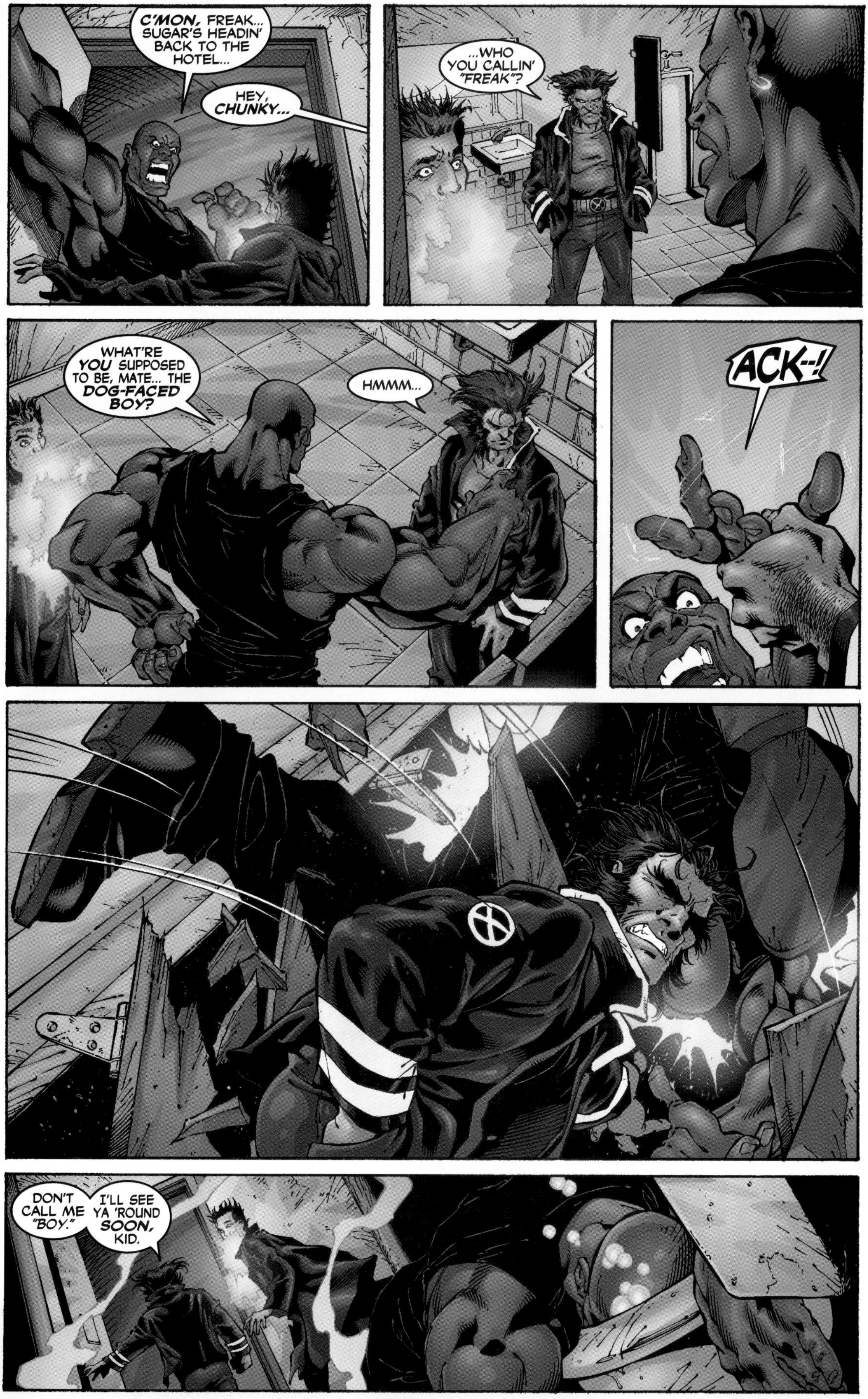
C'MON, FREAK... SUGAR'S HEADIN' BACK TO THE HOTEL...
HEY, CHUNKY...
...WHO YOU CALLIN' "FREAK"?
WHAT'RE YOU SUPPOSED TO BE, MATE... THE DOG-FACED BOY?
HMMM...
ACK--!
DON'T CALL ME "BOY."
I'LL SEE YA 'ROUND SOON, KID.

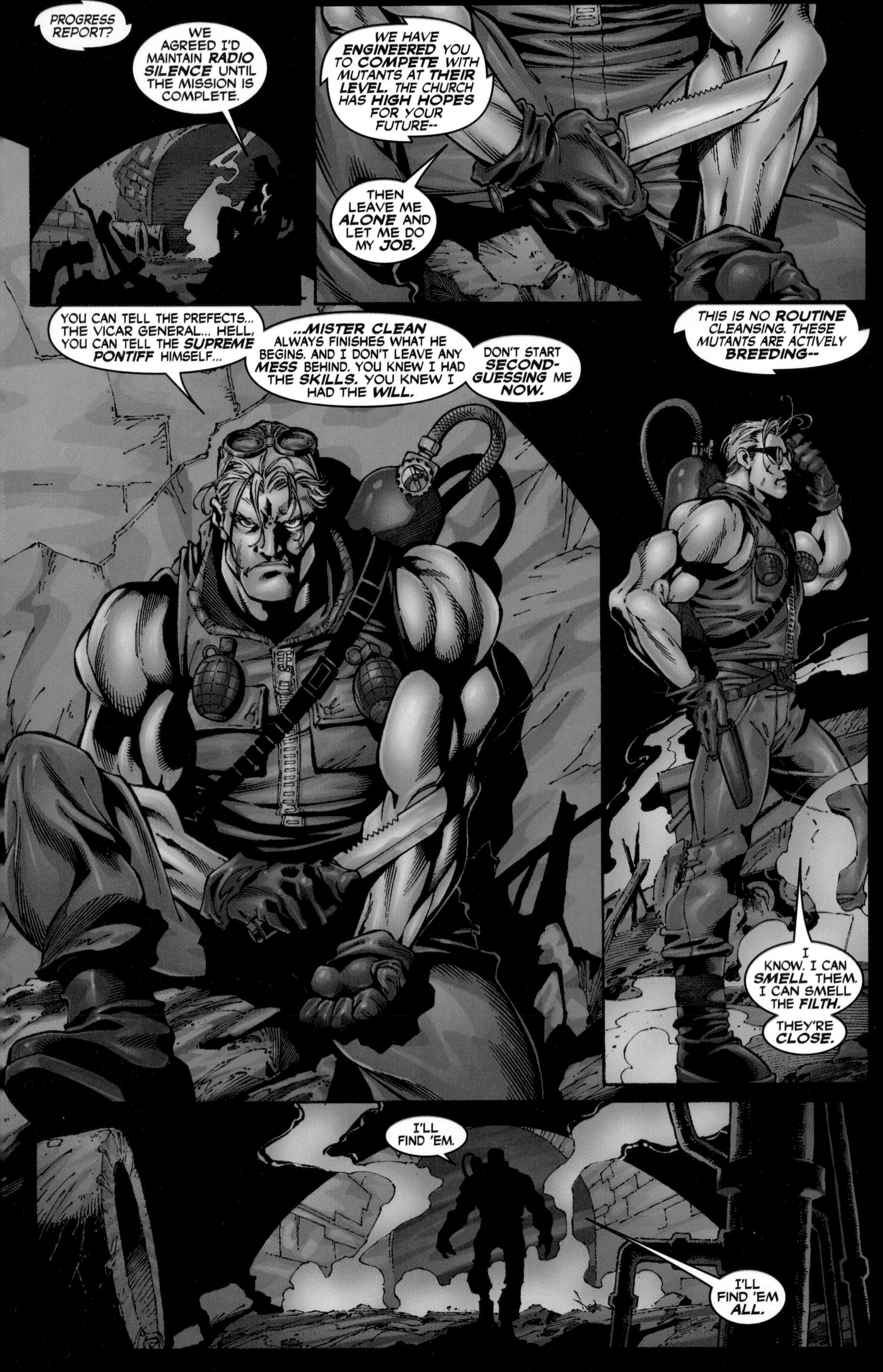
PROGRESS REPORT?
WE AGREED I'D MAINTAIN RADIO SILENCE UNTIL THE MISSION IS COMPLETE.
WE HAVE ENGINEERED YOU TO COMPETE WITH MUTANTS AT THEIR LEVEL. THE CHURCH HAS HIGH HOPES FOR YOUR FUTURE--
THEN LEAVE ME ALONE AND LET ME DO MY JOB.
YOU CAN TELL THE PREFECTS... THE VICAR GENERAL... HELL, YOU CAN TELL THE SUPREME PONTIFF HIMSELF...
...MISTER CLEAN ALWAYS FINISHES WHAT HE BEGINS, AND I DON'T LEAVE ANY MESS BEHIND. YOU KNEW I HAD THE SKILLS. YOU KNEW I HAD THE WILL.
DON'T START SECOND-GUESSING ME NOW.
THIS IS NO ROUTINE CLEANSING. THESE MUTANTS ARE ACTIVELY BREEDING--
I KNOW. I CAN SMELL THEM. I CAN SMELL THE FILTH.
THEY'RE CLOSE.
I'LL FIND 'EM.
I'LL FIND 'EM ALL.

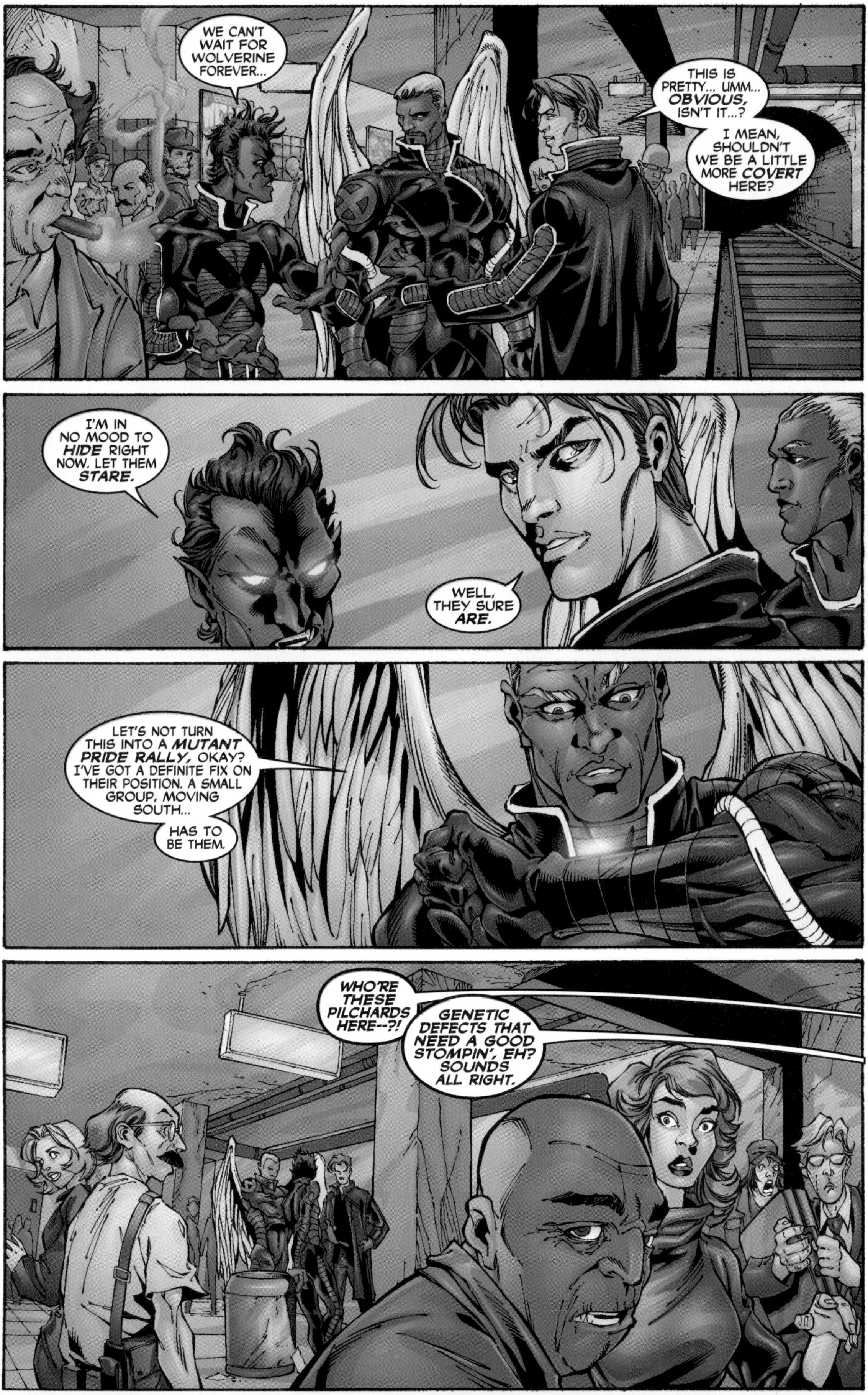
WE CAN'T WAIT FOR WOLVERINE FOREVER...
THIS IS PRETTY... UMM... OBVIOUS, ISN'T IT...?
I MEAN, SHOULDN'T WE BE A LITTLE MORE COVERT HERE?
I'M IN NO MOOD TO HIDE RIGHT NOW. LET THEM STARE.
WELL, THEY SURE ARE.
LET'S NOT TURN THIS INTO A MUTANT PRIDE RALLY, OKAY? I'VE GOT A DEFINITE FIX ON THEIR POSITION. A SMALL GROUP, MOVING SOUTH...
HAS TO BE THEM.
WHO'RE THESE PILCHARDS HERE--?!
GENETIC DEFECTS THAT NEED A GOOD STOMPIN', EH? SOUNDS ALL RIGHT.

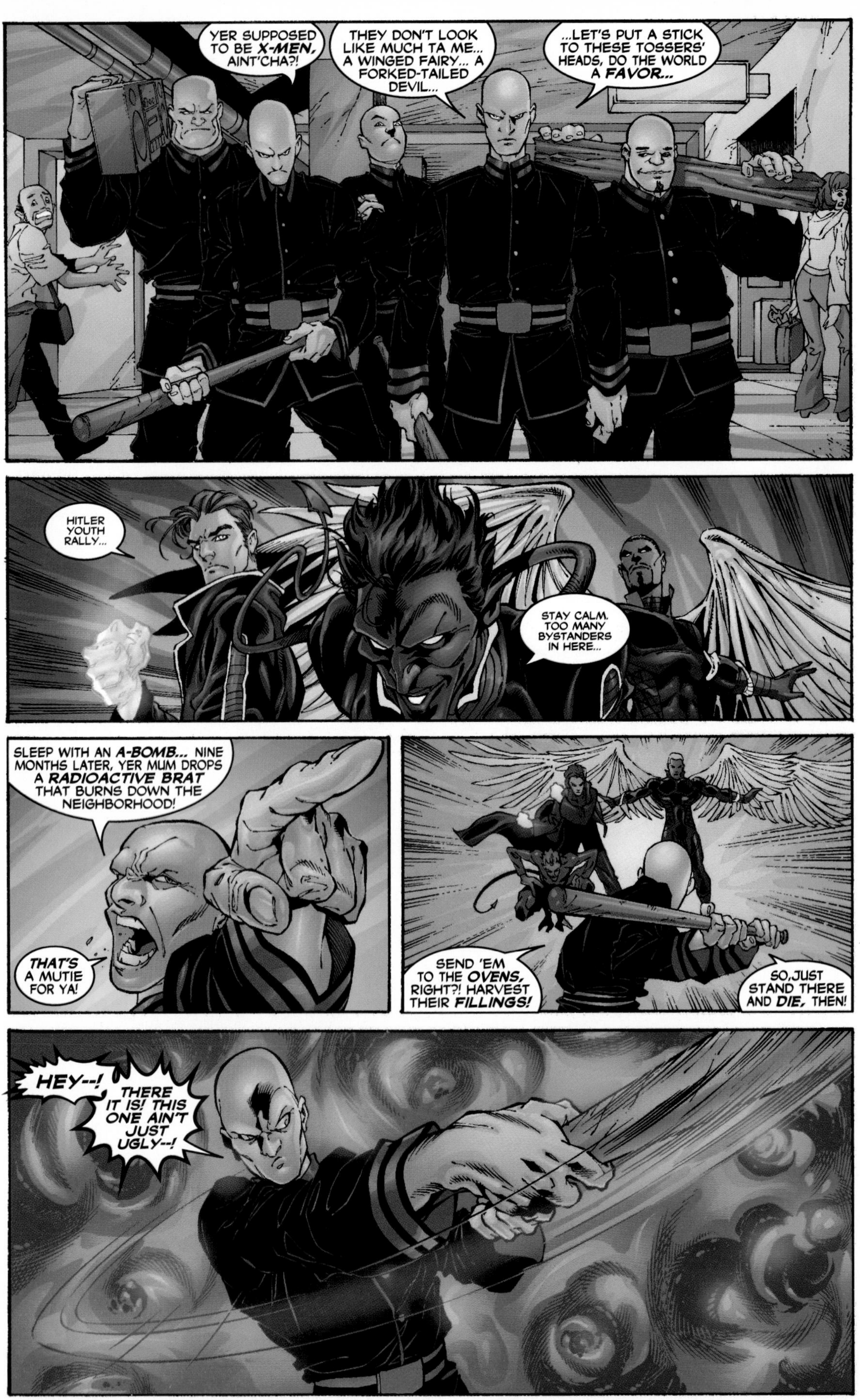
YER SUPPOSED TO BE X-MEN, AINT'CHA?!
THEY DON'T LOOK LIKE MUCH TA ME... A WINGED FAIRY... A FORKED-TAILED DEVIL...
...LET'S PUT A STICK TO THESE TOSSERS' HEADS, DO THE WORLD A FAVOR...
HITLER YOUTH RALLY...
STAY CALM. TOO MANY BYSTANDERS IN HERE...
SLEEP WITH AN A-BOMB... NINE MONTHS LATER, YER MUM DROPS A RADIOACTIVE BRAT THAT BURNS DOWN THE NEIGHBORHOOD!
THAT'S A MUTIE FOR YA!
SEND 'EM TO THE OVENS, RIGHT?! HARVEST THEIR FILLINGS!
SO, JUST STAND THERE AND DIE, THEN!
HEY--!
THERE IT IS! THIS ONE AIN'T JUST UGLY--!

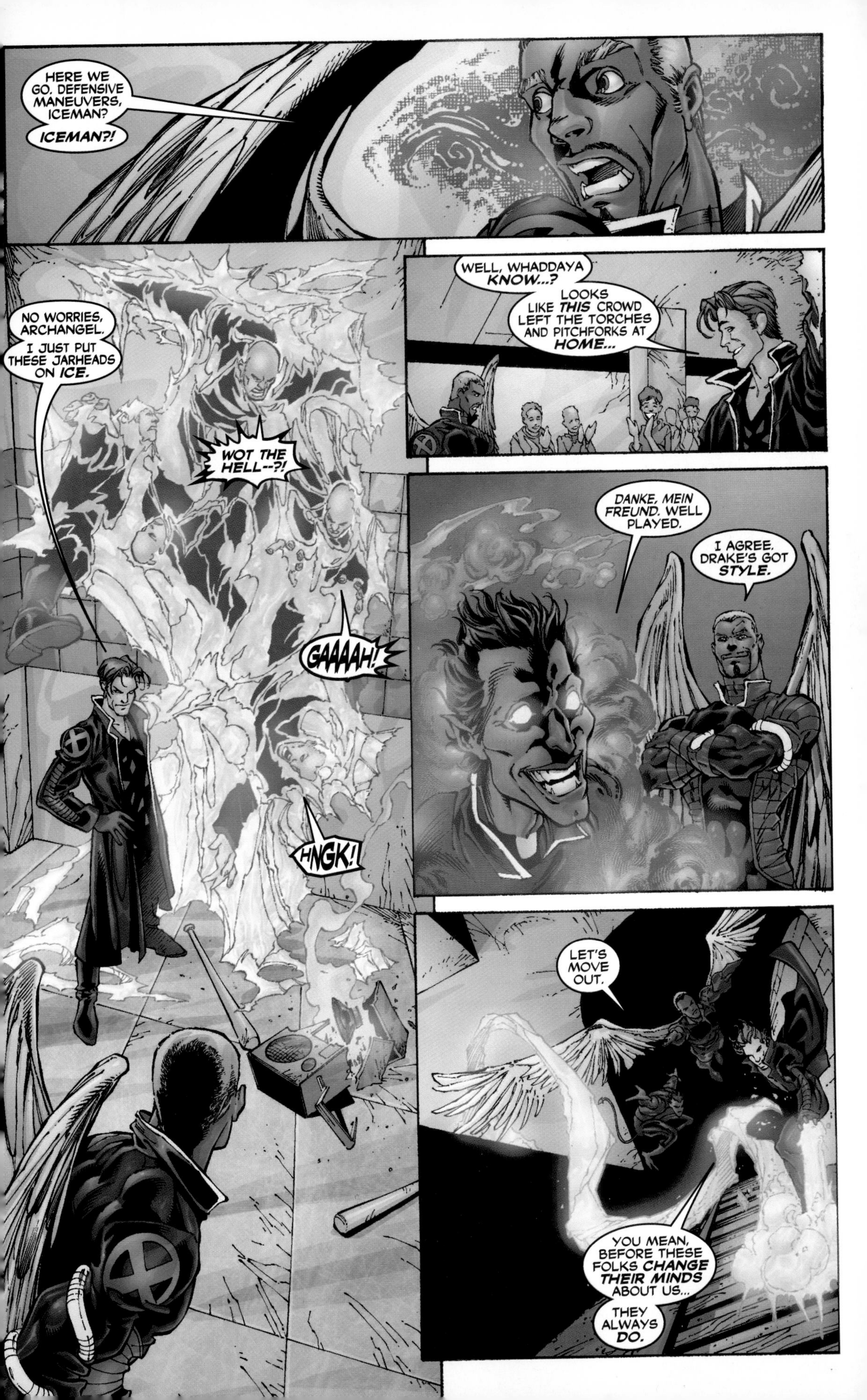
HERE WE GO. DEFENSIVE MANEUVERS, ICEMAN? ICEMAN?!
NO WORRIES, ARCHANGEL.
I JUST PUT THESE JARHEADS ON ICE.
WOT THE HELL--?!
GAAAAH!
HNGK!
WELL, WHADDAYA KNOW...?
LOOKS LIKE THIS CROWD LEFT THE TORCHES AND PITCHFORKS AT HOME...
DANKE, MEIN FREUND. WELL PLAYED.
I AGREE. DRAKE'S GOT STYLE.
LET'S MOVE OUT.
YOU MEAN, BEFORE THESE FOLKS CHANGE THEIR MINDS ABOUT US...
THEY ALWAYS DO.

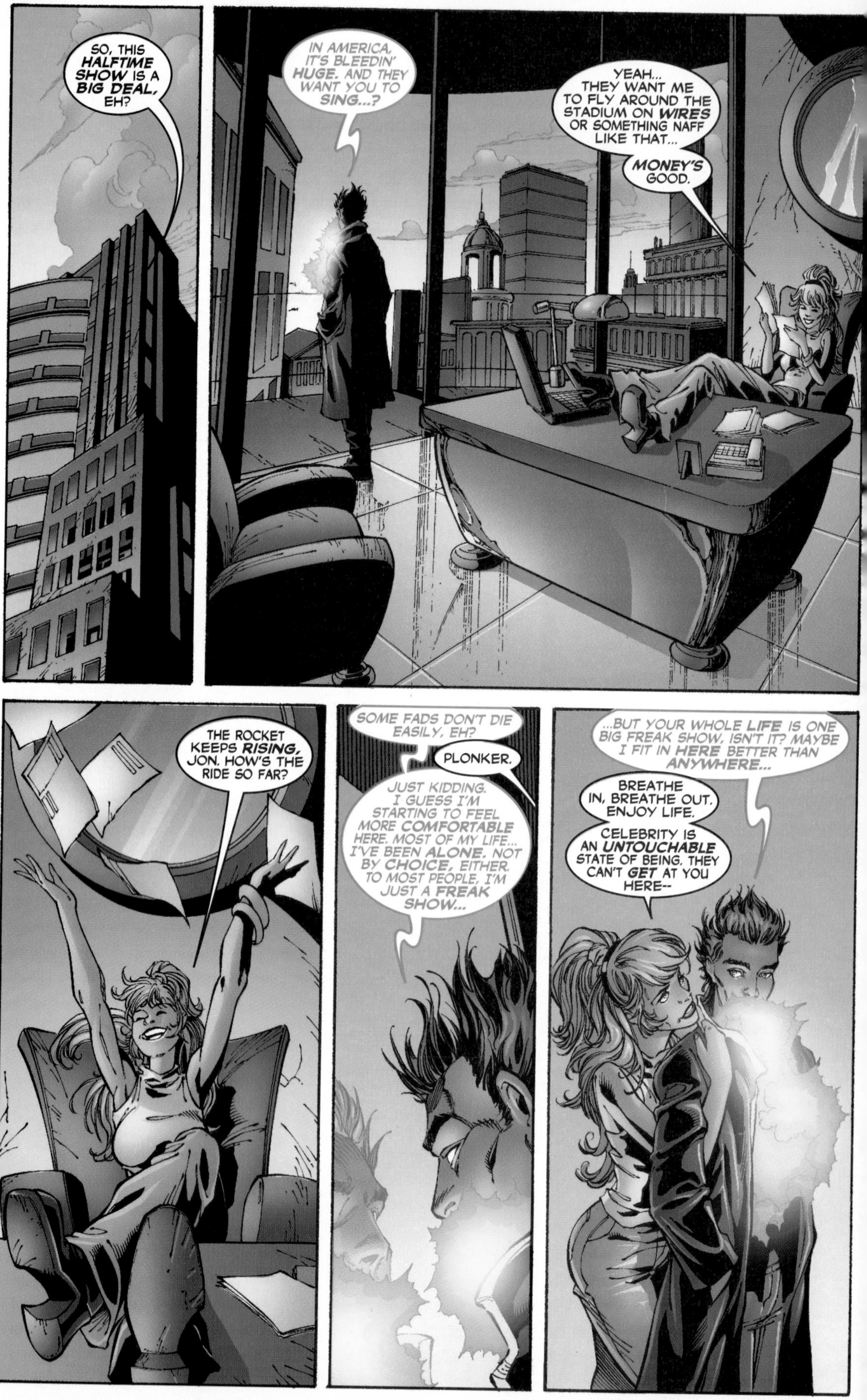
SO, THIS HALFTIME SHOW IS A BIG DEAL, EH?
IN AMERICA, IT'S BLEEDIN' HUGE. AND THEY WANT YOU TO SING...?
YEAH... THEY WANT ME TO FLY AROUND THE STADIUM ON WIRES OR SOMETHING NAFF LIKE THAT...
MONEY'S GOOD.
THE ROCKET KEEPS RISING, JON. HOW'S THE RIDE SO FAR?
SOME FADS DON'T DIE EASILY, EH?
PLONKER.
JUST KIDDING. I GUESS I'M STARTING TO FEEL MORE COMFORTABLE HERE. MOST OF MY LIFE... I'VE BEEN ALONE. NOT BY CHOICE, EITHER. TO MOST PEOPLE, I'M JUST A FREAK SHOW...
...BUT YOUR WHOLE LIFE IS ONE BIG FREAK SHOW, ISN'T IT? MAYBE I FIT IN HERE BETTER THAN ANYWHERE...
BREATHE IN, BREATHE OUT. ENJOY LIFE.
CELEBRITY IS AN UNTOUCHABLE STATE OF BEING. THEY CAN'T GET AT YOU HERE--

BLOODY HELL! WE'RE DONE FOR!

SIM! WHAT THE HELL HAVE YOU GOT YOUR KNICKERS IN A WAD FOR?!

HERE'S WHY!

YOU COULDN'T STAY OUT OF THIS *MONSTROSITY'S* PANTS AND *NOW* THEY'RE OUT TO *CRUCIFY* YOU!

I *TOLD* YOU NO GOOD WOULD COME OF THIS!

SOD OFF, SIM! THEY'VE BEEN ON MY CASE ABOUT THIS SINCE *DAY ONE!* IT'S BEEN GOOD FOR *BUSINESS,* HASN'T IT?!

WHAT'S SO DIFFERENT ABOUT THIS--

The Planet

SE EXCLUSIVE!

SUGA
PREGNA
WITH MUTANT'S
BABY!
HER OB/S
OUT

HIFI HOODLUMS DISRUPT POWERS WEDDING!!!

CRIMELAB STUDIOS JURIST

OH.

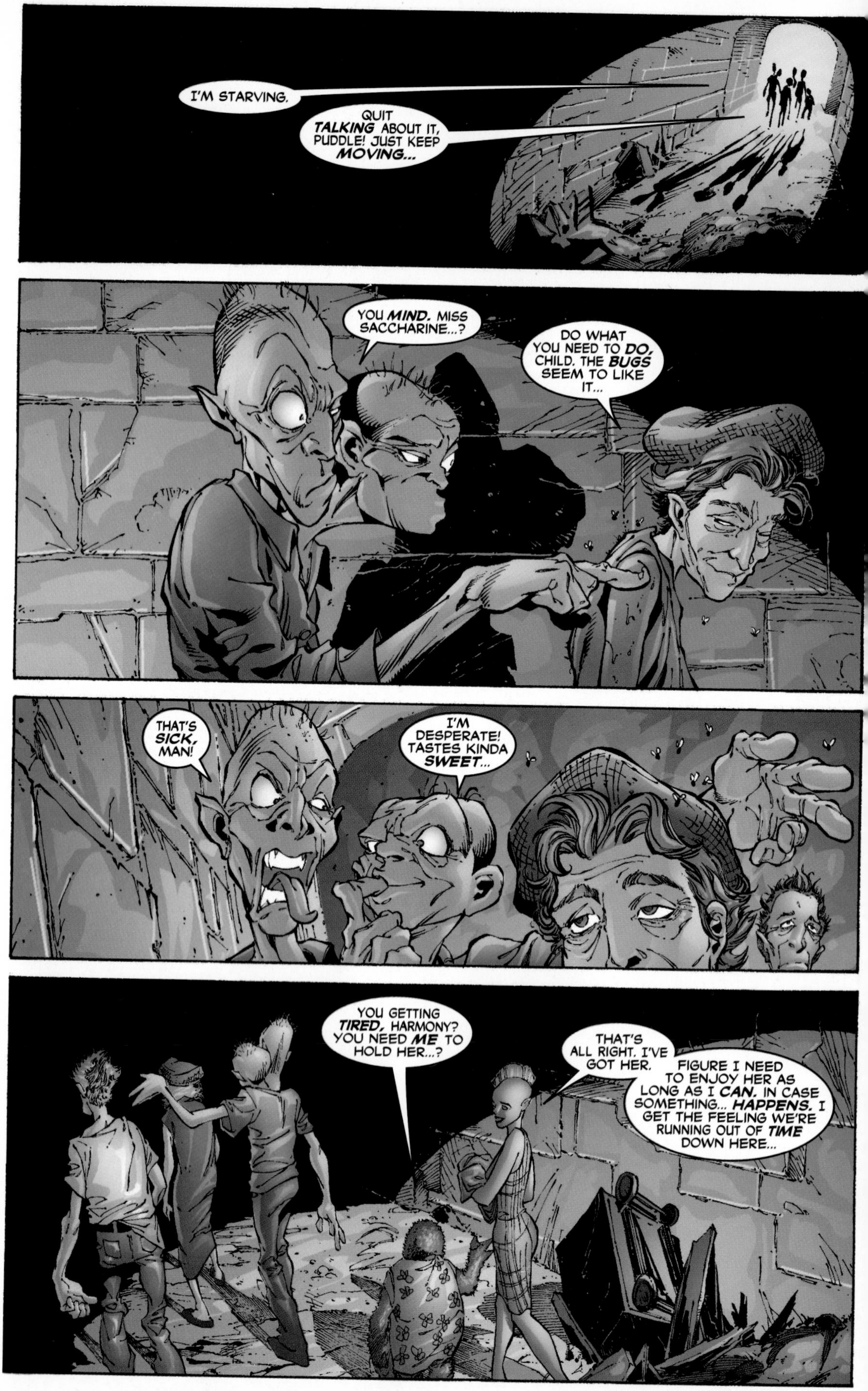
I'M STARVING.
QUIT *TALKING* ABOUT IT, PUDDLE! JUST KEEP *MOVING...*
YOU *MIND*, MISS SACCHARINE...?
DO WHAT YOU NEED TO *DO*, CHILD. THE *BUGS* SEEM TO LIKE IT...
THAT'S *SICK*, MAN!
I'M DESPERATE! TASTES KINDA *SWEET*...
YOU GETTING *TIRED*, HARMONY? YOU NEED *ME* TO HOLD HER...?
THAT'S ALL RIGHT. I'VE GOT HER.
FIGURE I NEED TO ENJOY HER AS LONG AS I *CAN*. IN CASE SOMETHING... *HAPPENS*. I GET THE FEELING WE'RE RUNNING OUT OF *TIME* DOWN HERE...

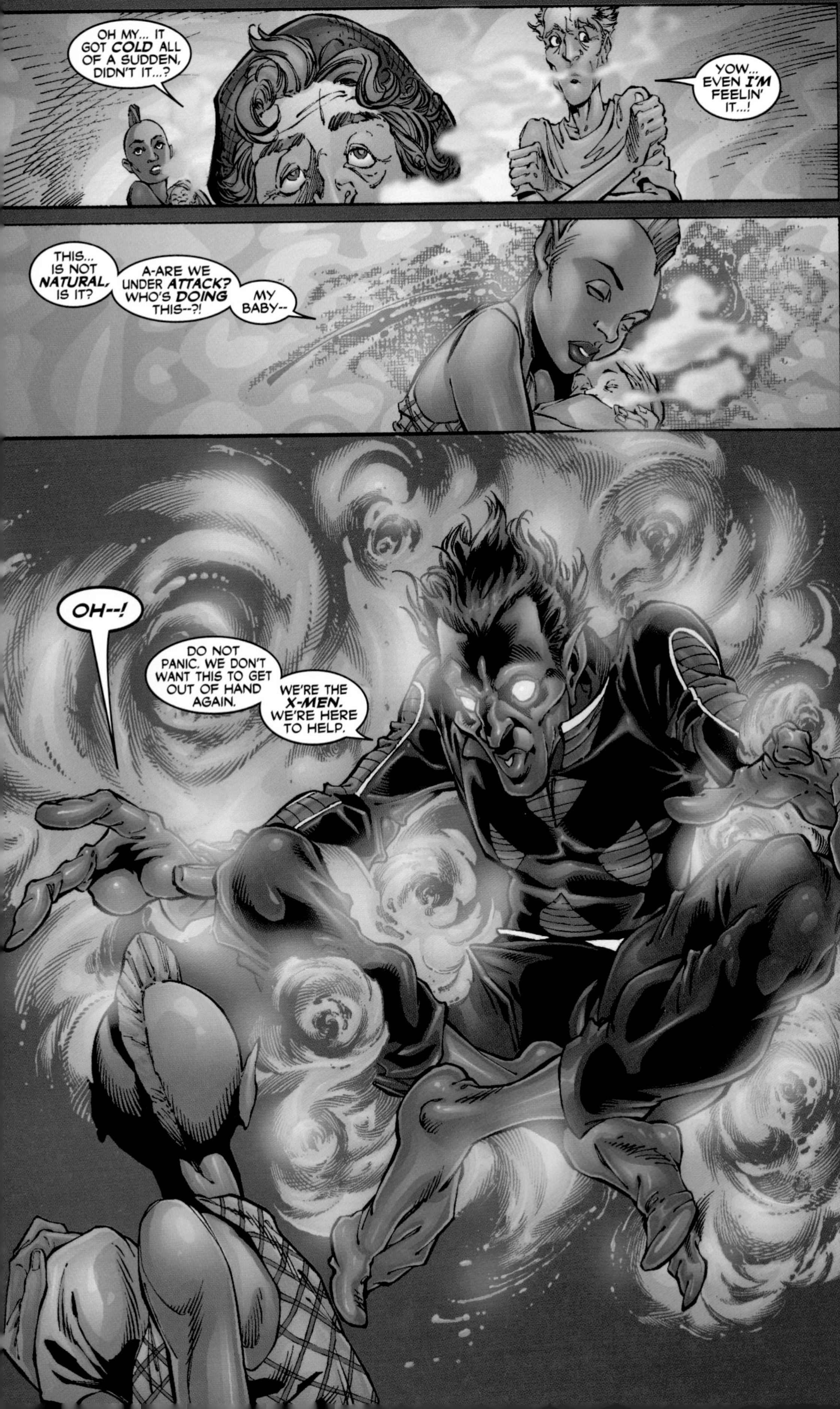
OH MY... IT GOT COLD ALL OF A SUDDEN, DIDN'T IT...?
YOW... EVEN I'M FEELIN' IT...!
THIS... IS NOT NATURAL, IS IT?
A-ARE WE UNDER ATTACK? WHO'S DOING THIS--?!
MY BABY--
OH--!
DO NOT PANIC. WE DON'T WANT THIS TO GET OUT OF HAND AGAIN.
WE'RE THE X-MEN. WE'RE HERE TO HELP.

THE CLASH

PART FIVE: UNCANNY X-MEN #398

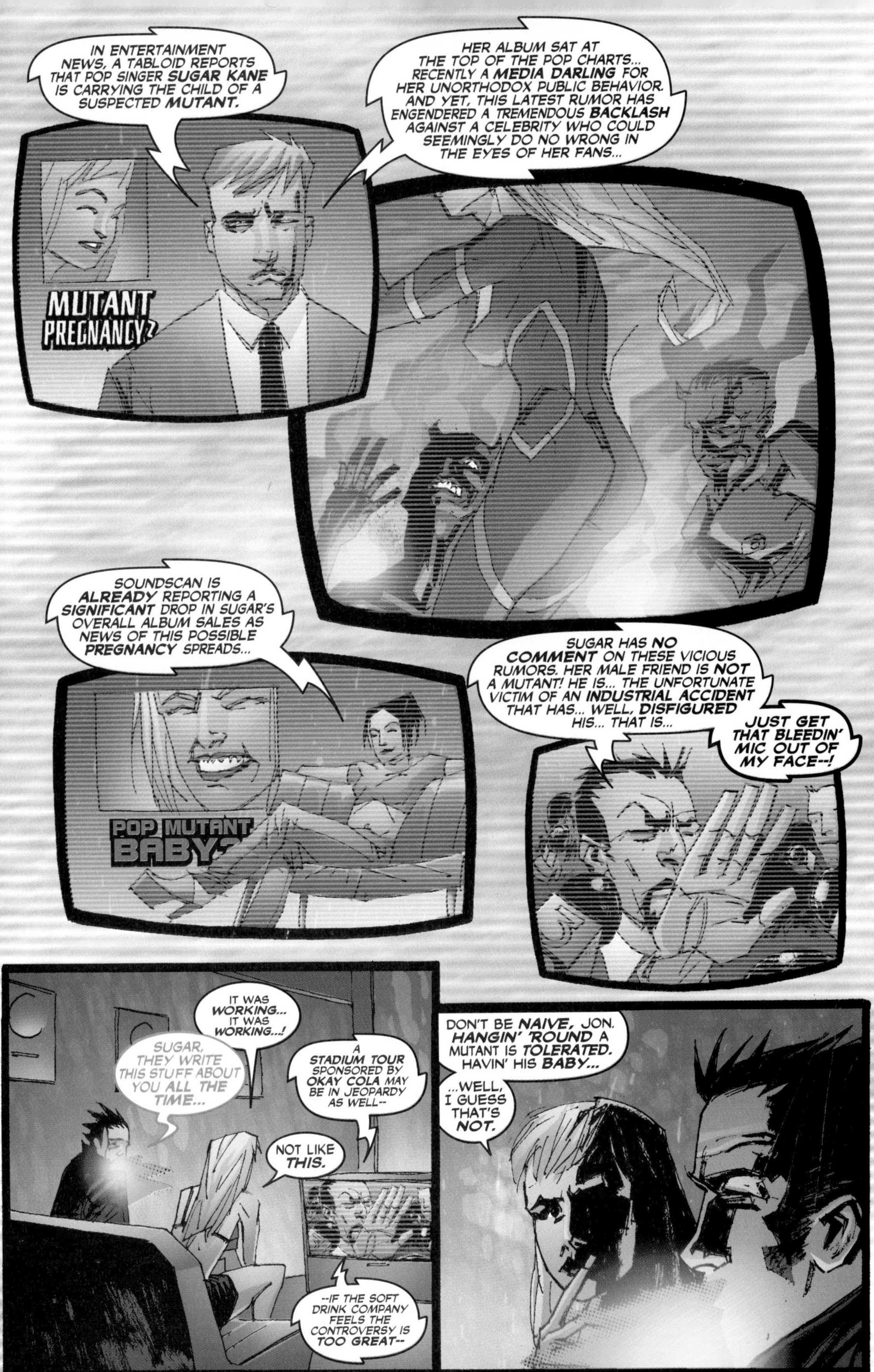
IN ENTERTAINMENT NEWS, A TABLOID REPORTS THAT POP SINGER SUGAR KANE IS CARRYING THE CHILD OF A SUSPECTED MUTANT.
MUTANT PREGNANCY?
HER ALBUM SAT AT THE TOP OF THE POP CHARTS... RECENTLY A MEDIA DARLING FOR HER UNORTHODOX PUBLIC BEHAVIOR. AND YET, THIS LATEST RUMOR HAS ENGENDERED A TREMENDOUS BACKLASH AGAINST A CELEBRITY WHO COULD SEEMINGLY DO NO WRONG IN THE EYES OF HER FANS...
SOUNDSCAN IS ALREADY REPORTING A SIGNIFICANT DROP IN SUGAR'S OVERALL ALBUM SALES AS NEWS OF THIS POSSIBLE PREGNANCY SPREADS...
POP MUTANT BABY?
SUGAR HAS NO COMMENT ON THESE VICIOUS RUMORS. HER MALE FRIEND IS NOT A MUTANT! HE IS... THE UNFORTUNATE VICTIM OF AN INDUSTRIAL ACCIDENT THAT HAS... WELL, DISFIGURED HIS... THAT IS...
JUST GET THAT BLEEDIN' MIC OUT OF MY FACE--!
IT WAS WORKING... IT WAS WORKING...!
SUGAR, THEY WRITE THIS STUFF ABOUT YOU ALL THE TIME...
A STADIUM TOUR SPONSORED BY OKAY COLA MAY BE IN JEOPARDY AS WELL--
NOT LIKE THIS.
--IF THE SOFT DRINK COMPANY FEELS THE CONTROVERSY IS TOO GREAT--
DON'T BE NAIVE, JON. HANGIN' 'ROUND A MUTANT IS TOLERATED. HAVIN' HIS BABY...
...WELL, I GUESS THAT'S NOT.

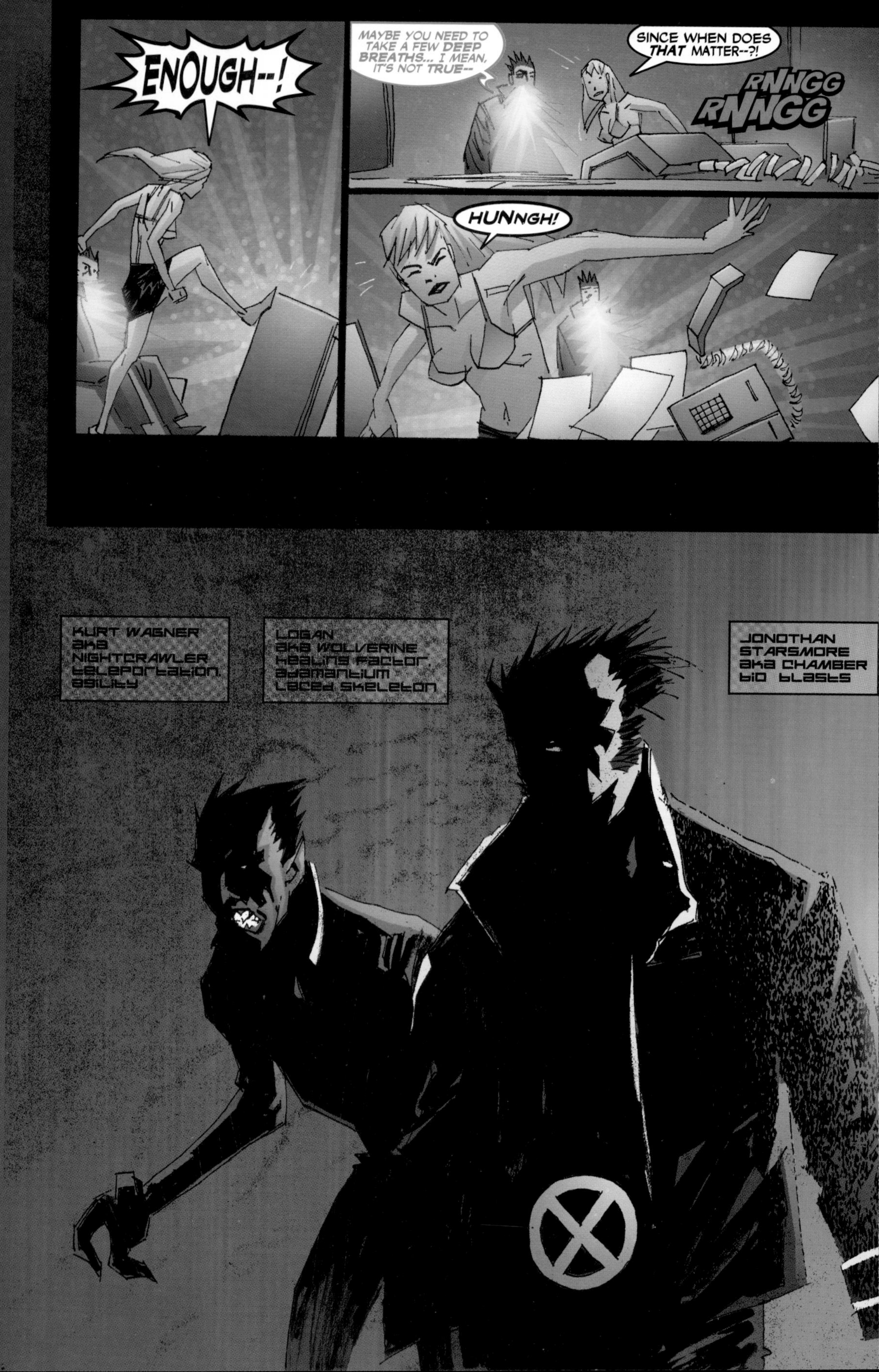
ENOUGH--!
MAYBE YOU NEED TO TAKE A FEW DEEP BREATHS... I MEAN, IT'S NOT TRUE--
SINCE WHEN DOES THAT MATTER--?!
RNNGG RNNGG
HUNNGH!
KURT WAGNER aka NIGHTCRAWLER teleportation, agility
LOGAN aka WOLVERINE healing factor, adamantium laced skeleton
JONOTHAN STARSMORE aka CHAMBER bio blasts

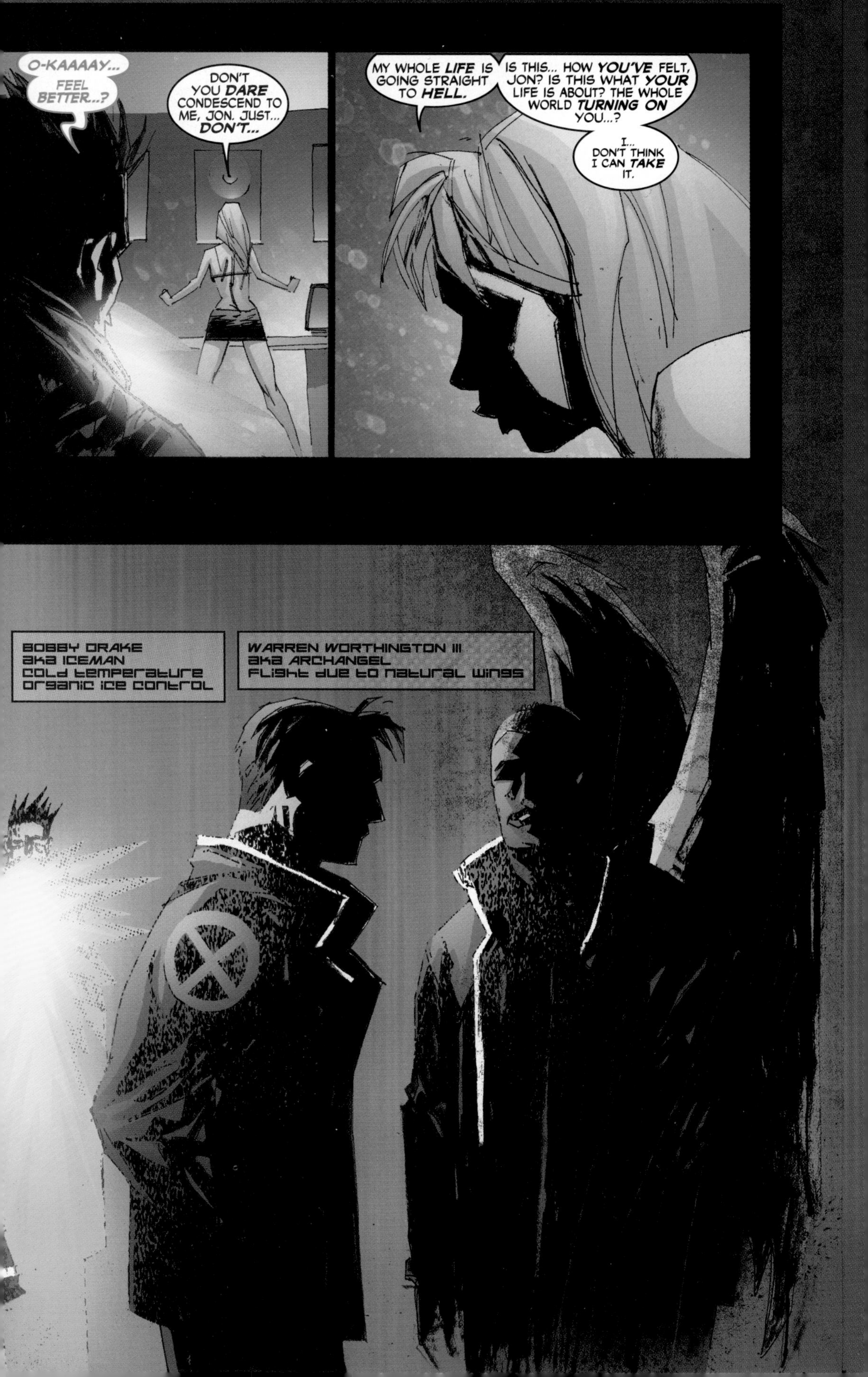
O-KAAAAY... FEEL BETTER...?
DON'T YOU DARE CONDESCEND TO ME, JON. JUST... DON'T...
MY WHOLE LIFE IS GOING STRAIGHT TO HELL.
IS THIS... HOW YOU'VE FELT, JON? IS THIS WHAT YOUR LIFE IS ABOUT? THE WHOLE WORLD TURNING ON YOU...?
I... DON'T THINK I CAN TAKE IT.
BOBBY DRAKE AKA ICEMAN COLD TEMPERATURE ORGANIC ICE CONTROL
WARREN WORTHINGTON III AKA ARCHANGEL FLIGHT DUE TO NATURAL WINGS

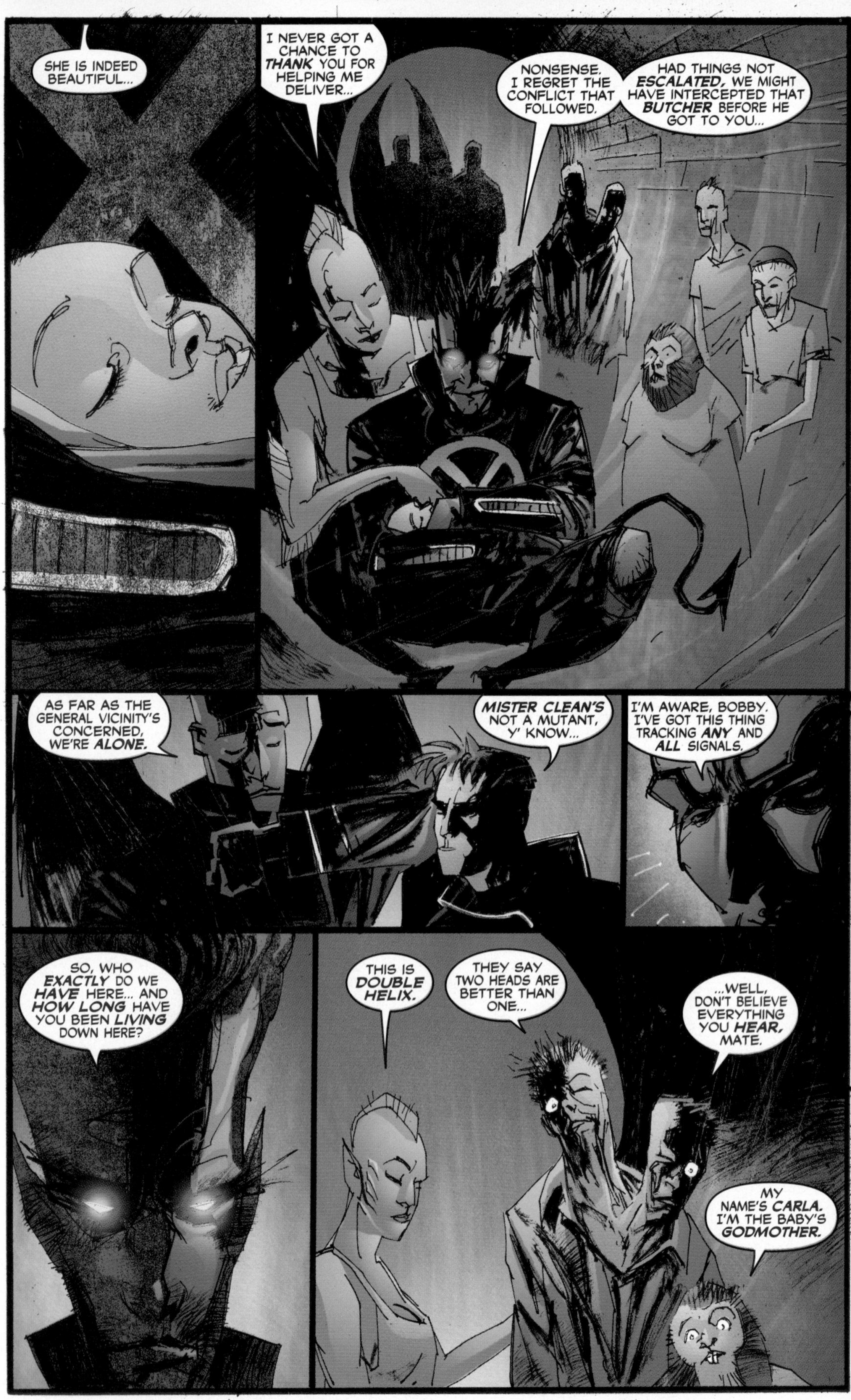
SHE IS INDEED BEAUTIFUL...
I NEVER GOT A CHANCE TO THANK YOU FOR HELPING ME DELIVER...
NONSENSE. I REGRET THE CONFLICT THAT FOLLOWED.
HAD THINGS NOT ESCALATED, WE MIGHT HAVE INTERCEPTED THAT BUTCHER BEFORE HE GOT TO YOU...
AS FAR AS THE GENERAL VICINITY'S CONCERNED, WE'RE ALONE.
MISTER CLEAN'S NOT A MUTANT, Y' KNOW...
I'M AWARE, BOBBY. I'VE GOT THIS THING TRACKING ANY AND ALL SIGNALS.
SO, WHO EXACTLY DO WE HAVE HERE... AND HOW LONG HAVE YOU BEEN LIVING DOWN HERE?
THIS IS DOUBLE HELIX.
THEY SAY TWO HEADS ARE BETTER THAN ONE...
...WELL, DON'T BELIEVE EVERYTHING YOU HEAR, MATE.
MY NAME'S CARLA. I'M THE BABY'S GODMOTHER.

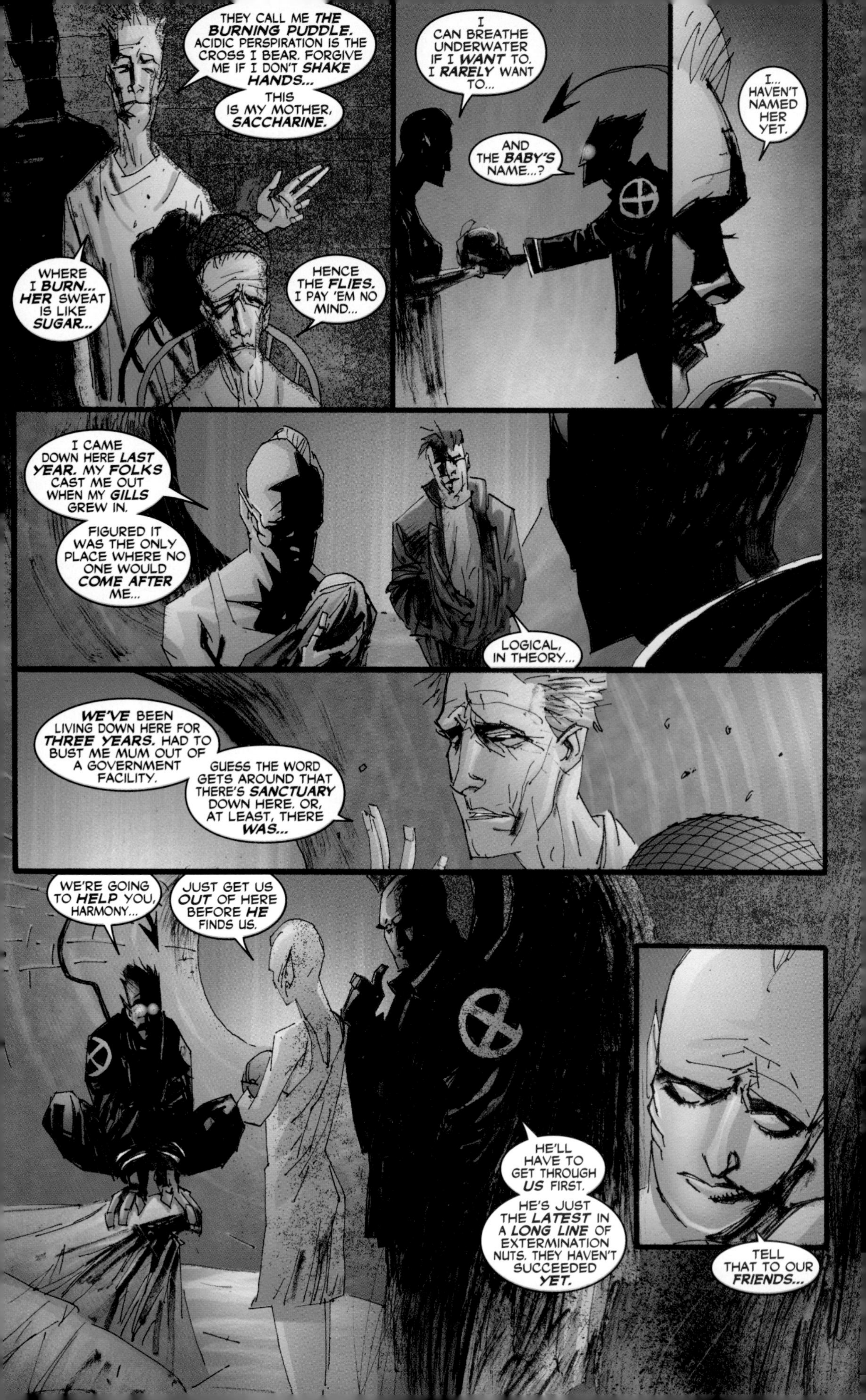
THEY CALL ME THE BURNING PUDDLE. ACIDIC PERSPIRATION IS THE CROSS I BEAR. FORGIVE ME IF I DON'T SHAKE HANDS...
THIS IS MY MOTHER, SACCHARINE.
WHERE I BURN... HER SWEAT IS LIKE SUGAR...
HENCE THE FLIES. I PAY 'EM NO MIND...
I CAN BREATHE UNDERWATER IF I WANT TO. I RARELY WANT TO...
AND THE BABY'S NAME...?
I... HAVEN'T NAMED HER YET.
I CAME DOWN HERE LAST YEAR. MY FOLKS CAST ME OUT WHEN MY GILLS GREW IN.
FIGURED IT WAS THE ONLY PLACE WHERE NO ONE WOULD COME AFTER ME...
LOGICAL, IN THEORY...
WE'VE BEEN LIVING DOWN HERE FOR THREE YEARS. HAD TO BUST ME MUM OUT OF A GOVERNMENT FACILITY.
GUESS THE WORD GETS AROUND THAT THERE'S SANCTUARY DOWN HERE. OR, AT LEAST, THERE WAS...
WE'RE GOING TO HELP YOU, HARMONY...
JUST GET US OUT OF HERE BEFORE HE FINDS US.
HE'LL HAVE TO GET THROUGH US FIRST.
HE'S JUST THE LATEST IN A LONG LINE OF EXTERMINATION NUTS. THEY HAVEN'T SUCCEEDED YET.
TELL THAT TO OUR FRIENDS...

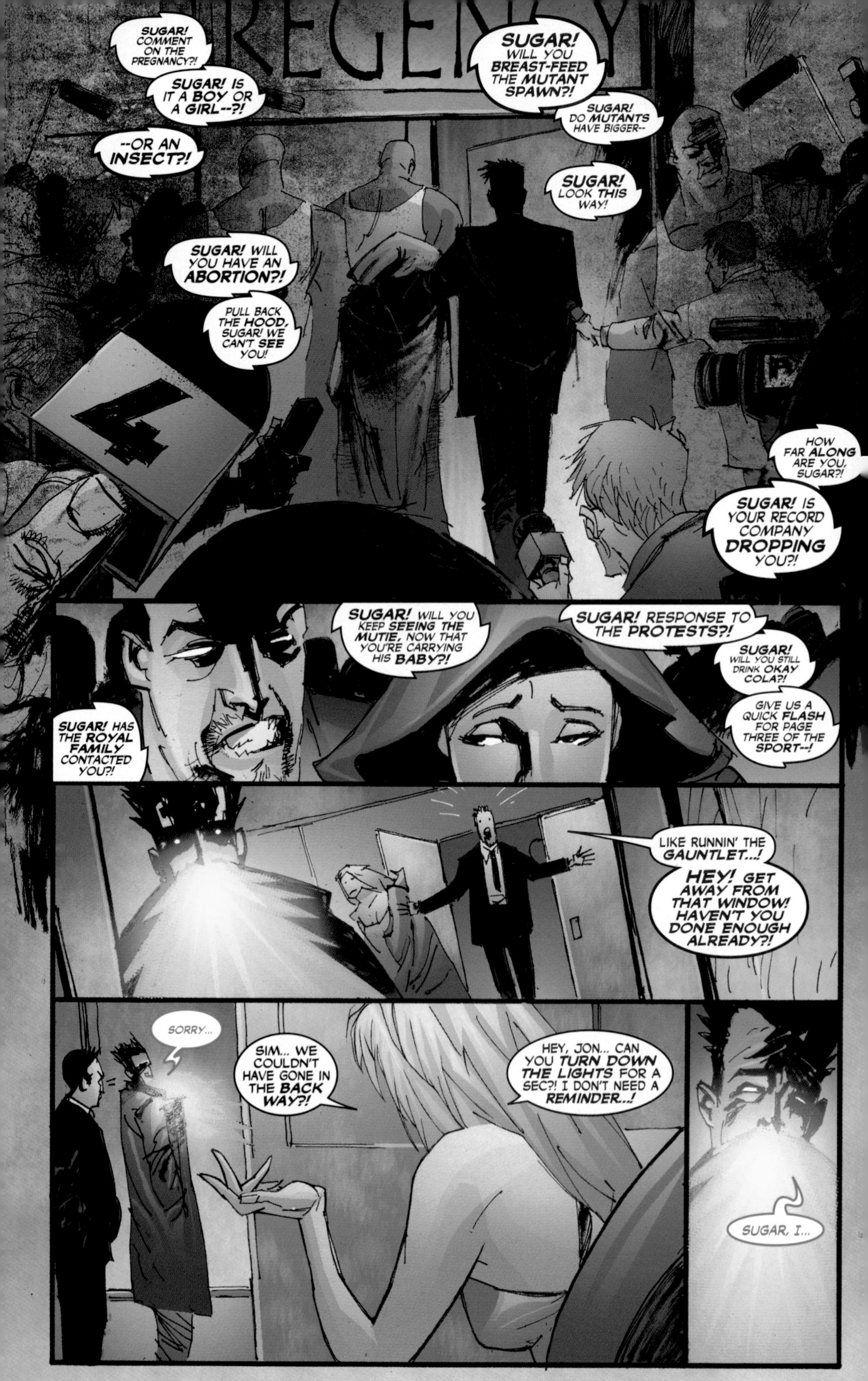
REGENCY
SUGAR! COMMENT ON THE PREGNANCY?!
SUGAR! IS IT A BOY OR A GIRL--?!
--OR AN INSECT?!
SUGAR! WILL YOU BREAST-FEED THE MUTANT SPAWN?!
SUGAR! DO MUTANTS HAVE BIGGER--
SUGAR! LOOK THIS WAY!
SUGAR! WILL YOU HAVE AN ABORTION?!
PULL BACK THE HOOD, SUGAR! WE CAN'T SEE YOU!
4
HOW FAR ALONG ARE YOU, SUGAR?!
SUGAR! IS YOUR RECORD COMPANY DROPPING YOU?!
SUGAR! WILL YOU KEEP SEEING THE MUTIE, NOW THAT YOU'RE CARRYING HIS BABY?!
SUGAR! RESPONSE TO THE PROTESTS?!
SUGAR! WILL YOU STILL DRINK OKAY COLA?!
GIVE US A QUICK FLASH FOR PAGE THREE OF THE SPORT--!
SUGAR! HAS THE ROYAL FAMILY CONTACTED YOU?!
LIKE RUNNIN' THE GAUNTLET...!
HEY! GET AWAY FROM THAT WINDOW! HAVEN'T YOU DONE ENOUGH ALREADY?!
SORRY...
SIM... WE COULDN'T HAVE GONE IN THE BACK WAY?!
HEY, JON... CAN YOU TURN DOWN THE LIGHTS FOR A SEC?! I DON'T NEED A REMINDER...!
SUGAR, I...

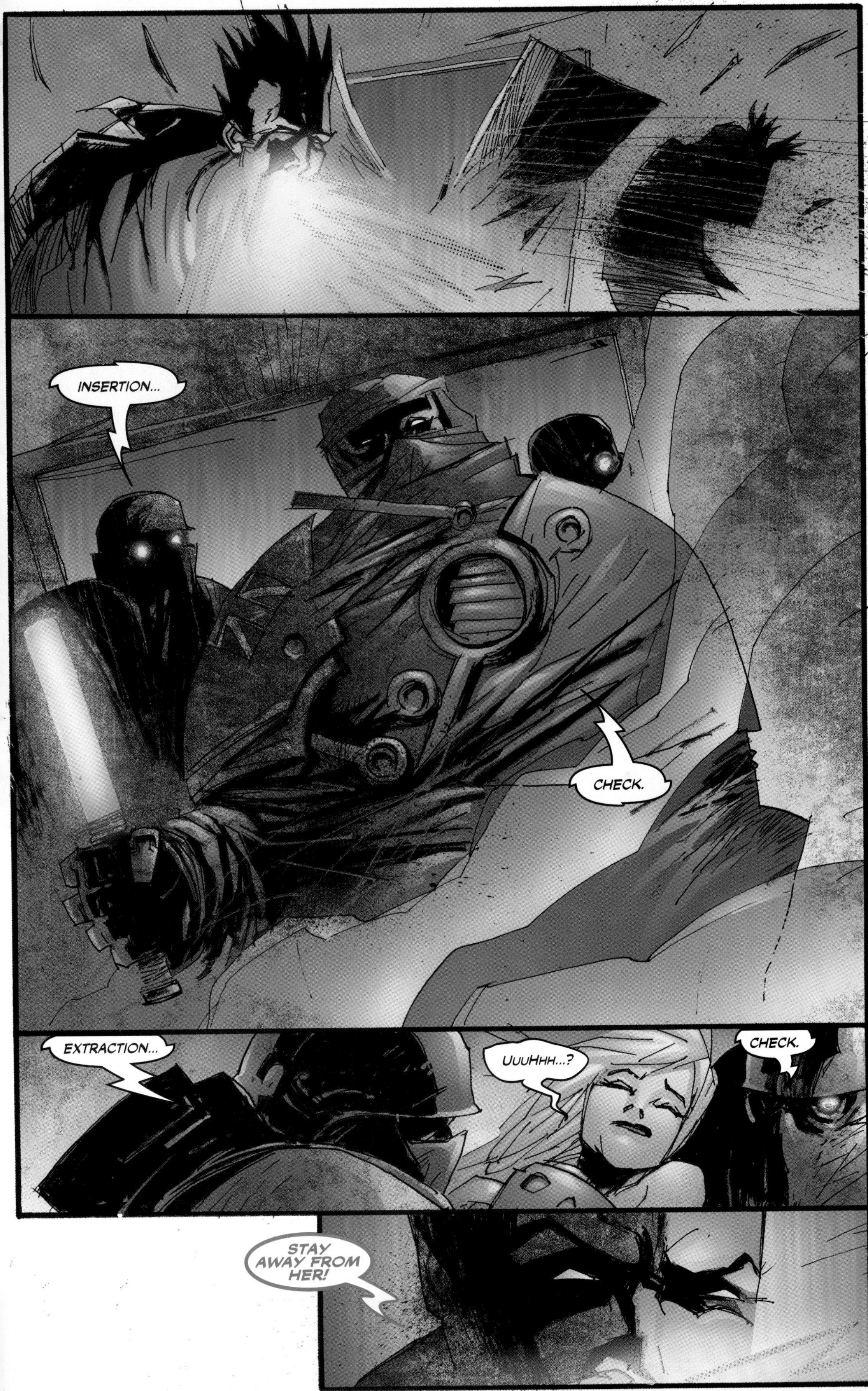
INSERTION...
CHECK.
EXTRACTION...
UuuHhh...?
CHECK.
STAY AWAY FROM HER!

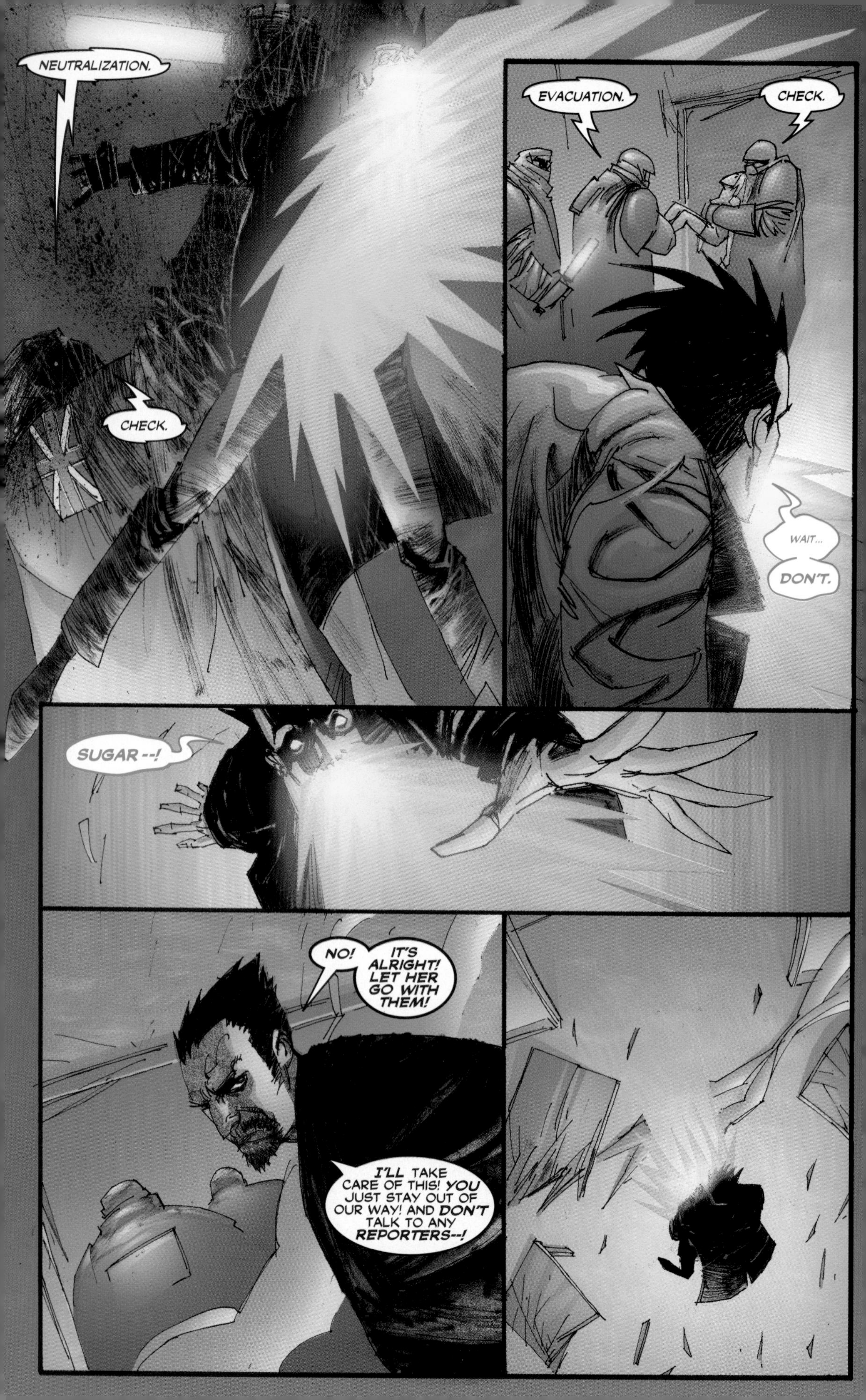
NEUTRALIZATION.
CHECK.
EVACUATION.
CHECK.
WAIT... DON'T.
SUGAR--!
NO! IT'S ALRIGHT! LET HER GO WITH THEM!
I'LL TAKE CARE OF THIS! YOU JUST STAY OUT OF OUR WAY! AND DON'T TALK TO ANY REPORTERS--!

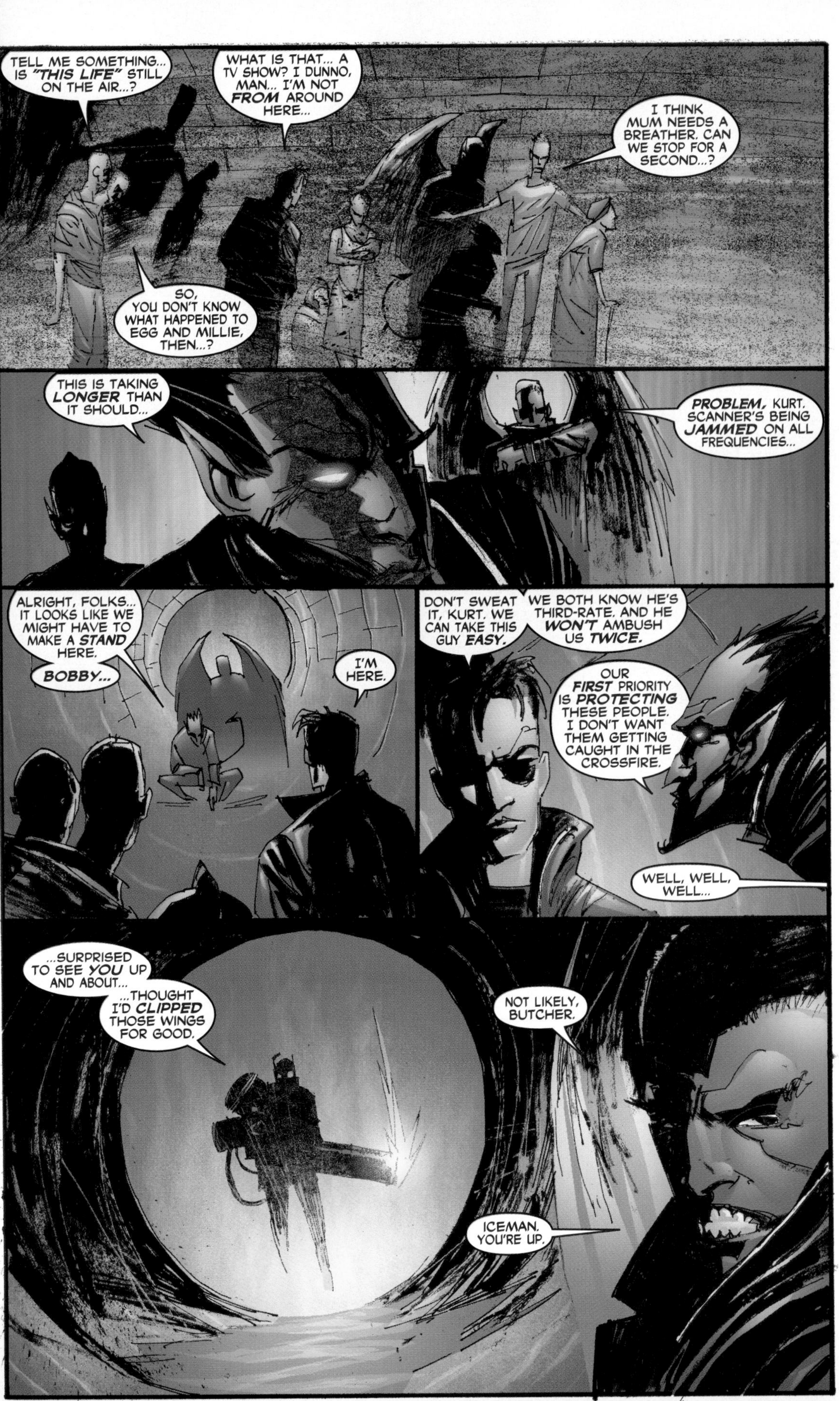
TELL ME SOMETHING... IS "THIS LIFE" STILL ON THE AIR...?
WHAT IS THAT... A TV SHOW? I DUNNO, MAN... I'M NOT FROM AROUND HERE...
I THINK MUM NEEDS A BREATHER. CAN WE STOP FOR A SECOND...?
SO, YOU DON'T KNOW WHAT HAPPENED TO EGG AND MILLIE, THEN...?
THIS IS TAKING LONGER THAN IT SHOULD...
PROBLEM, KURT. SCANNER'S BEING JAMMED ON ALL FREQUENCIES...
ALRIGHT, FOLKS... IT LOOKS LIKE WE MIGHT HAVE TO MAKE A STAND HERE.
BOBBY...
I'M HERE.
DON'T SWEAT IT, KURT. WE CAN TAKE THIS GUY EASY.
WE BOTH KNOW HE'S THIRD-RATE, AND HE WON'T AMBUSH US TWICE.
OUR FIRST PRIORITY IS PROTECTING THESE PEOPLE. I DON'T WANT THEM GETTING CAUGHT IN THE CROSSFIRE.
WELL, WELL, WELL...
...SURPRISED TO SEE YOU UP AND ABOUT...
...THOUGHT I'D CLIPPED THOSE WINGS FOR GOOD.
NOT LIKELY, BUTCHER.
ICEMAN. YOU'RE UP.

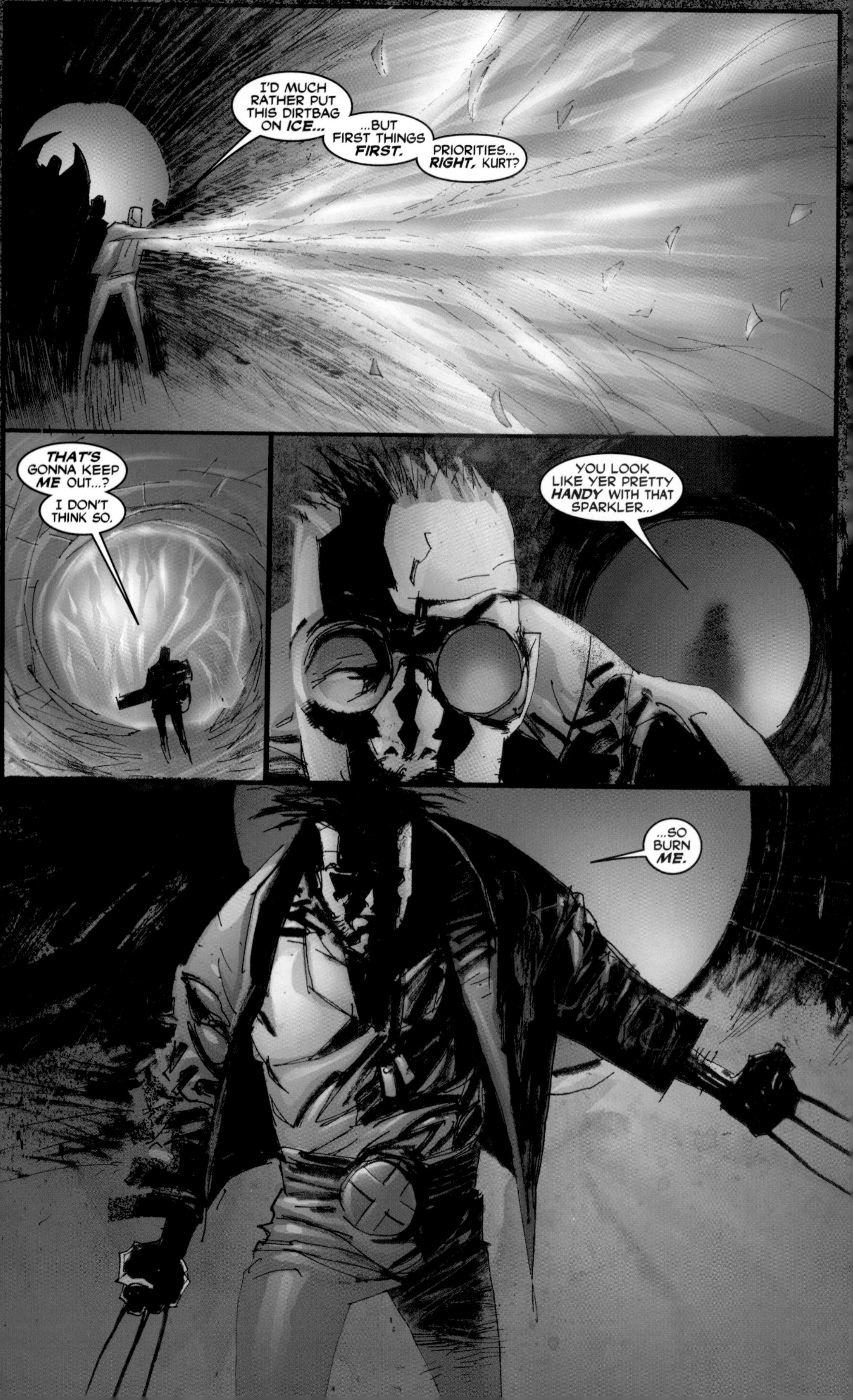
I'D MUCH RATHER PUT THIS DIRTBAG ON ICE...
...BUT FIRST THINGS FIRST.
PRIORITIES... RIGHT, KURT?
THAT'S GONNA KEEP ME OUT...?
I DON'T THINK SO.
YOU LOOK LIKE YER PRETTY HANDY WITH THAT SPARKLER...
...SO BURN ME.

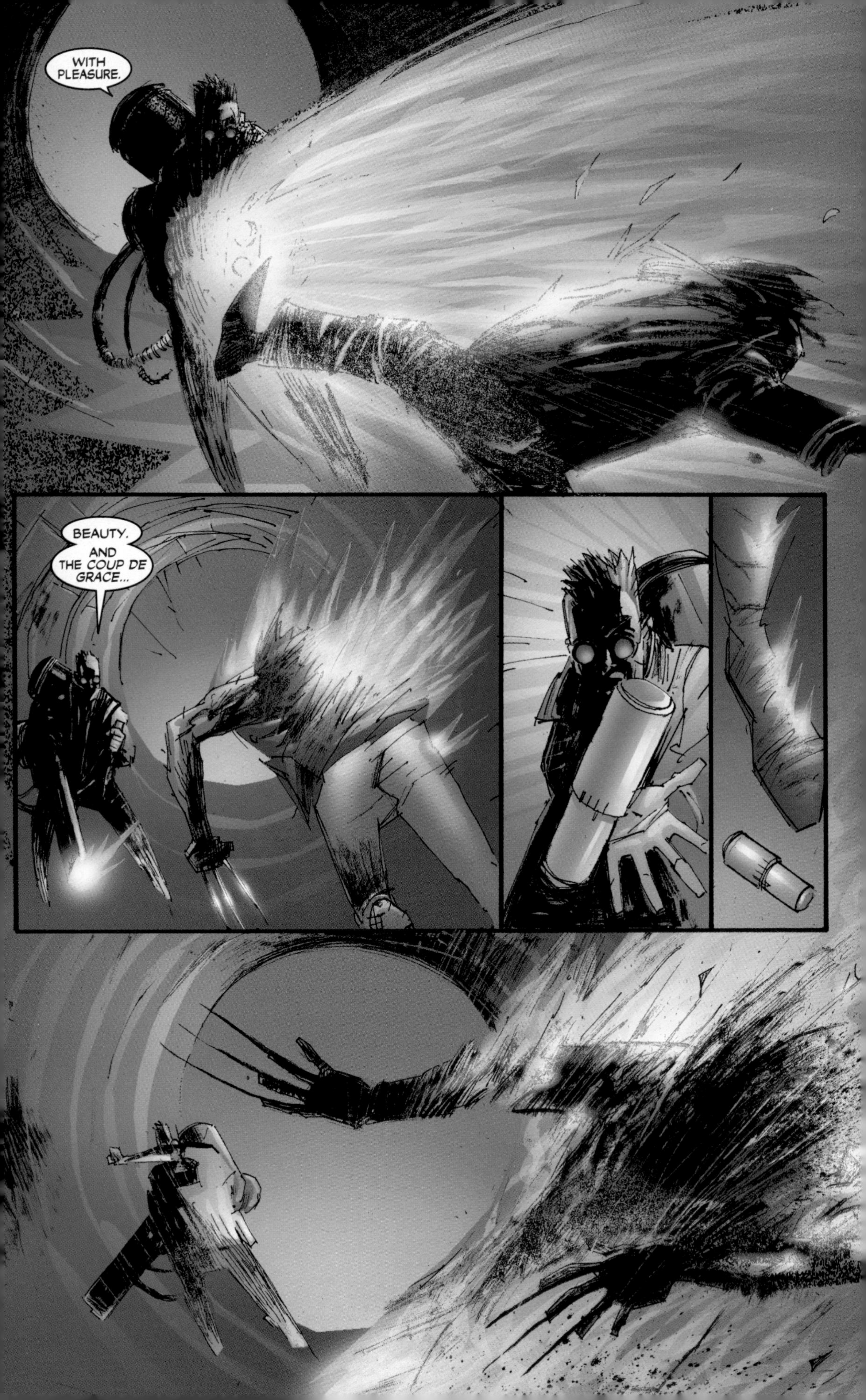
WITH PLEASURE.
BEAUTY.
AND THE *COUP DE GRACE*...

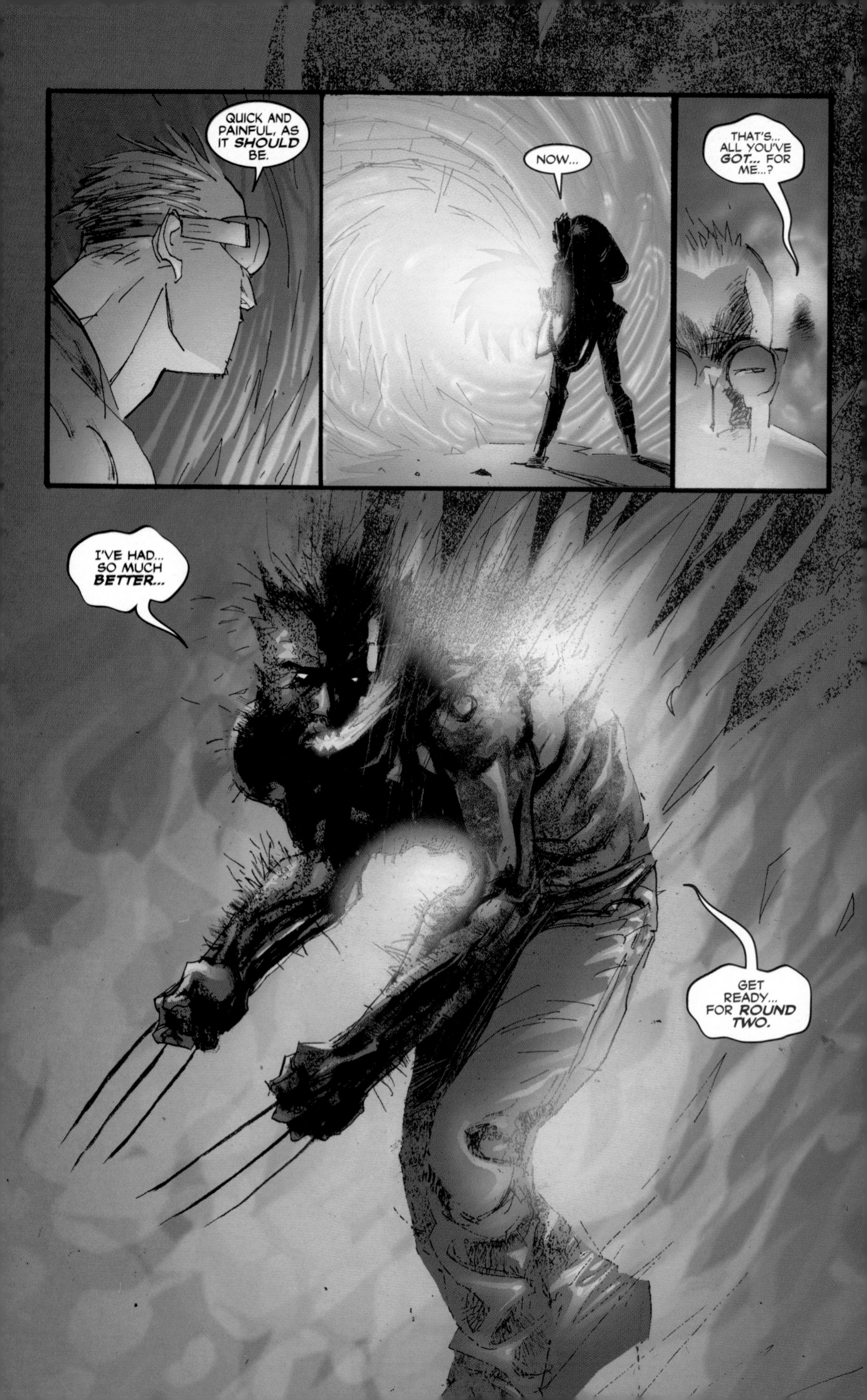
QUICK AND PAINFUL, AS IT SHOULD BE.
NOW...
THAT'S... ALL YOU'VE GOT... FOR ME...?
I'VE HAD... SO MUCH BETTER...
GET READY... FOR ROUND TWO.

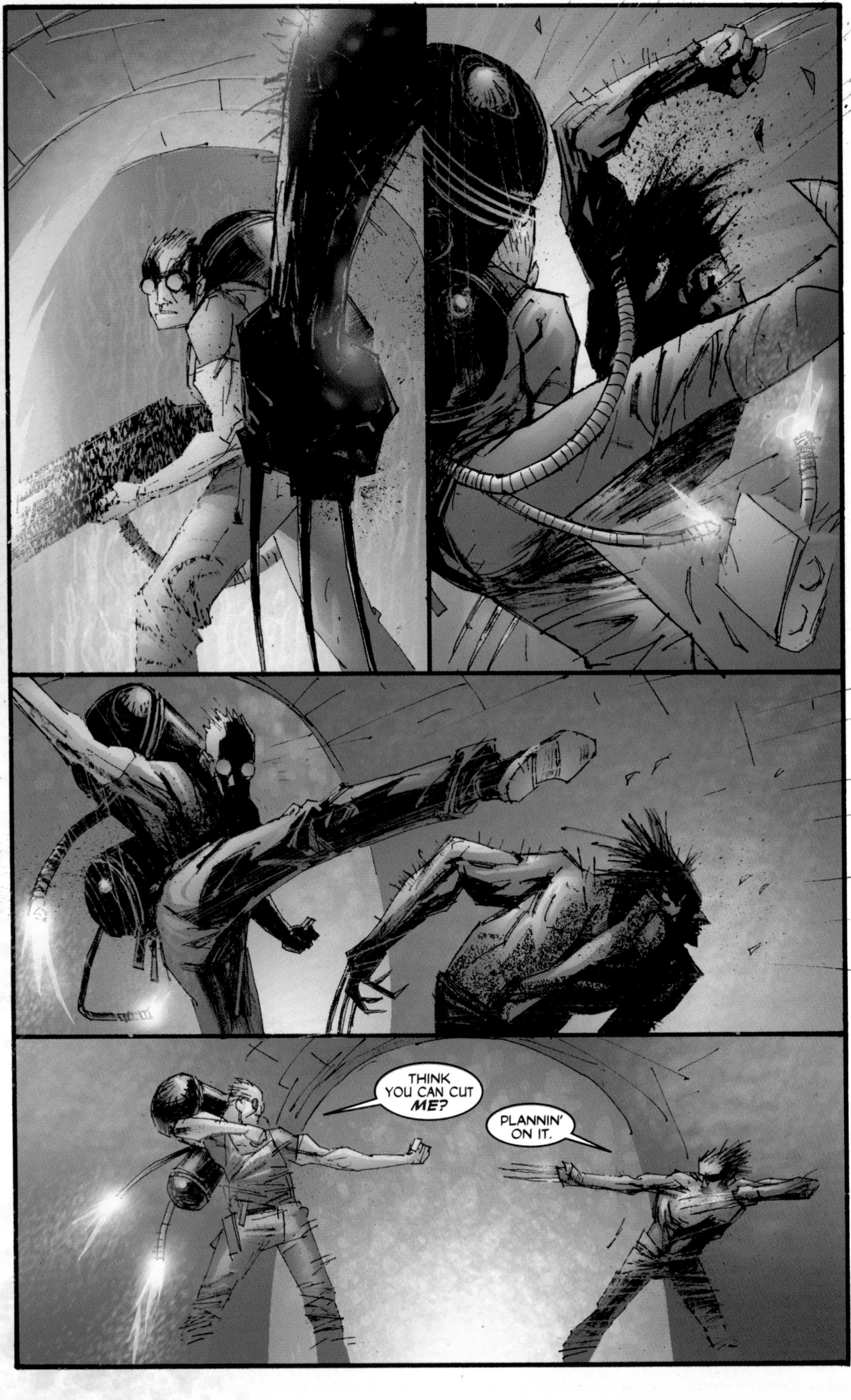
THINK YOU CAN CUT *ME?*
PLANNIN' ON IT.

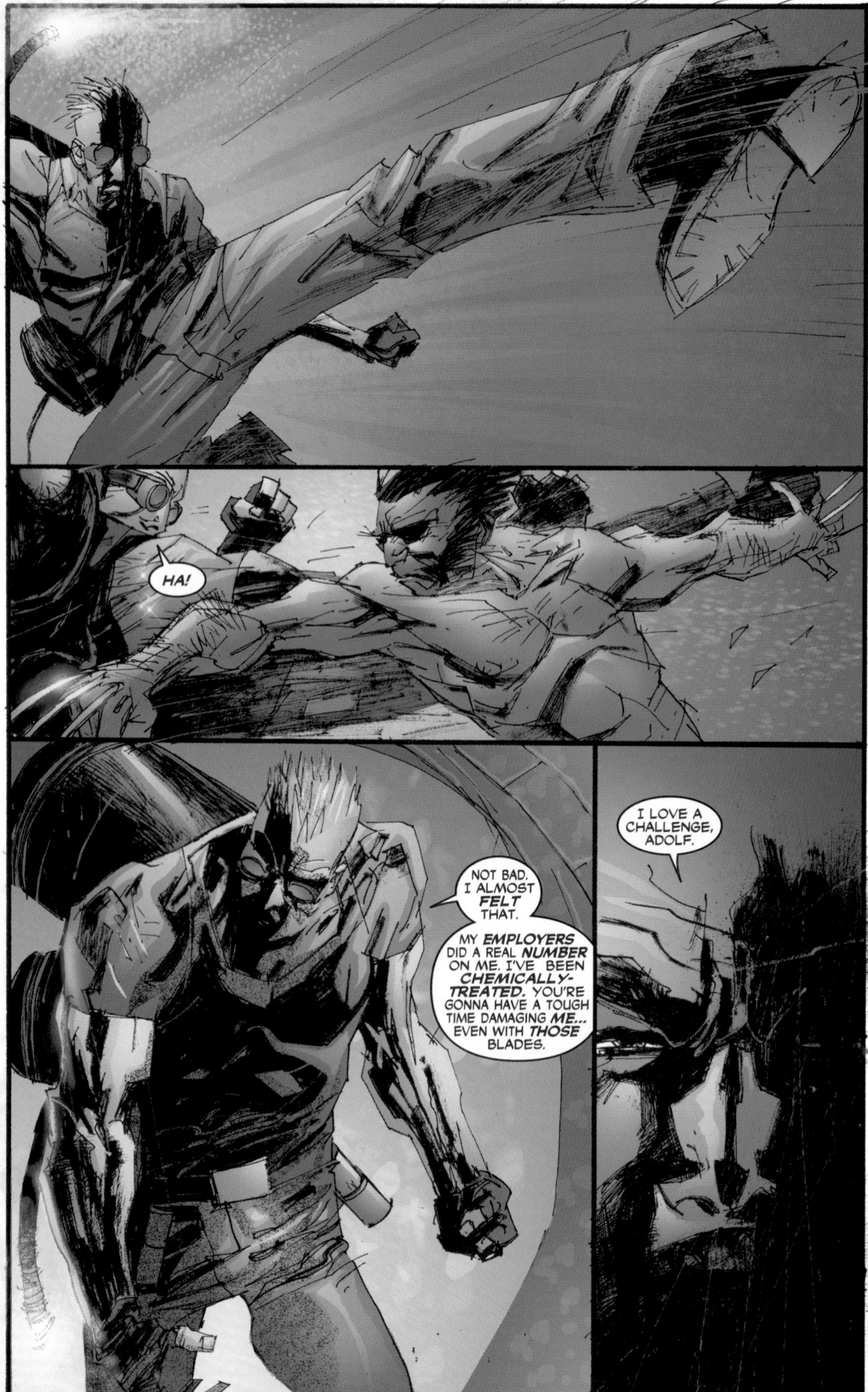
HA!
NOT BAD. I ALMOST FELT THAT.
MY EMPLOYERS DID A REAL NUMBER ON ME. I'VE BEEN CHEMICALLY-TREATED. YOU'RE GONNA HAVE A TOUGH TIME DAMAGING ME... EVEN WITH THOSE BLADES.
I LOVE A CHALLENGE, ADOLF.

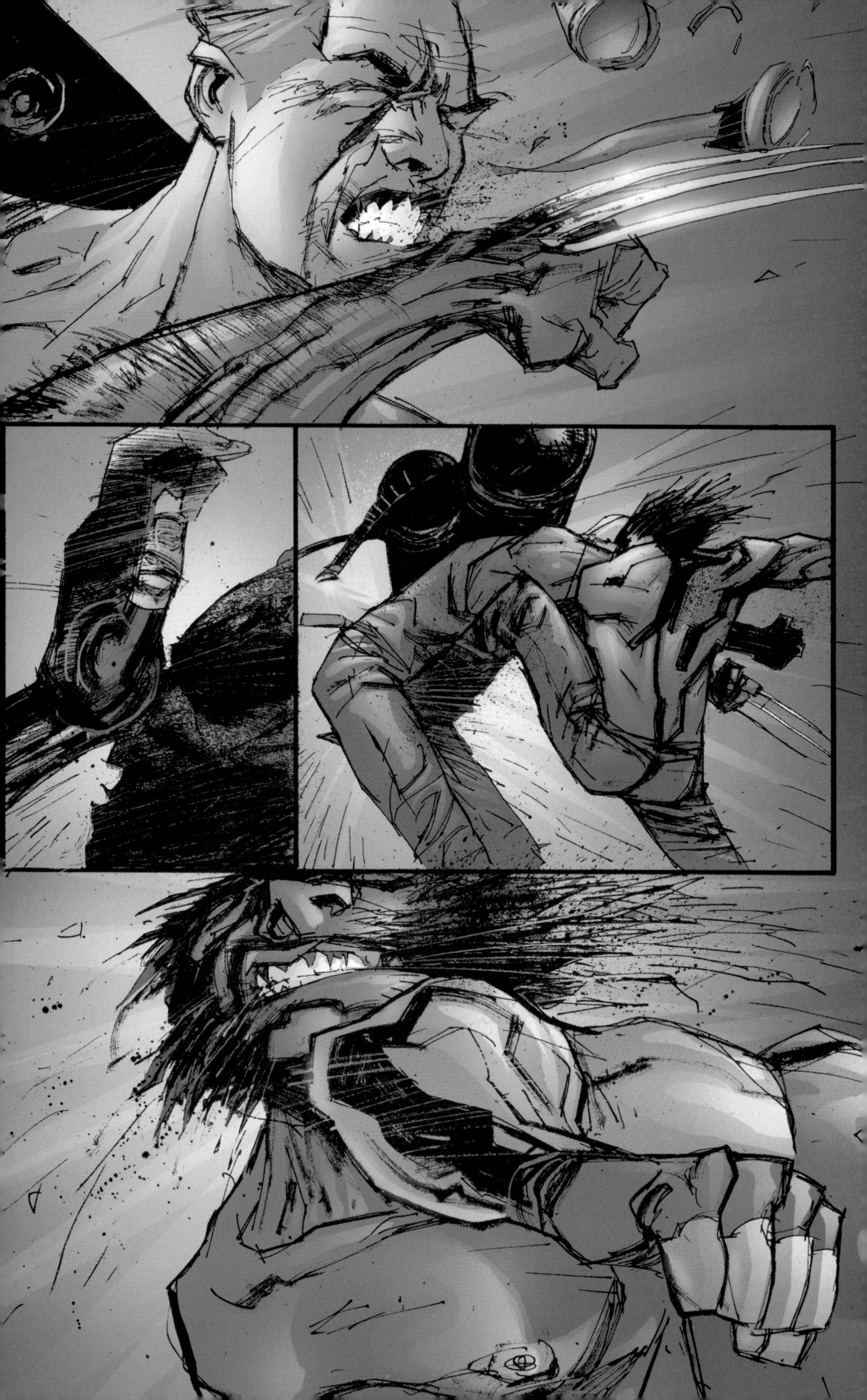

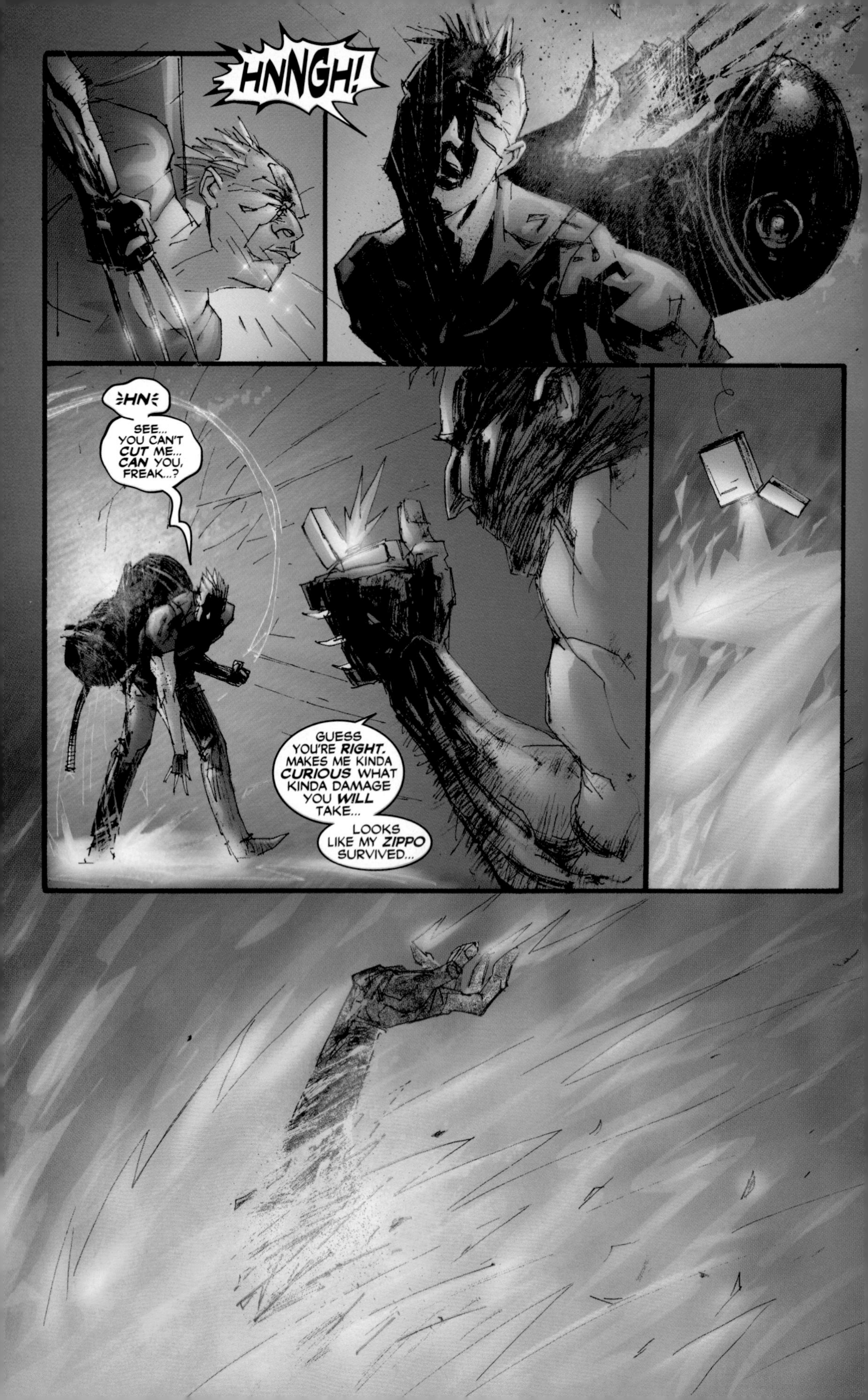
HNNGH!
HN
SEE... YOU CAN'T CUT ME... CAN YOU, FREAK...?
GUESS YOU'RE RIGHT. MAKES ME KINDA CURIOUS WHAT KINDA DAMAGE YOU WILL TAKE...
LOOKS LIKE MY ZIPPO SURVIVED...

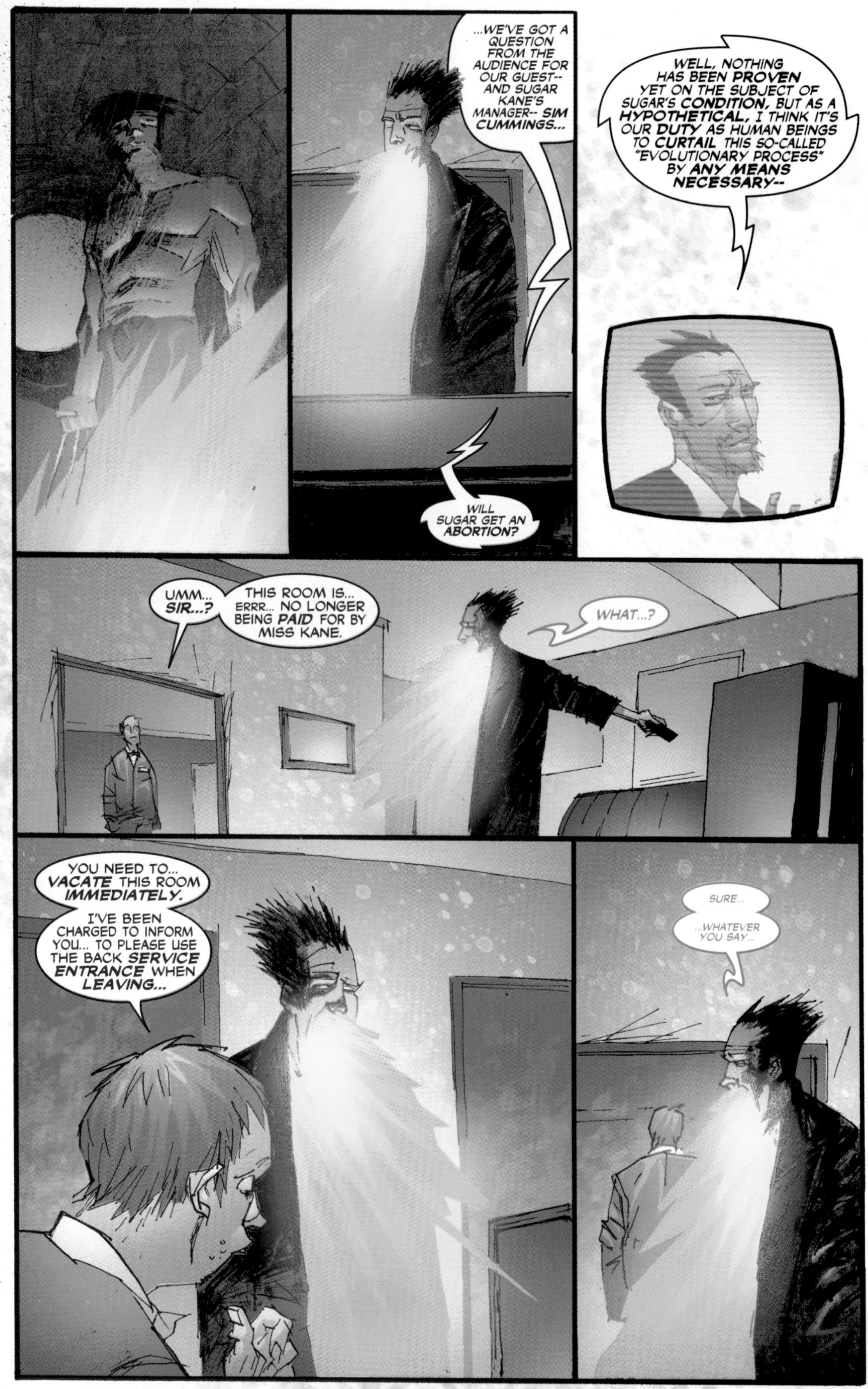
...WE'VE GOT A QUESTION FROM THE AUDIENCE FOR OUR GUEST-- AND SUGAR KANE'S MANAGER-- SIM CUMMINGS...
WELL, NOTHING HAS BEEN PROVEN YET ON THE SUBJECT OF SUGAR'S CONDITION, BUT AS A HYPOTHETICAL, I THINK IT'S OUR DUTY AS HUMAN BEINGS TO CURTAIL THIS SO-CALLED "EVOLUTIONARY PROCESS" BY ANY MEANS NECESSARY--
WILL SUGAR GET AN ABORTION?
UMM... SIR...?
THIS ROOM IS... ERRR... NO LONGER BEING PAID FOR BY MISS KANE.
WHAT...?
YOU NEED TO... VACATE THIS ROOM IMMEDIATELY.
I'VE BEEN CHARGED TO INFORM YOU... TO PLEASE USE THE BACK SERVICE ENTRANCE WHEN LEAVING...
SURE...
...WHATEVER YOU SAY...

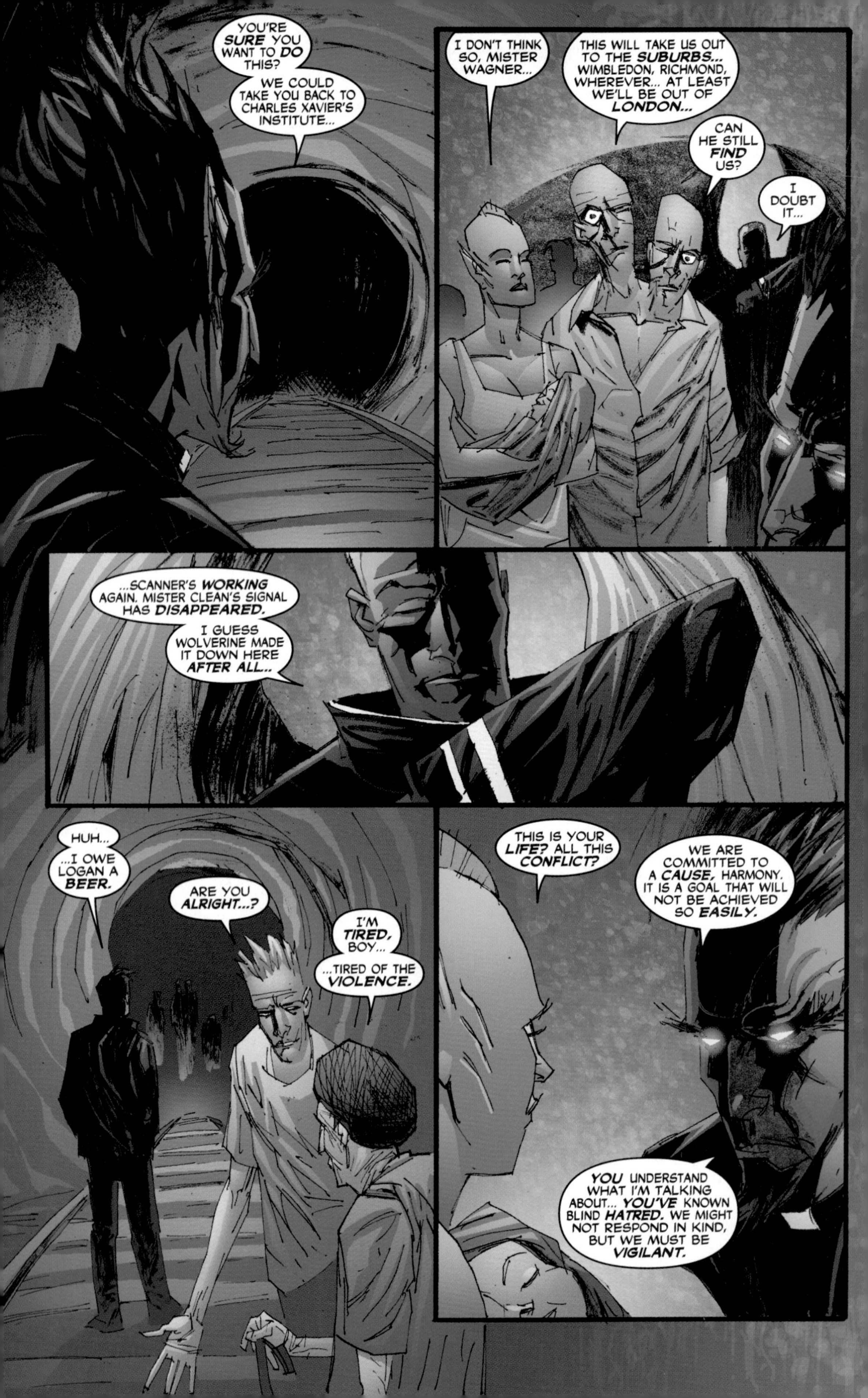
YOU'RE SURE YOU WANT TO DO THIS?
WE COULD TAKE YOU BACK TO CHARLES XAVIER'S INSTITUTE...
I DON'T THINK SO, MISTER WAGNER...
THIS WILL TAKE US OUT TO THE SUBURBS... WIMBLEDON, RICHMOND, WHEREVER... AT LEAST WE'LL BE OUT OF LONDON...
CAN HE STILL FIND US?
I DOUBT IT...
...SCANNER'S WORKING AGAIN. MISTER CLEAN'S SIGNAL HAS DISAPPEARED.
I GUESS WOLVERINE MADE IT DOWN HERE AFTER ALL...
HUH...
...I OWE LOGAN A BEER.
ARE YOU ALRIGHT...?
I'M TIRED, BOY...
...TIRED OF THE VIOLENCE.
THIS IS YOUR LIFE? ALL THIS CONFLICT?
WE ARE COMMITTED TO A CAUSE, HARMONY. IT IS A GOAL THAT WILL NOT BE ACHIEVED SO EASILY.
YOU UNDERSTAND WHAT I'M TALKING ABOUT... YOU'VE KNOWN BLIND HATRED. WE MIGHT NOT RESPOND IN KIND, BUT WE MUST BE VIGILANT.

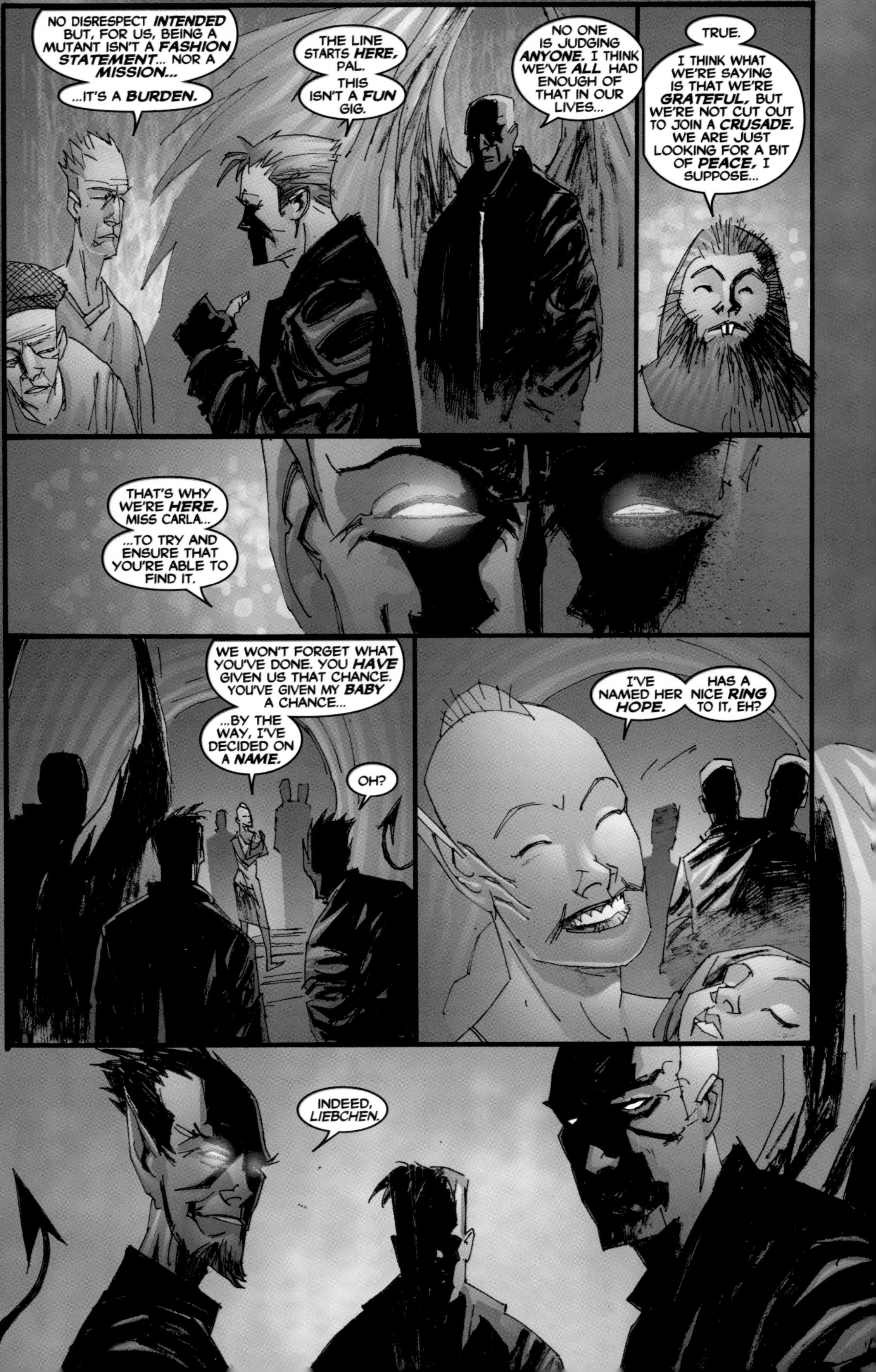

NO DISRESPECT INTENDED BUT, FOR US, BEING A MUTANT ISN'T A FASHION STATEMENT... NOR A MISSION...
...IT'S A BURDEN.
THE LINE STARTS HERE, PAL.
THIS ISN'T A FUN GIG.
NO ONE IS JUDGING ANYONE. I THINK WE'VE ALL HAD ENOUGH OF THAT IN OUR LIVES...
TRUE.
I THINK WHAT WE'RE SAYING IS THAT WE'RE GRATEFUL, BUT WE'RE NOT CUT OUT TO JOIN A CRUSADE. WE ARE JUST LOOKING FOR A BIT OF PEACE, I SUPPOSE...
THAT'S WHY WE'RE HERE, MISS CARLA...
...TO TRY AND ENSURE THAT YOU'RE ABLE TO FIND IT.
WE WON'T FORGET WHAT YOU'VE DONE. YOU HAVE GIVEN US THAT CHANCE. YOU'VE GIVEN MY BABY A CHANCE...
...BY THE WAY, I'VE DECIDED ON A NAME.
OH?
I'VE NAMED HER HOPE.
HAS A NICE RING TO IT, EH?
INDEED, LIEBCHEN.

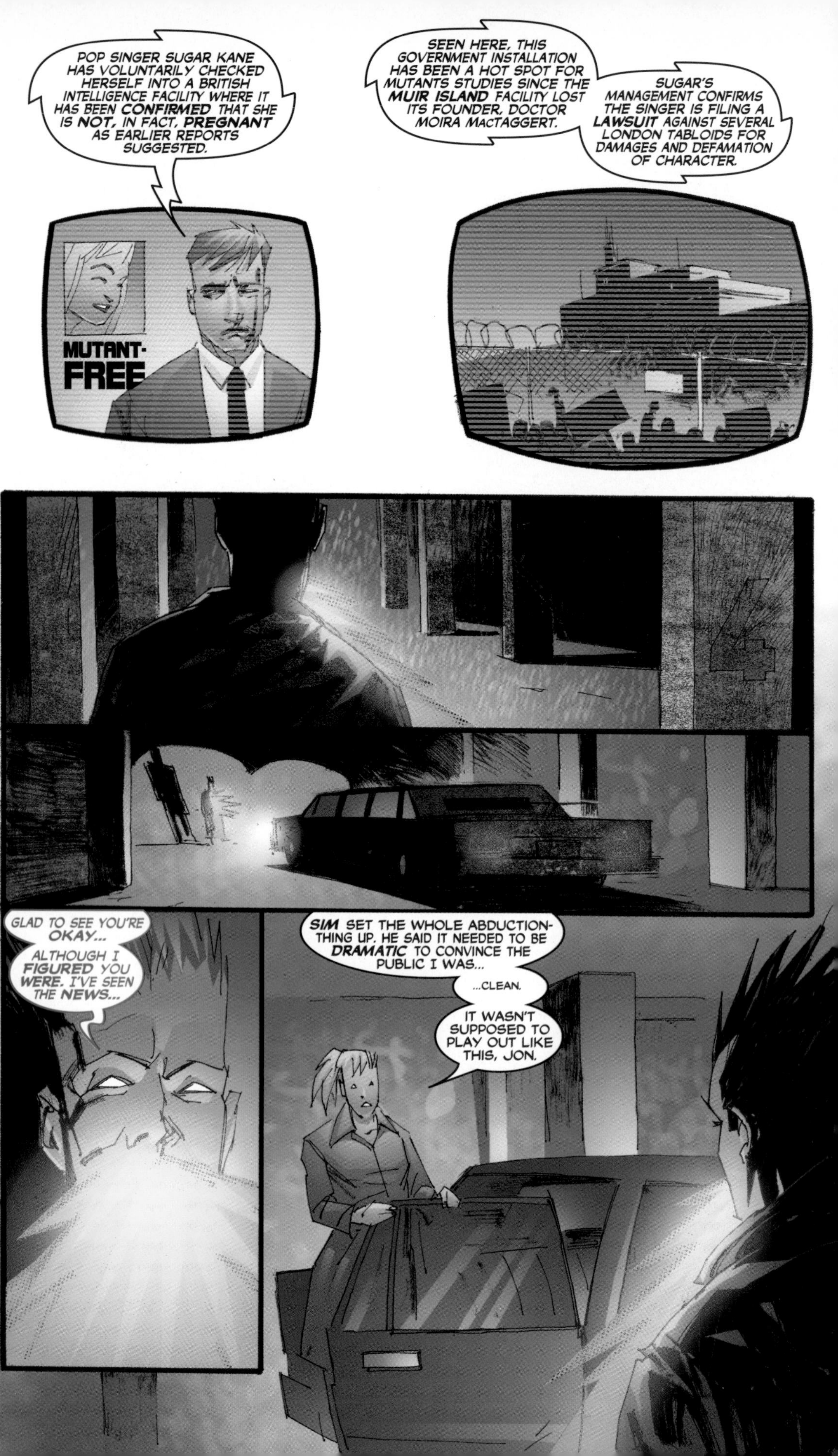
POP SINGER SUGAR KANE HAS VOLUNTARILY CHECKED HERSELF INTO A BRITISH INTELLIGENCE FACILITY WHERE IT HAS BEEN CONFIRMED THAT SHE IS NOT, IN FACT, PREGNANT AS EARLIER REPORTS SUGGESTED.
MUTANT-FREE
SEEN HERE, THIS GOVERNMENT INSTALLATION HAS BEEN A HOT SPOT FOR MUTANTS STUDIES SINCE THE MUIR ISLAND FACILITY LOST ITS FOUNDER, DOCTOR MOIRA MacTAGGERT.
SUGAR'S MANAGEMENT CONFIRMS THE SINGER IS FILING A LAWSUIT AGAINST SEVERAL LONDON TABLOIDS FOR DAMAGES AND DEFAMATION OF CHARACTER.
GLAD TO SEE YOU'RE OKAY...
ALTHOUGH I FIGURED YOU WERE. I'VE SEEN THE NEWS...
SIM SET THE WHOLE ABDUCTION-THING UP. HE SAID IT NEEDED TO BE DRAMATIC TO CONVINCE THE PUBLIC I WAS...
...CLEAN.
IT WASN'T SUPPOSED TO PLAY OUT LIKE THIS, JON.

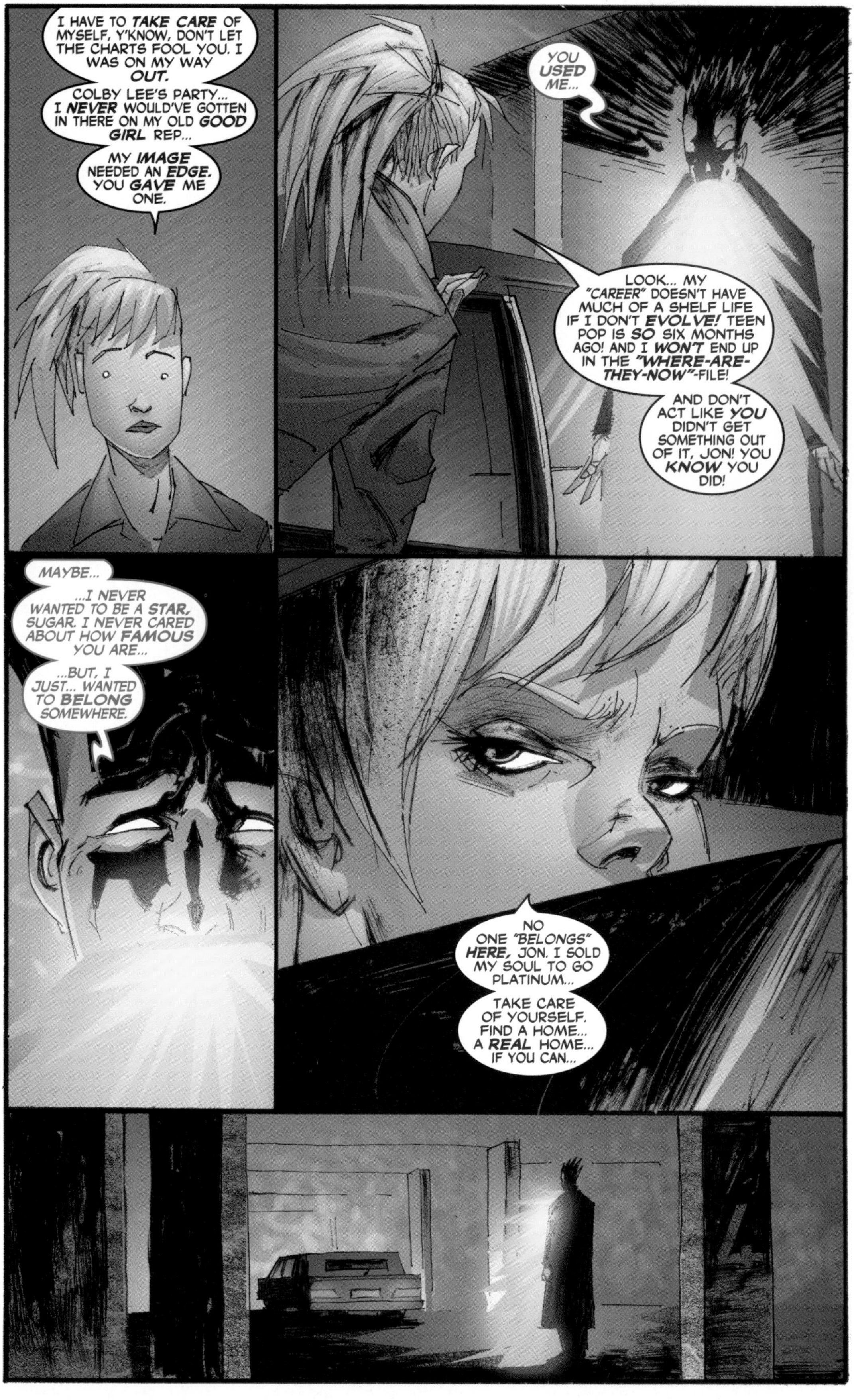
I HAVE TO TAKE CARE OF MYSELF, Y'KNOW, DON'T LET THE CHARTS FOOL YOU. I WAS ON MY WAY OUT.
COLBY LEE'S PARTY... I NEVER WOULD'VE GOTTEN IN THERE ON MY OLD GOOD GIRL REP...
MY IMAGE NEEDED AN EDGE. YOU GAVE ME ONE.
YOU USED ME...
LOOK... MY "CAREER" DOESN'T HAVE MUCH OF A SHELF LIFE IF I DON'T EVOLVE! TEEN POP IS SO SIX MONTHS AGO! AND I WON'T END UP IN THE "WHERE-ARE-THEY-NOW"-FILE!
AND DON'T ACT LIKE YOU DIDN'T GET SOMETHING OUT OF IT, JON! YOU KNOW YOU DID!
MAYBE...
...I NEVER WANTED TO BE A STAR, SUGAR. I NEVER CARED ABOUT HOW FAMOUS YOU ARE...
...BUT, I JUST... WANTED TO BELONG SOMEWHERE.
NO ONE "BELONGS" HERE, JON. I SOLD MY SOUL TO GO PLATINUM...
TAKE CARE OF YOURSELF. FIND A HOME... A REAL HOME... IF YOU CAN...

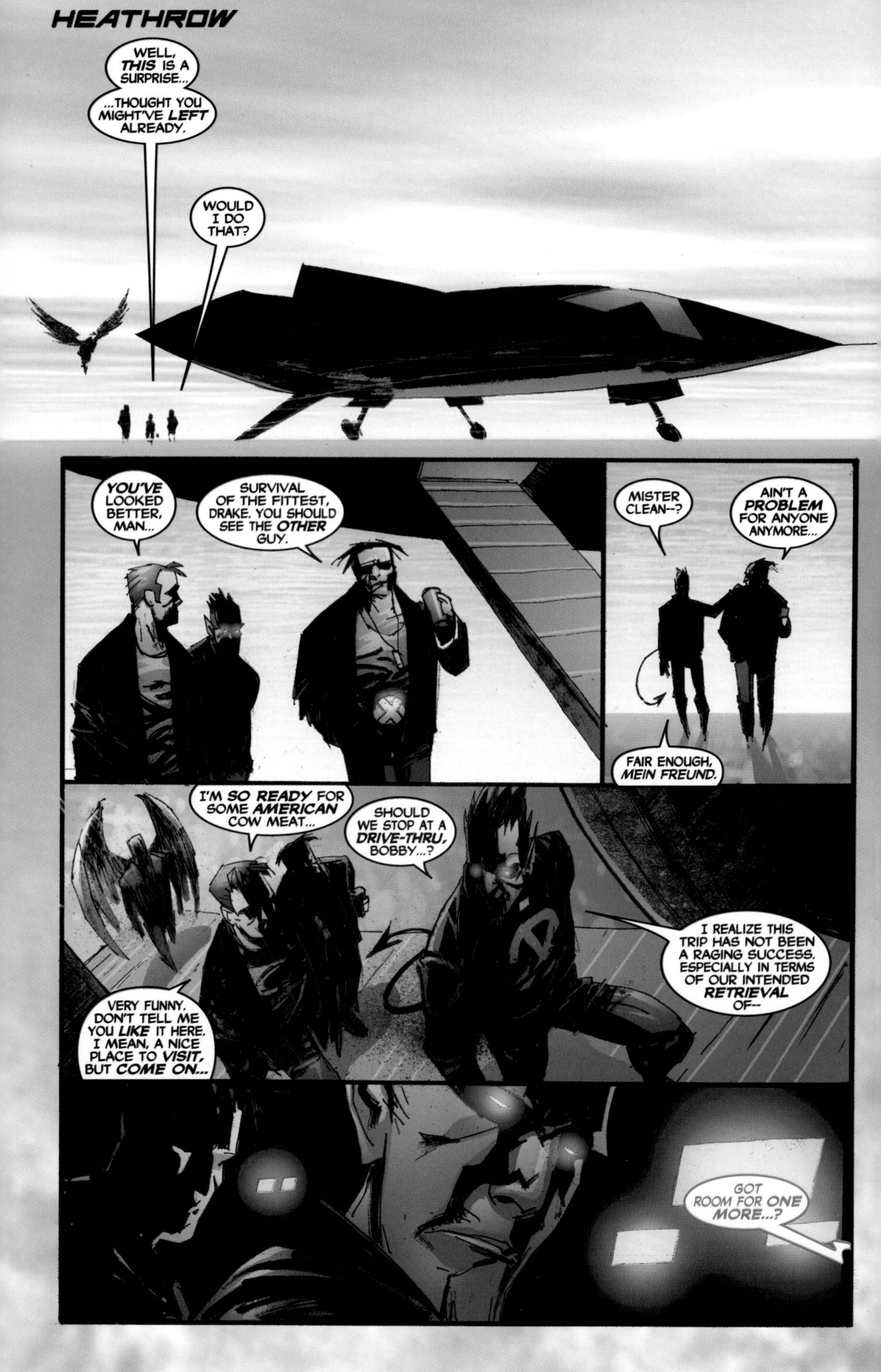
HEATHROW
WELL, THIS IS A SURPRISE...
...THOUGHT YOU MIGHT'VE LEFT ALREADY.
WOULD I DO THAT?
YOU'VE LOOKED BETTER, MAN...
SURVIVAL OF THE FITTEST, DRAKE. YOU SHOULD SEE THE OTHER GUY.
MISTER CLEAN--?
AIN'T A PROBLEM FOR ANYONE ANYMORE...
FAIR ENOUGH, MEIN FREUND.
I'M SO READY FOR SOME AMERICAN COW MEAT...
SHOULD WE STOP AT A DRIVE-THRU, BOBBY...?
VERY FUNNY. DON'T TELL ME YOU LIKE IT HERE. I MEAN, A NICE PLACE TO VISIT, BUT COME ON...
I REALIZE THIS TRIP HAS NOT BEEN A RAGING SUCCESS, ESPECIALLY IN TERMS OF OUR INTENDED RETRIEVAL OF--
GOT ROOM FOR ONE MORE...?

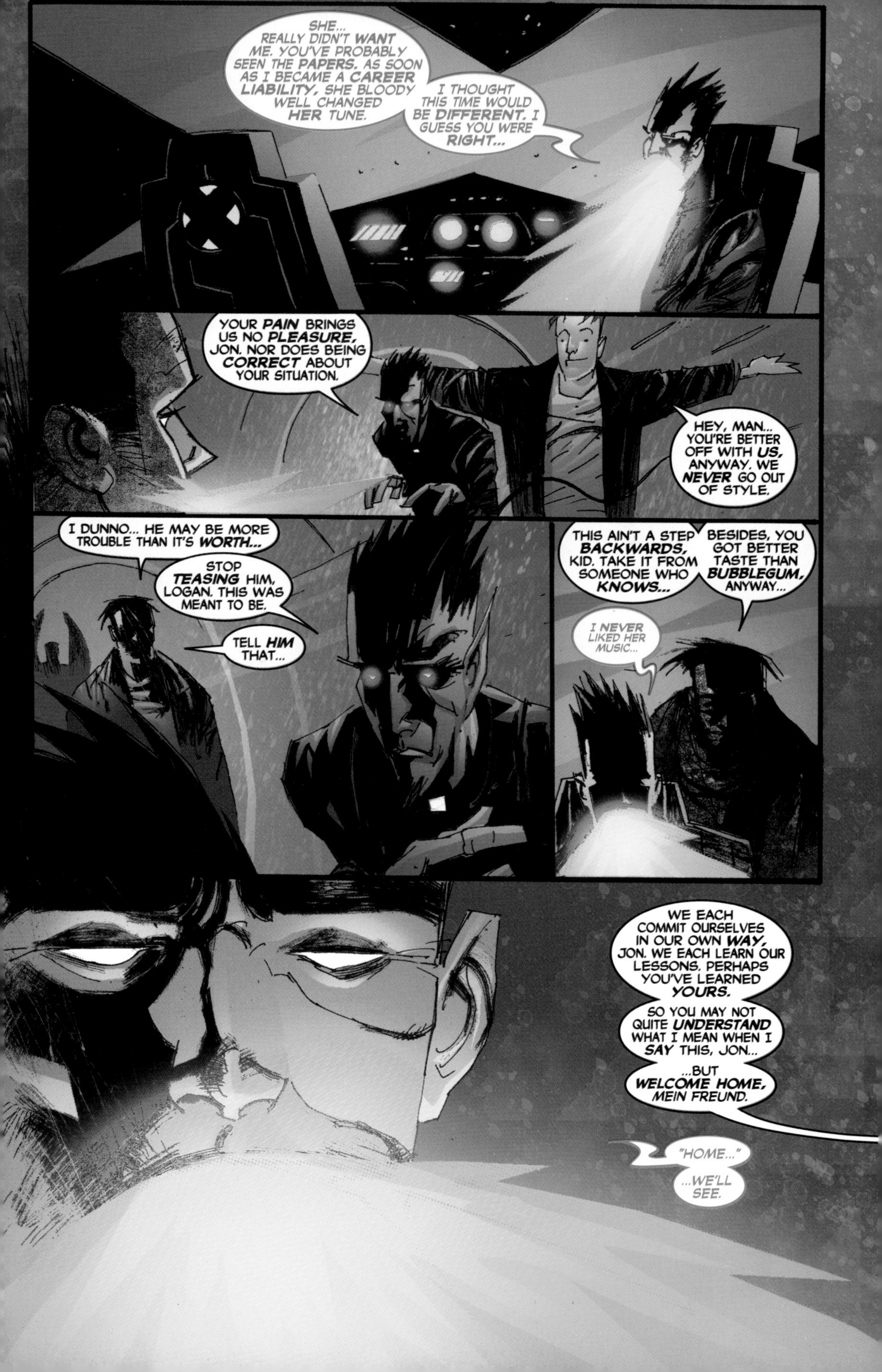
SHE... REALLY DIDN'T WANT ME. YOU'VE PROBABLY SEEN THE PAPERS. AS SOON AS I BECAME A CAREER LIABILITY, SHE BLOODY WELL CHANGED HER TUNE.
I THOUGHT THIS TIME WOULD BE DIFFERENT. I GUESS YOU WERE RIGHT...
YOUR PAIN BRINGS US NO PLEASURE, JON. NOR DOES BEING CORRECT ABOUT YOUR SITUATION.
HEY, MAN... YOU'RE BETTER OFF WITH US, ANYWAY. WE NEVER GO OUT OF STYLE.
I DUNNO... HE MAY BE MORE TROUBLE THAN IT'S WORTH...
STOP TEASING HIM, LOGAN. THIS WAS MEANT TO BE.
TELL HIM THAT...
THIS AIN'T A STEP BACKWARDS, KID. TAKE IT FROM SOMEONE WHO KNOWS...
BESIDES, YOU GOT BETTER TASTE THAN BUBBLEGUM, ANYWAY...
I NEVER LIKED HER MUSIC...
WE EACH COMMIT OURSELVES IN OUR OWN WAY, JON. WE EACH LEARN OUR LESSONS. PERHAPS YOU'VE LEARNED YOURS.
SO YOU MAY NOT QUITE UNDERSTAND WHAT I MEAN WHEN I SAY THIS, JON...
...BUT WELCOME HOME, MEIN FREUND.
"HOME..."
...WE'LL SEE.

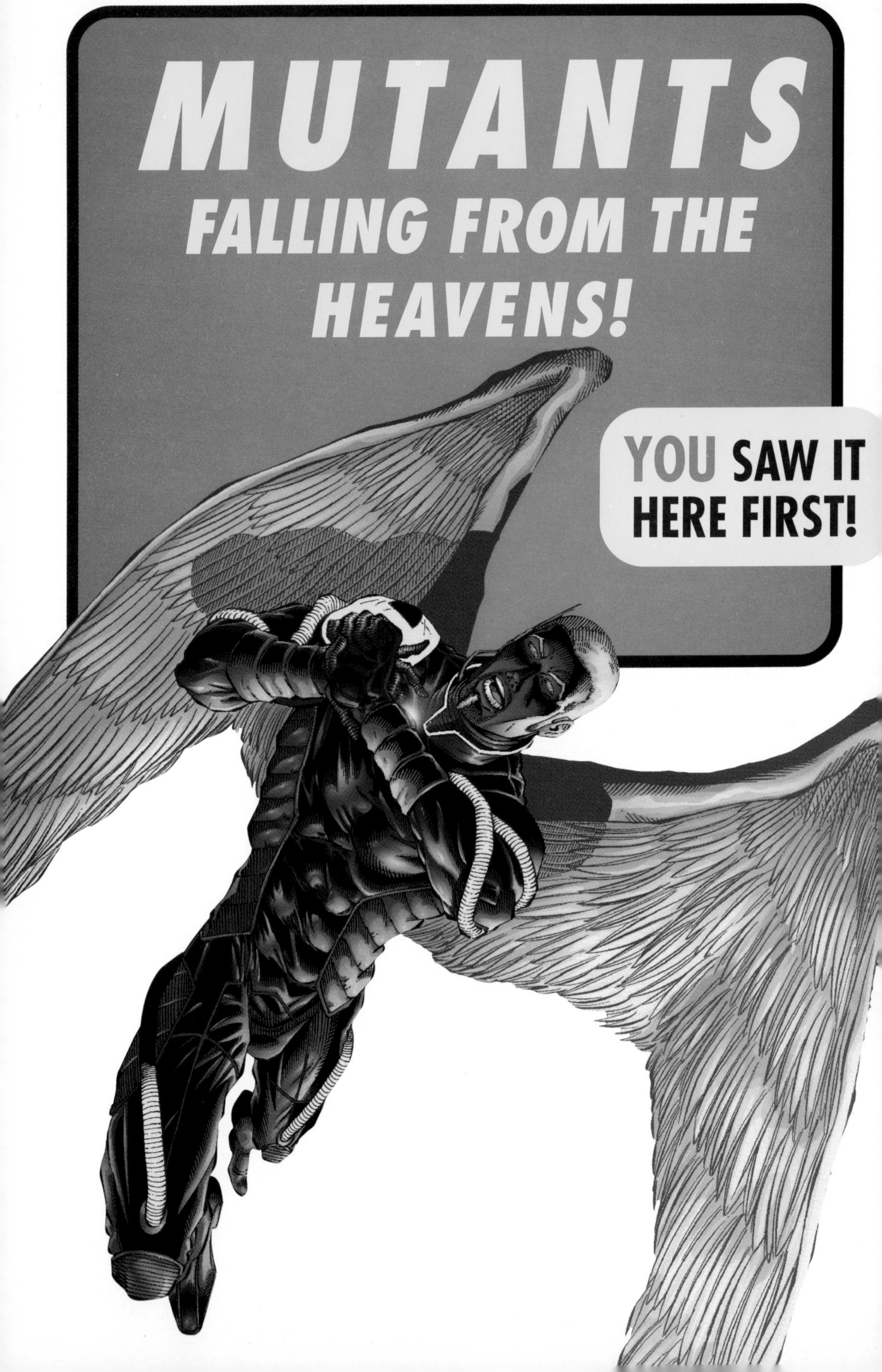
MUTANTS
FALLING FROM THE HEAVENS!
YOU SAW IT HERE FIRST!

FOR UNLAWFUL CARNAL KNOWLEDGE

-RANEY-

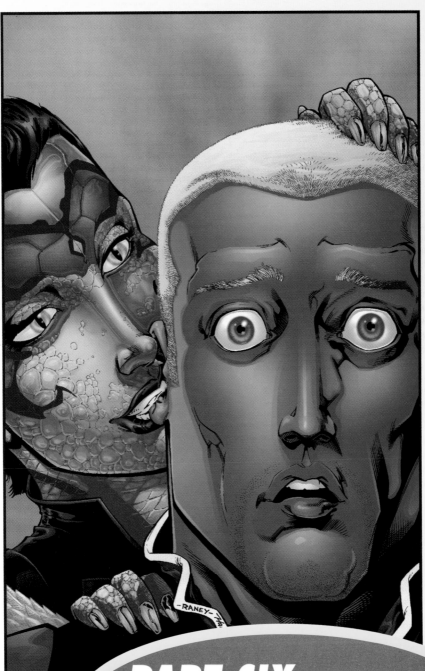

PART SIX:
UNCANNY X-MEN #399

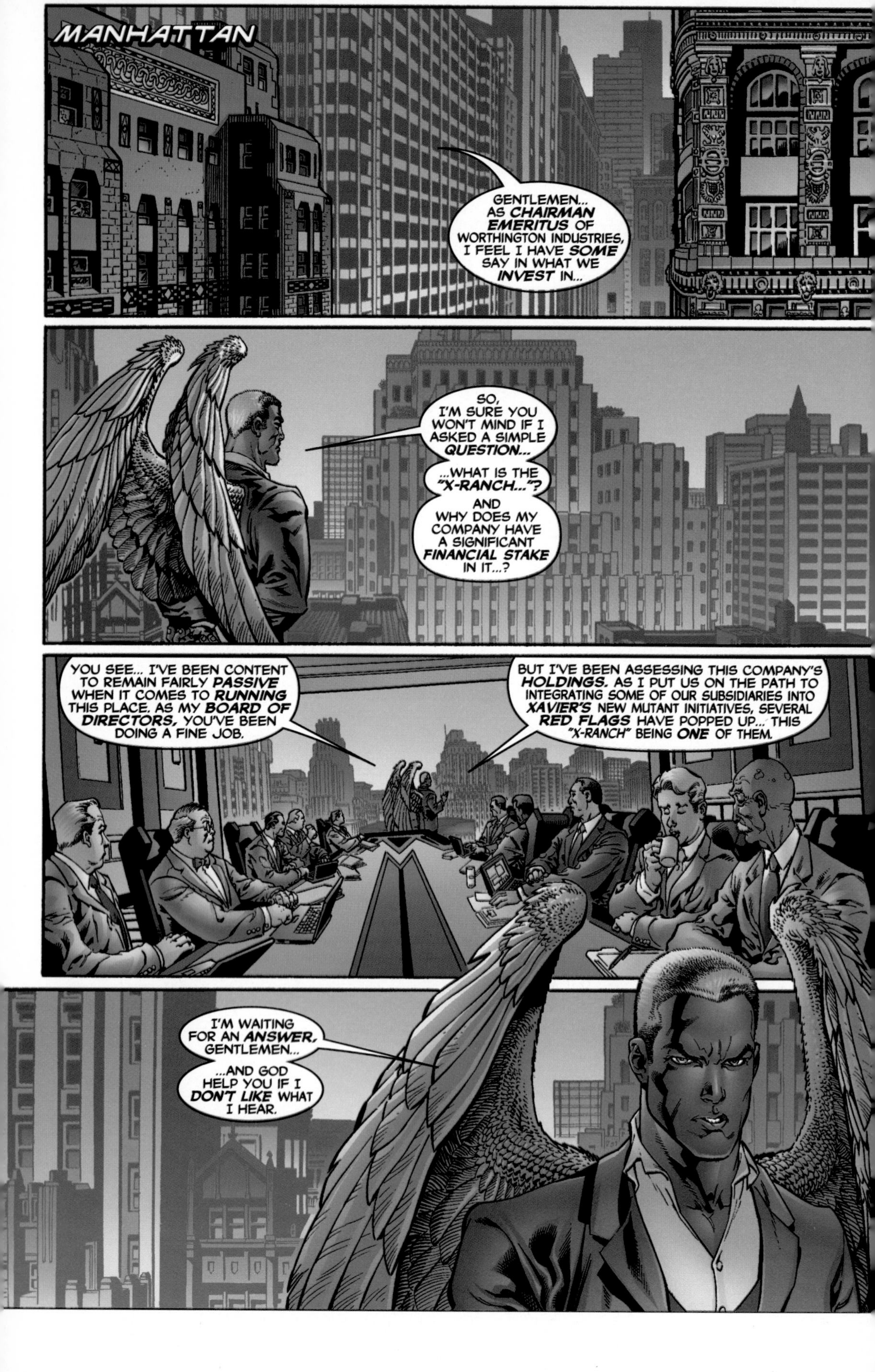
MANHATTAN
GENTLEMEN... AS CHAIRMAN EMERITUS OF WORTHINGTON INDUSTRIES, I FEEL I HAVE SOME SAY IN WHAT WE INVEST IN...
SO, I'M SURE YOU WON'T MIND IF I ASKED A SIMPLE QUESTION...
...WHAT IS THE "X-RANCH..."?
AND WHY DOES MY COMPANY HAVE A SIGNIFICANT FINANCIAL STAKE IN IT...?
YOU SEE... I'VE BEEN CONTENT TO REMAIN FAIRLY PASSIVE WHEN IT COMES TO RUNNING THIS PLACE. AS MY BOARD OF DIRECTORS, YOU'VE BEEN DOING A FINE JOB.
BUT I'VE BEEN ASSESSING THIS COMPANY'S HOLDINGS. AS I PUT US ON THE PATH TO INTEGRATING SOME OF OUR SUBSIDIARIES INTO XAVIER'S NEW MUTANT INITIATIVES, SEVERAL RED FLAGS HAVE POPPED UP... THIS "X-RANCH" BEING ONE OF THEM.
I'M WAITING FOR AN ANSWER, GENTLEMEN...
...AND GOD HELP YOU IF I DON'T LIKE WHAT I HEAR.

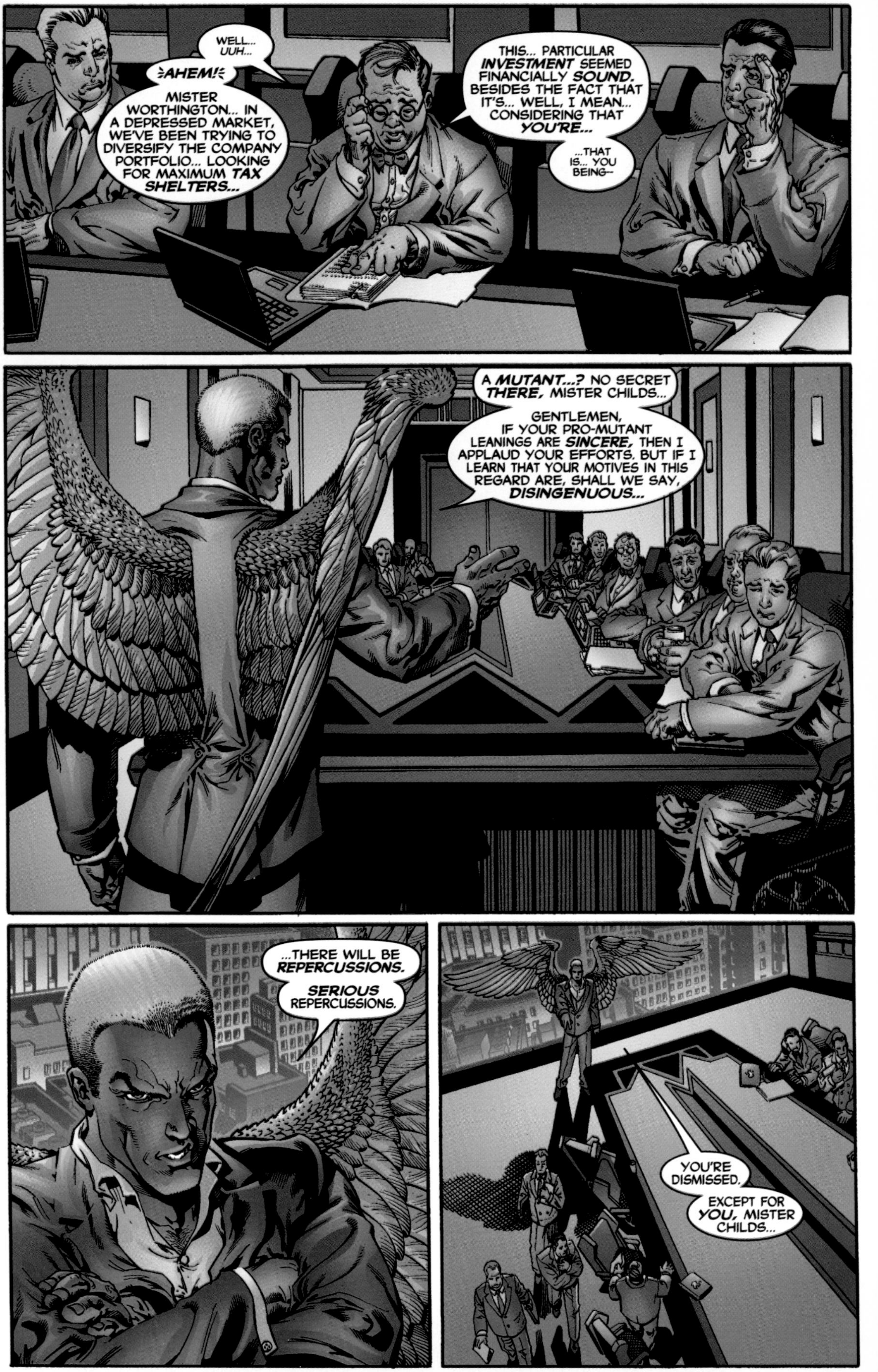
WELL... UUH...
AHEM!
MISTER WORTHINGTON... IN A DEPRESSED MARKET, WE'VE BEEN TRYING TO DIVERSIFY THE COMPANY PORTFOLIO... LOOKING FOR MAXIMUM TAX SHELTERS...
THIS... PARTICULAR INVESTMENT SEEMED FINANCIALLY SOUND. BESIDES THE FACT THAT IT'S... WELL, I MEAN... CONSIDERING THAT YOU'RE...
...THAT IS... YOU BEING--
A MUTANT...? NO SECRET THERE, MISTER CHILDS...
GENTLEMEN, IF YOUR PRO-MUTANT LEANINGS ARE SINCERE, THEN I APPLAUD YOUR EFFORTS. BUT IF I LEARN THAT YOUR MOTIVES IN THIS REGARD ARE, SHALL WE SAY, DISINGENUOUS...
...THERE WILL BE REPERCUSSIONS.
SERIOUS REPERCUSSIONS.
YOU'RE DISMISSED.
EXCEPT FOR YOU, MISTER CHILDS...

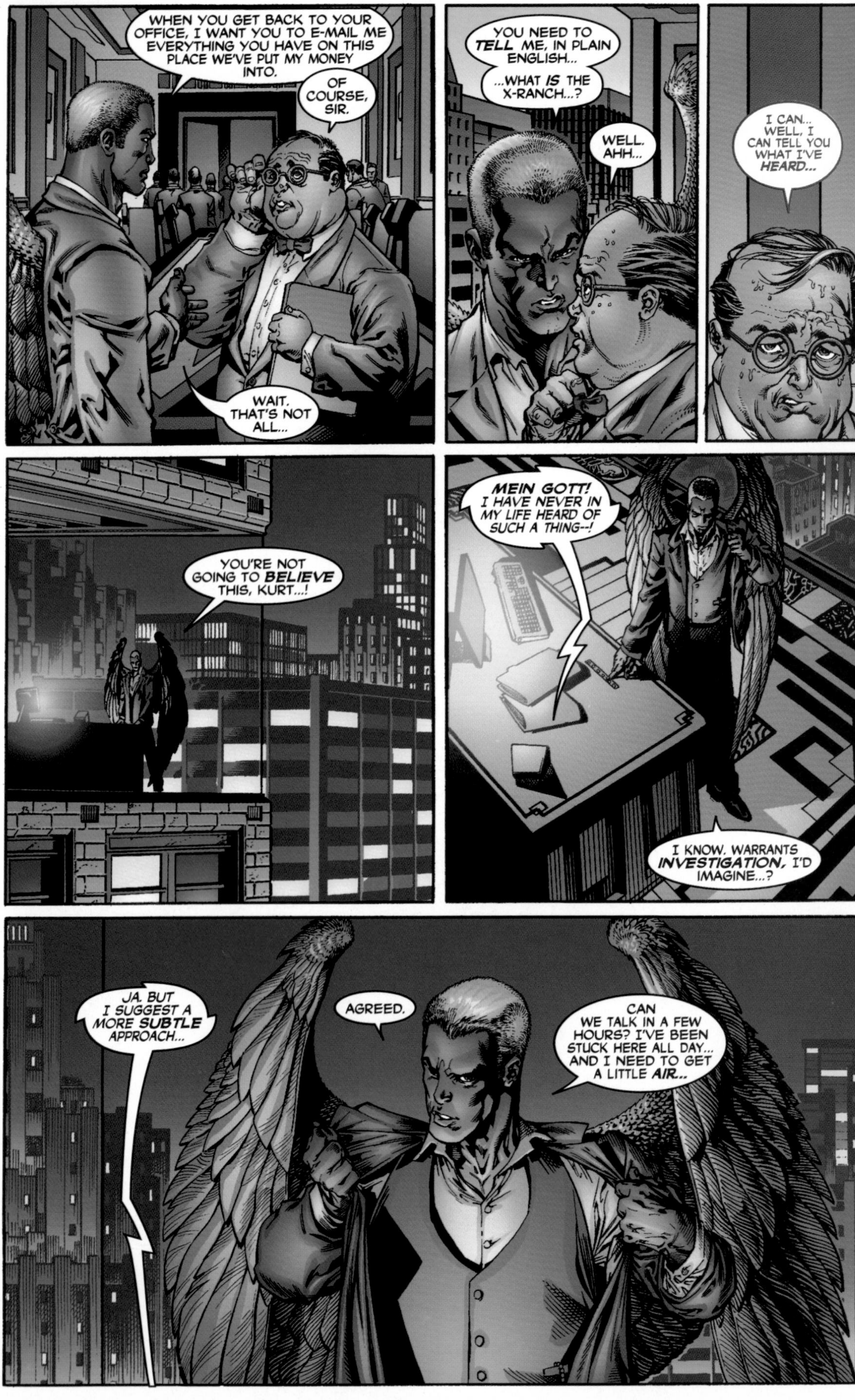
WHEN YOU GET BACK TO YOUR OFFICE, I WANT YOU TO E-MAIL ME EVERYTHING YOU HAVE ON THIS PLACE WE'VE PUT MY MONEY INTO.
OF COURSE, SIR.
WAIT. THAT'S NOT ALL...
YOU NEED TO TELL ME, IN PLAIN ENGLISH...
...WHAT IS THE X-RANCH...?
WELL. AHH...
I CAN... WELL, I CAN TELL YOU WHAT I'VE HEARD...
YOU'RE NOT GOING TO BELIEVE THIS, KURT...!
MEIN GOTT! I HAVE NEVER IN MY LIFE HEARD OF SUCH A THING--!
I KNOW. WARRANTS INVESTIGATION, I'D IMAGINE...?
JA. BUT I SUGGEST A MORE SUBTLE APPROACH...
AGREED.
CAN WE TALK IN A FEW HOURS? I'VE BEEN STUCK HERE ALL DAY... AND I NEED TO GET A LITTLE AIR...

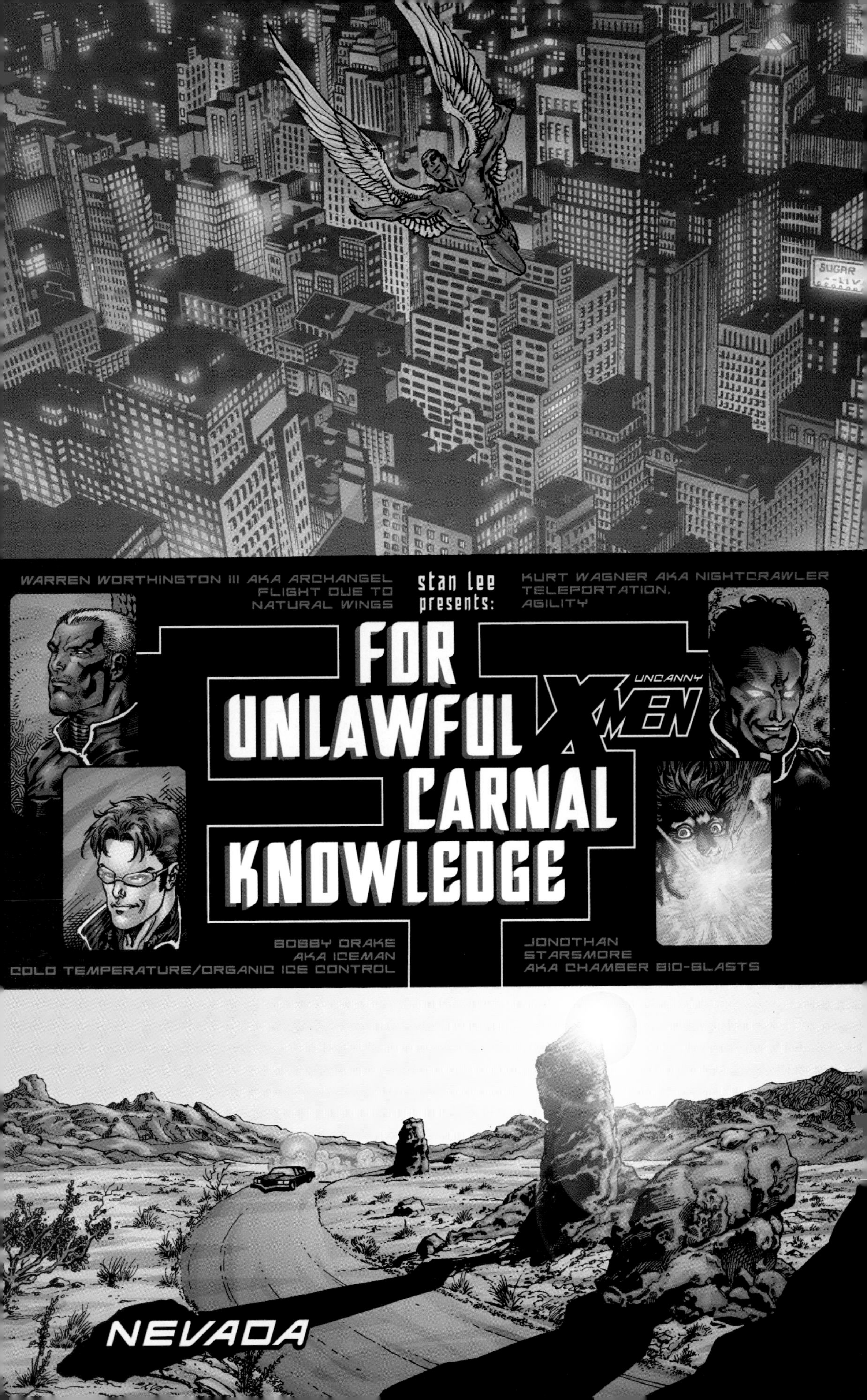
SUGAR
WARREN WORTHINGTON III AKA ARCHANGEL
FLIGHT DUE TO
NATURAL WINGS
stan lee presents:
KURT WAGNER AKA NIGHTCRAWLER
TELEPORTATION,
AGILITY
FOR UNLAWFUL CARNAL KNOWLEDGE
UNCANNY X-MEN
BOBBY DRAKE
AKA ICEMAN
COLD TEMPERATURE/ORGANIC ICE CONTROL
JONOTHAN
STARSMORE
AKA CHAMBER BIO-BLASTS
NEVADA

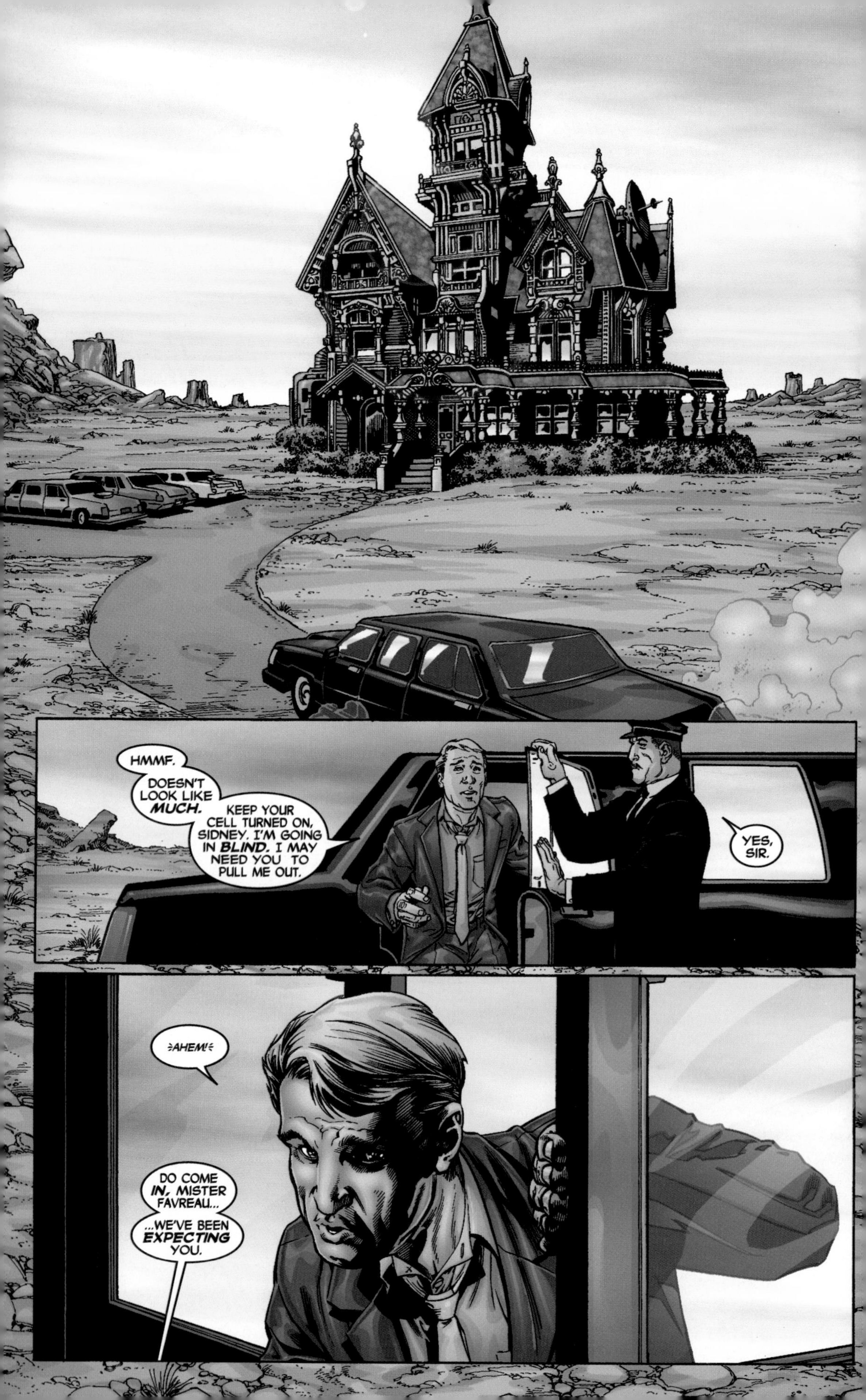
HMMF.
DOESN'T LOOK LIKE MUCH.
KEEP YOUR CELL TURNED ON, SIDNEY. I'M GOING IN BLIND. I MAY NEED YOU TO PULL ME OUT.
YES, SIR.
AHEM!
DO COME IN, MISTER FAVREAU...
...WE'VE BEEN EXPECTING YOU.

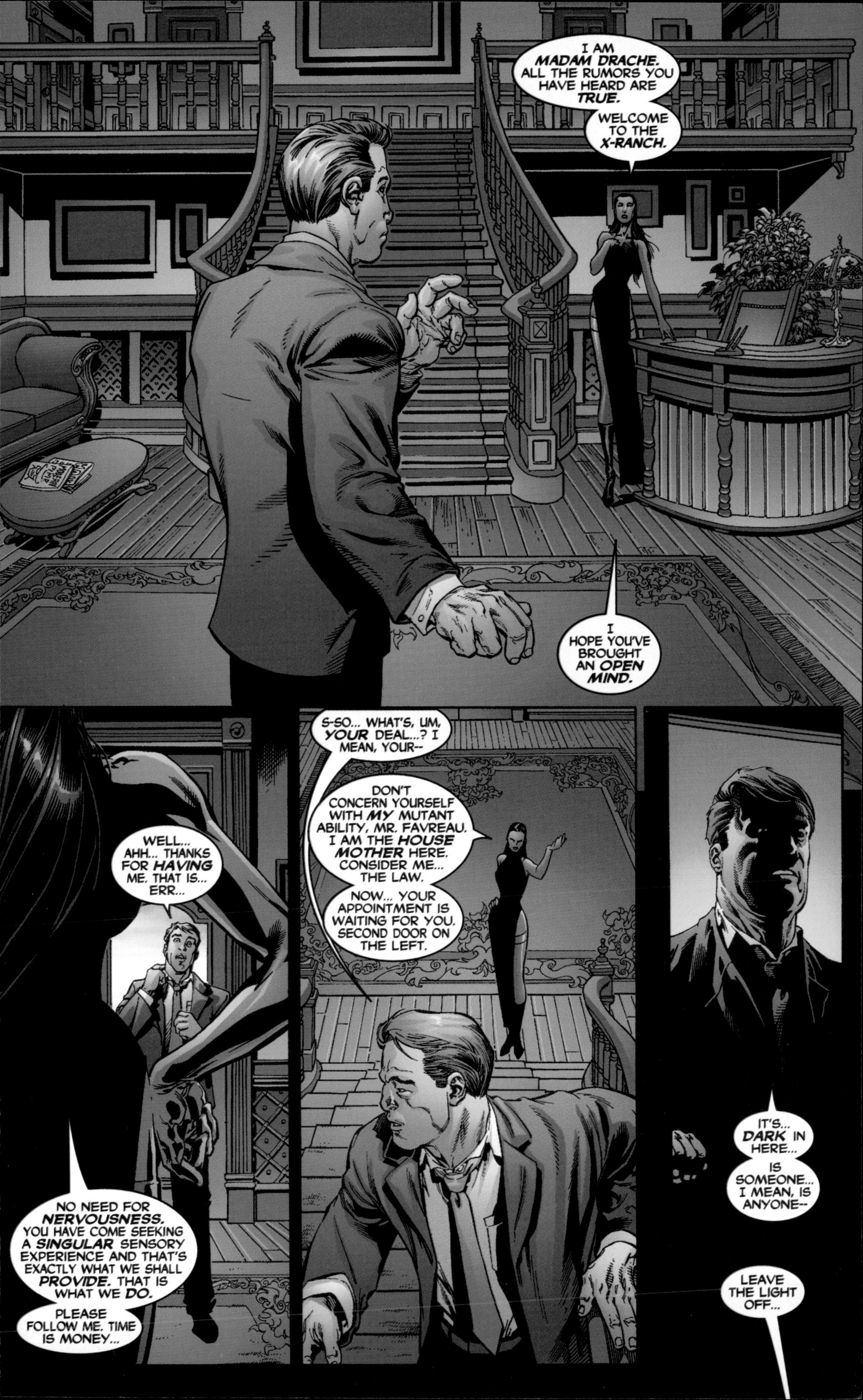
I AM MADAM DRACHE. ALL THE RUMORS YOU HAVE HEARD ARE TRUE.
WELCOME TO THE X-RANCH.
I HOPE YOU'VE BROUGHT AN OPEN MIND.
WELL... AHH... THANKS FOR HAVING ME. THAT IS... ERR...
NO NEED FOR NERVOUSNESS. YOU HAVE COME SEEKING A SINGULAR SENSORY EXPERIENCE AND THAT'S EXACTLY WHAT WE SHALL PROVIDE. THAT IS WHAT WE DO.
PLEASE FOLLOW ME. TIME IS MONEY...
S-SO... WHAT'S, UM, YOUR DEAL...? I MEAN, YOUR--
DON'T CONCERN YOURSELF WITH MY MUTANT ABILITY, MR. FAVREAU. I AM THE HOUSE MOTHER HERE. CONSIDER ME... THE LAW.
NOW... YOUR APPOINTMENT IS WAITING FOR YOU. SECOND DOOR ON THE LEFT.
IT'S... DARK IN HERE...
IS SOMEONE... I MEAN, IS ANYONE--
LEAVE THE LIGHT OFF...

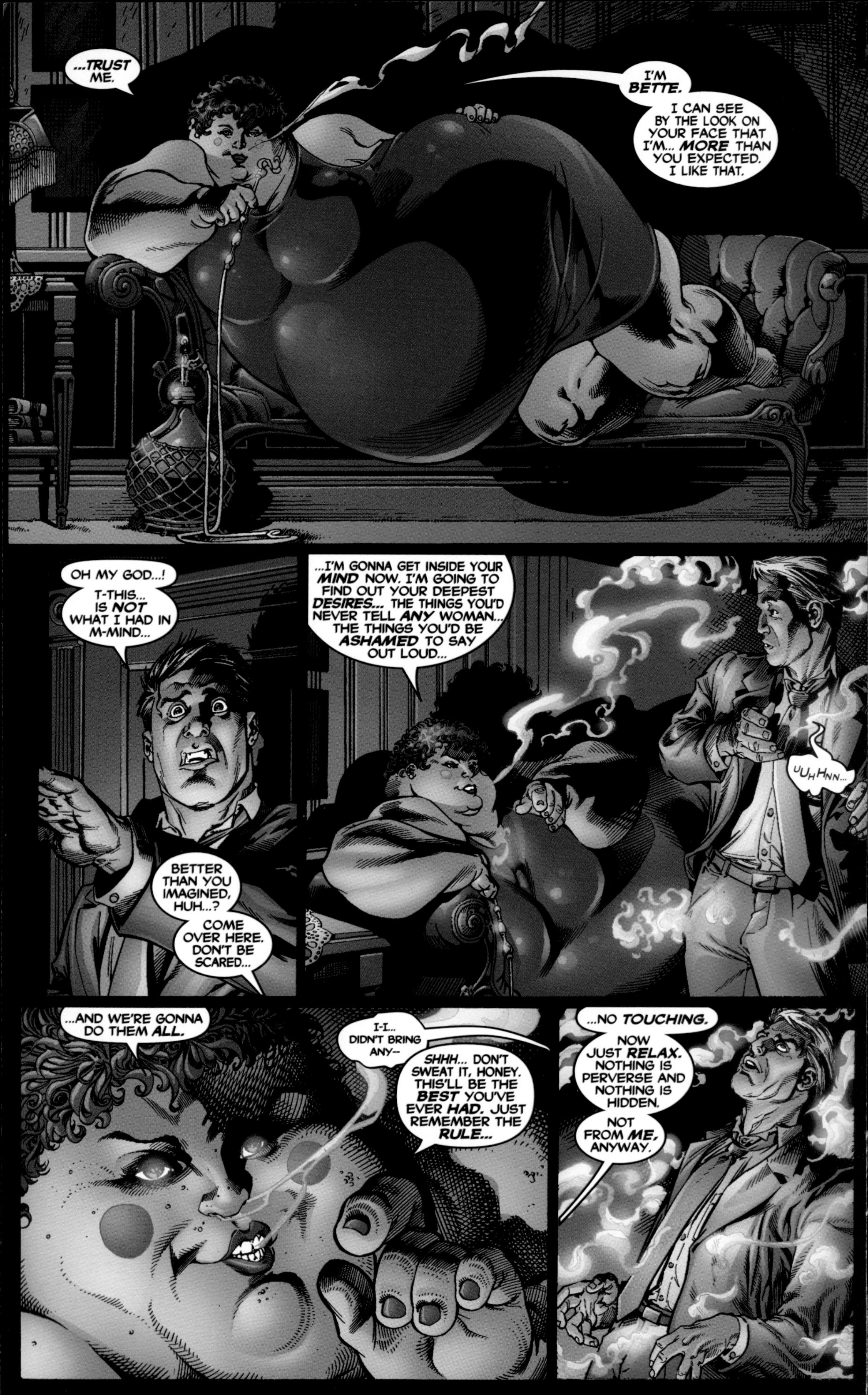
...TRUST ME.
I'M BETTE.
I CAN SEE BY THE LOOK ON YOUR FACE THAT I'M... MORE THAN YOU EXPECTED. I LIKE THAT.
OH MY GOD...!
T-THIS... IS NOT WHAT I HAD IN M-MIND...
BETTER THAN YOU IMAGINED, HUH...?
COME OVER HERE. DON'T BE SCARED...
...I'M GONNA GET INSIDE YOUR MIND NOW. I'M GOING TO FIND OUT YOUR DEEPEST DESIRES... THE THINGS YOU'D NEVER TELL ANY WOMAN... THE THINGS YOU'D BE ASHAMED TO SAY OUT LOUD...
UUHHNN...
...AND WE'RE GONNA DO THEM ALL.
I-I... DIDN'T BRING ANY--
SHHH... DON'T SWEAT IT, HONEY. THIS'LL BE THE BEST YOU'VE EVER HAD. JUST REMEMBER THE RULE...
...NO TOUCHING.
NOW JUST RELAX. NOTHING IS PERVERSE AND NOTHING IS HIDDEN.
NOT FROM ME, ANYWAY.

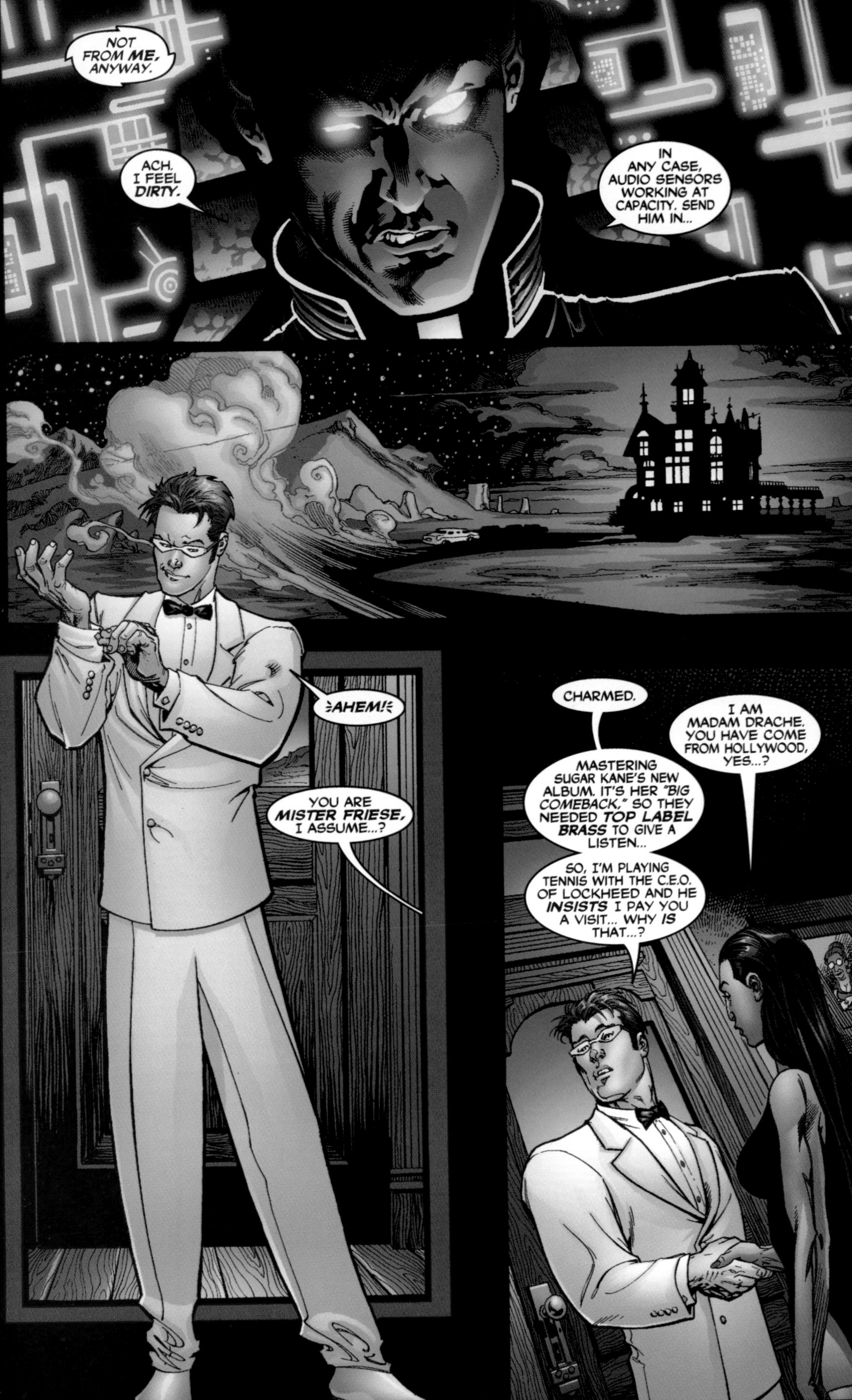
NOT FROM **ME,** ANYWAY.
ACH. I FEEL **DIRTY.**
IN ANY CASE, AUDIO SENSORS WORKING AT CAPACITY. SEND HIM IN...
AHEM!
YOU ARE **MISTER FRIESE,** I ASSUME...?
I AM MADAM DRACHE. YOU HAVE COME FROM HOLLYWOOD, YES...?
CHARMED.
MASTERING SUGAR KANE'S NEW ALBUM. IT'S HER "BIG COMEBACK," SO THEY NEEDED **TOP LABEL BRASS** TO GIVE A LISTEN...
SO, I'M PLAYING TENNIS WITH THE C.E.O. OF LOCKHEED AND HE **INSISTS** I PAY YOU A VISIT... WHY **IS** THAT...?

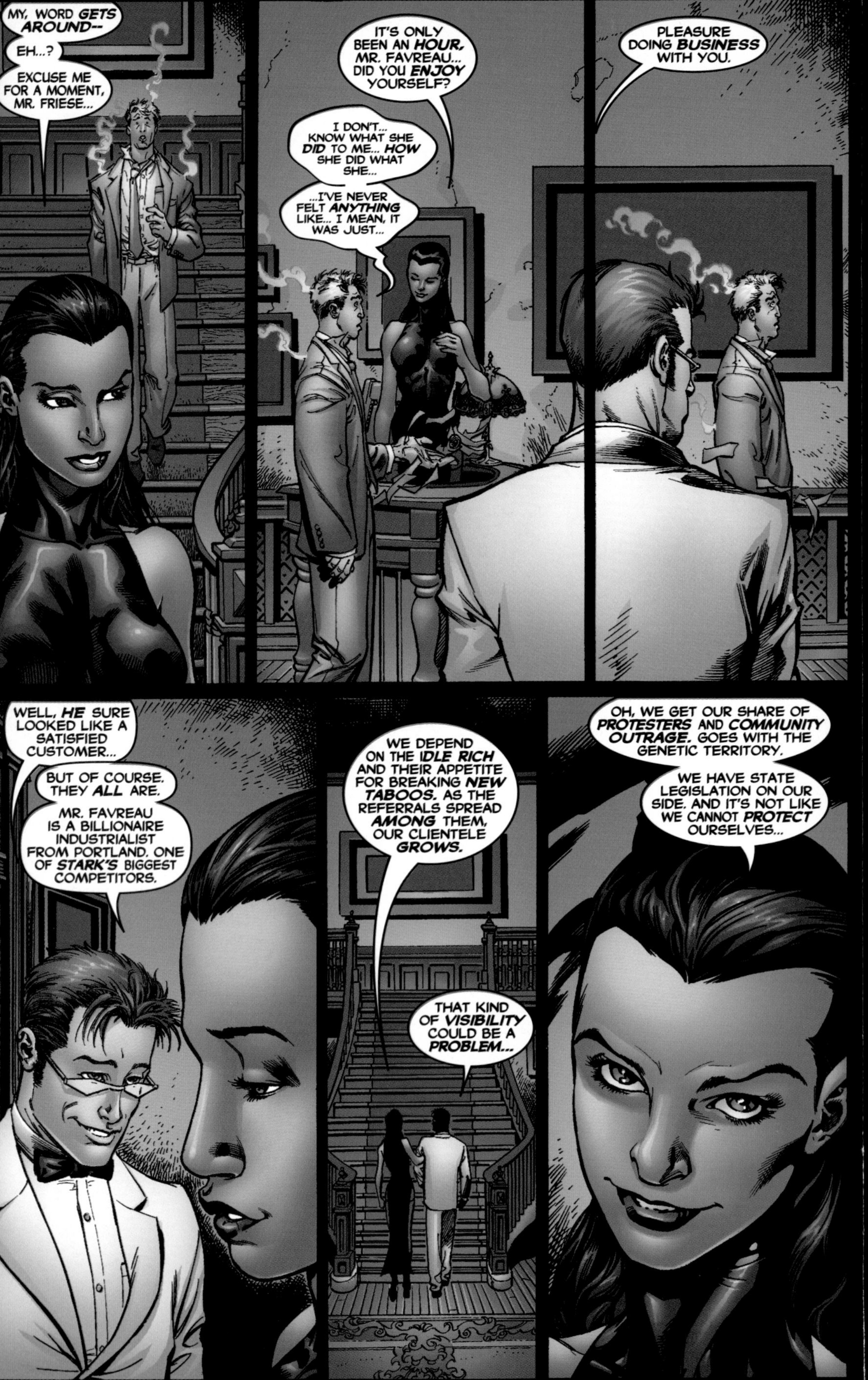
MY, WORD GETS AROUND--
EH...?
EXCUSE ME FOR A MOMENT, MR. FRIESE...
IT'S ONLY BEEN AN HOUR, MR. FAVREAU... DID YOU ENJOY YOURSELF?
I DON'T... KNOW WHAT SHE DID TO ME... HOW SHE DID WHAT SHE...
...I'VE NEVER FELT ANYTHING LIKE... I MEAN, IT WAS JUST...
PLEASURE DOING BUSINESS WITH YOU.
WELL, HE SURE LOOKED LIKE A SATISFIED CUSTOMER...
BUT OF COURSE. THEY ALL ARE.
MR. FAVREAU IS A BILLIONAIRE INDUSTRIALIST FROM PORTLAND. ONE OF STARK'S BIGGEST COMPETITORS.
WE DEPEND ON THE IDLE RICH AND THEIR APPETITE FOR BREAKING NEW TABOOS. AS THE REFERRALS SPREAD AMONG THEM, OUR CLIENTELE GROWS.
THAT KIND OF VISIBILITY COULD BE A PROBLEM...
OH, WE GET OUR SHARE OF PROTESTERS AND COMMUNITY OUTRAGE. GOES WITH THE GENETIC TERRITORY.
WE HAVE STATE LEGISLATION ON OUR SIDE. AND IT'S NOT LIKE WE CANNOT PROTECT OURSELVES...

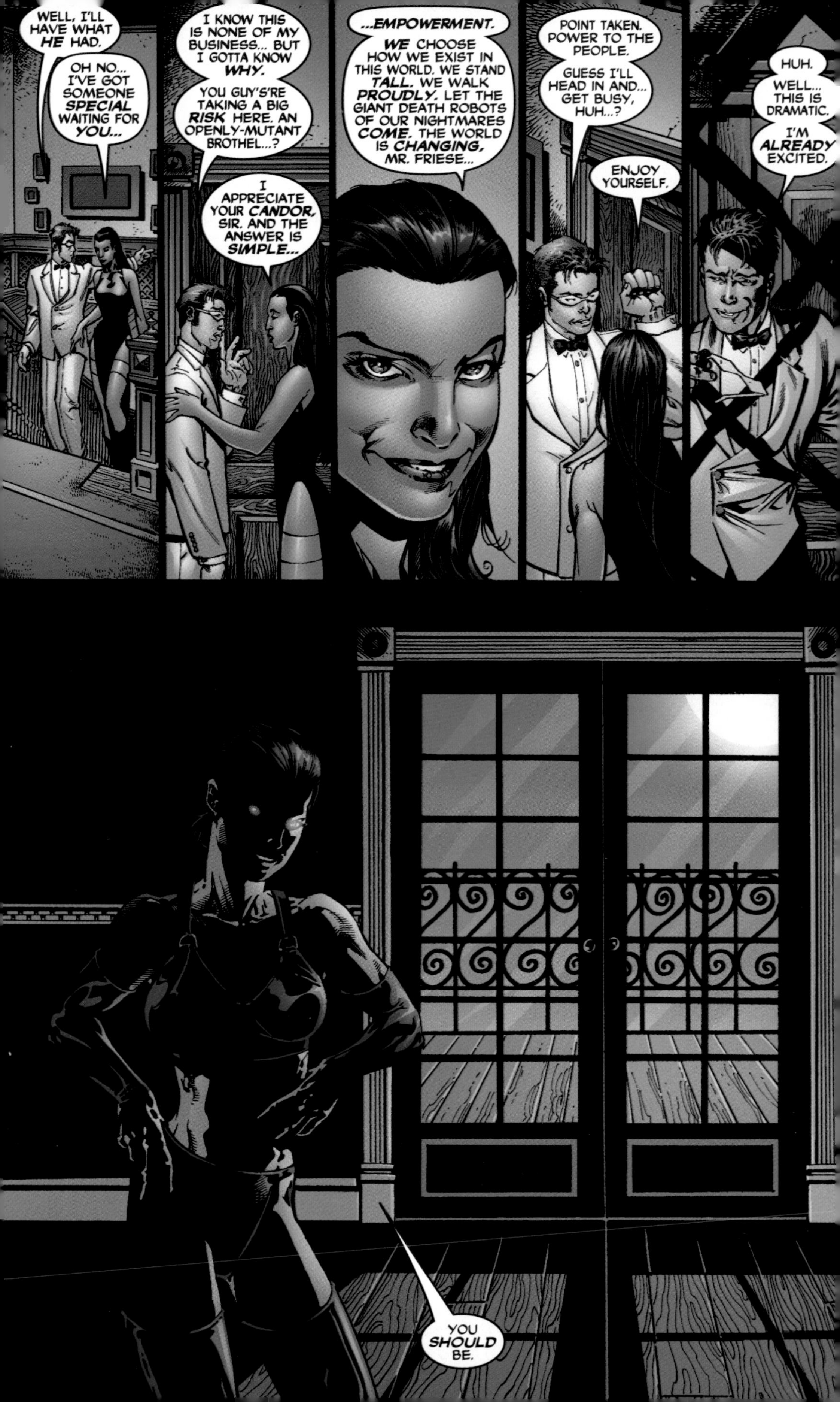
WELL, I'LL HAVE WHAT HE HAD.
OH NO... I'VE GOT SOMEONE SPECIAL WAITING FOR YOU...
I KNOW THIS IS NONE OF MY BUSINESS... BUT I GOTTA KNOW WHY.
YOU GUY'S'RE TAKING A BIG RISK HERE. AN OPENLY-MUTANT BROTHEL...?
I APPRECIATE YOUR CANDOR, SIR, AND THE ANSWER IS SIMPLE...
...EMPOWERMENT.
WE CHOOSE HOW WE EXIST IN THIS WORLD. WE STAND TALL. WE WALK PROUDLY. LET THE GIANT DEATH ROBOTS OF OUR NIGHTMARES COME. THE WORLD IS CHANGING, MR. FRIESE...
POINT TAKEN. POWER TO THE PEOPLE.
GUESS I'LL HEAD IN AND... GET BUSY, HUH...?
ENJOY YOURSELF.
HUH.
WELL... THIS IS DRAMATIC.
I'M ALREADY EXCITED.
YOU SHOULD BE.

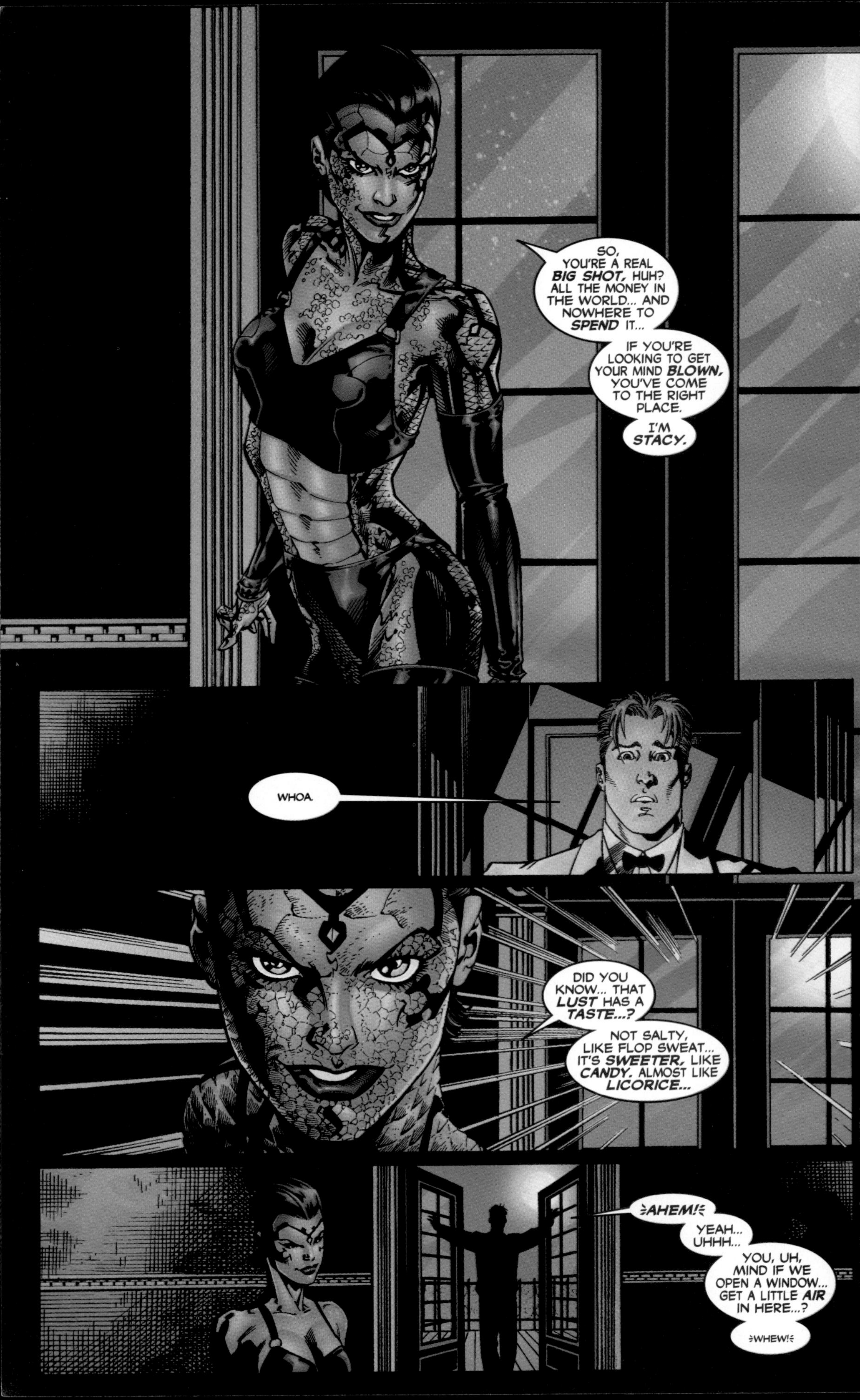
SO, YOU'RE A REAL BIG SHOT, HUH? ALL THE MONEY IN THE WORLD... AND NOWHERE TO SPEND IT...
IF YOU'RE LOOKING TO GET YOUR MIND BLOWN, YOU'VE COME TO THE RIGHT PLACE.
I'M STACY.
WHOA.
DID YOU KNOW... THAT LUST HAS A TASTE...?
NOT SALTY, LIKE FLOP SWEAT... IT'S SWEETER, LIKE CANDY. ALMOST LIKE LICORICE...
AHEM!
YEAH... UHHH...
YOU, UH, MIND IF WE OPEN A WINDOW... GET A LITTLE AIR IN HERE...?
WHEW!

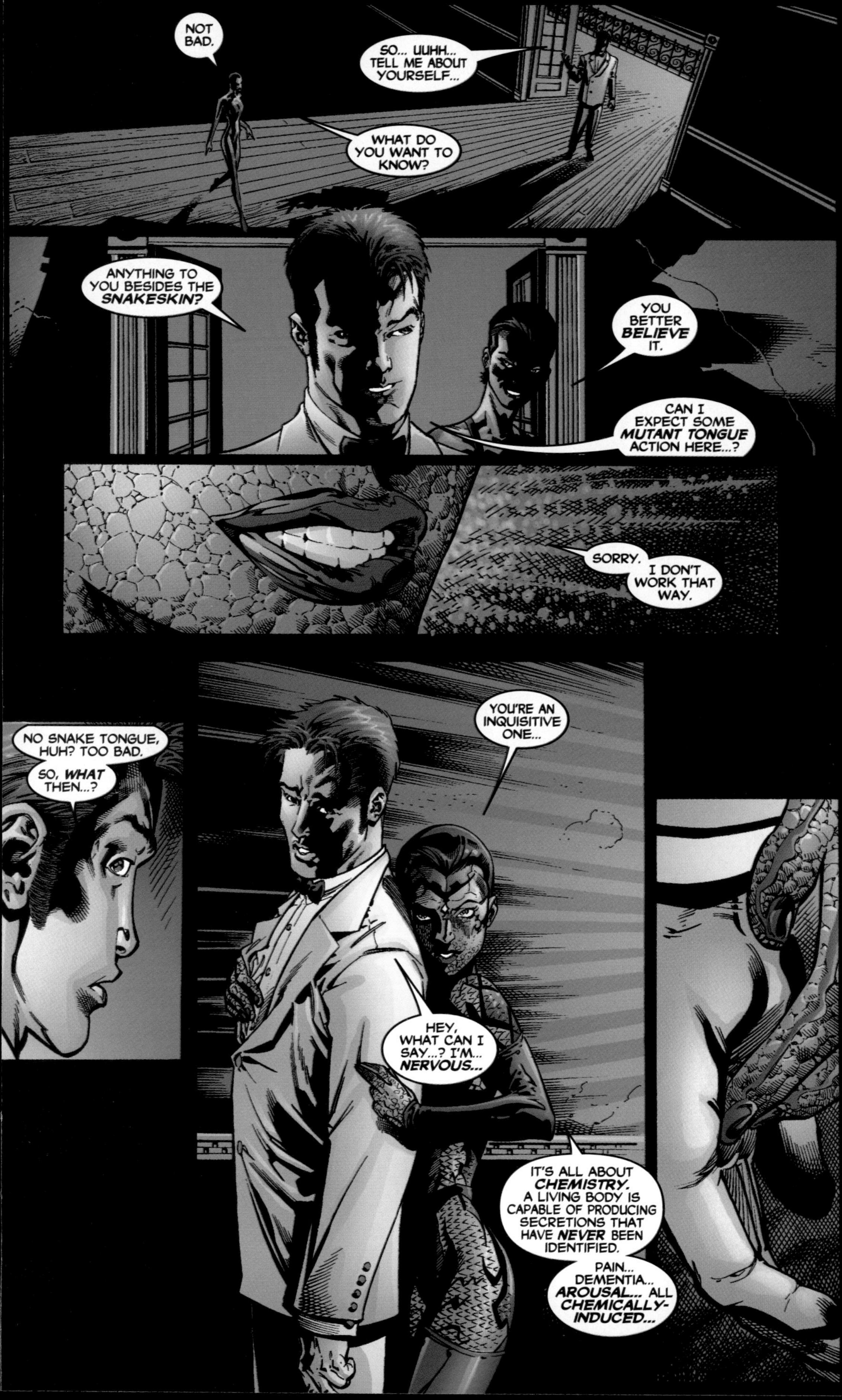
NOT BAD.
SO... UUHH... TELL ME ABOUT YOURSELF...
WHAT DO YOU WANT TO KNOW?
ANYTHING TO YOU BESIDES THE **SNAKESKIN?**
YOU BETTER **BELIEVE** IT.
CAN I EXPECT SOME **MUTANT TONGUE** ACTION HERE...?
SORRY. I DON'T WORK THAT WAY.
NO SNAKE TONGUE, HUH? TOO BAD.
SO, **WHAT** THEN...?
YOU'RE AN INQUISITIVE ONE...
HEY, WHAT CAN I SAY...? I'M... **NERVOUS...**
IT'S ALL ABOUT **CHEMISTRY.** A LIVING BODY IS CAPABLE OF PRODUCING SECRETIONS THAT HAVE **NEVER** BEEN IDENTIFIED.
PAIN... DEMENTIA... **AROUSAL... ALL CHEMICALLY-INDUCED...**

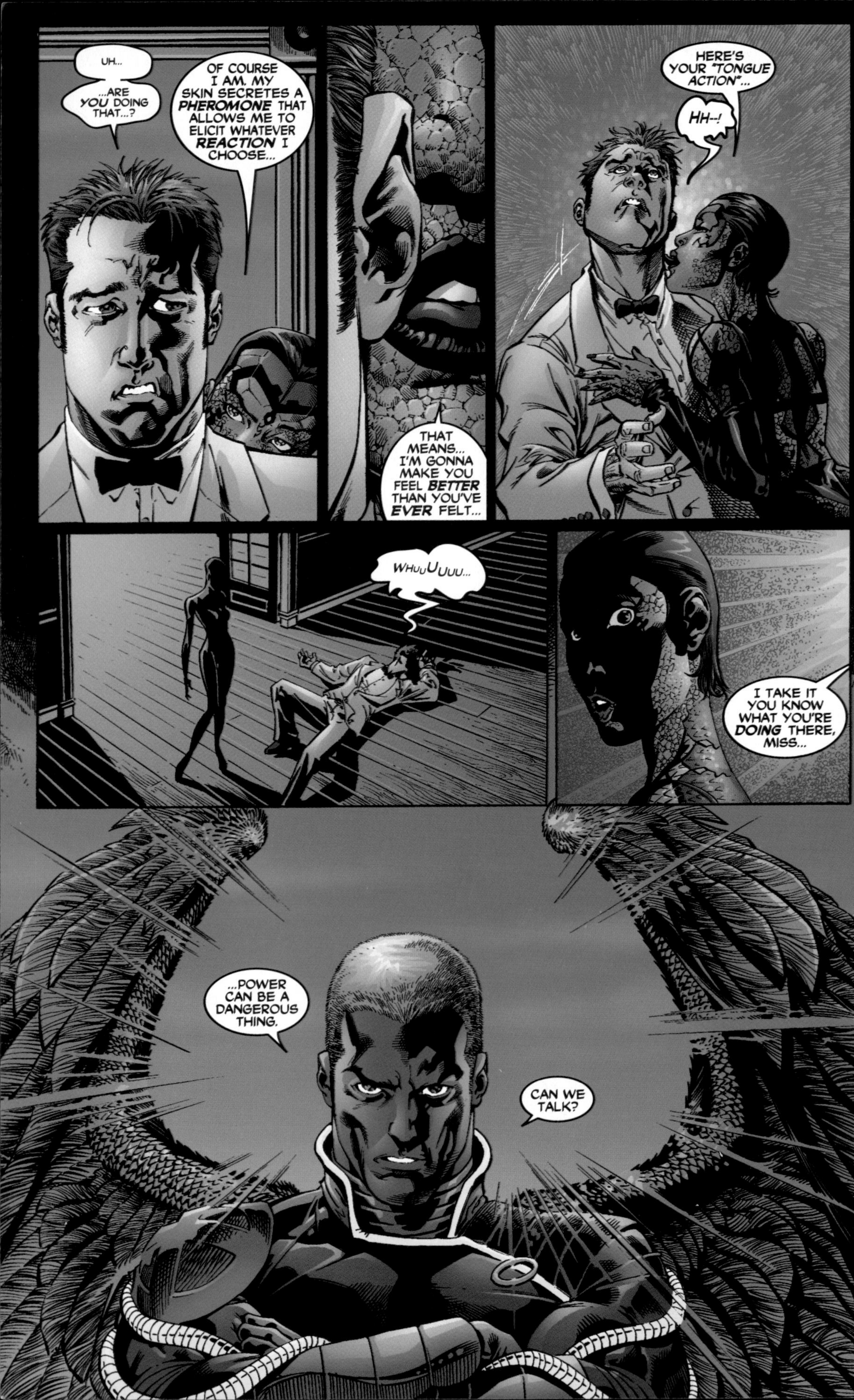
UH...
...ARE YOU DOING THAT...?
OF COURSE I AM. MY SKIN SECRETES A PHEROMONE THAT ALLOWS ME TO ELICIT WHATEVER REACTION I CHOOSE...
THAT MEANS... I'M GONNA MAKE YOU FEEL BETTER THAN YOU'VE EVER FELT...
HERE'S YOUR "TONGUE ACTION"...
HH--!
WHUUUUUU...
I TAKE IT YOU KNOW WHAT YOU'RE DOING THERE, MISS...
...POWER CAN BE A DANGEROUS THING.
CAN WE TALK?

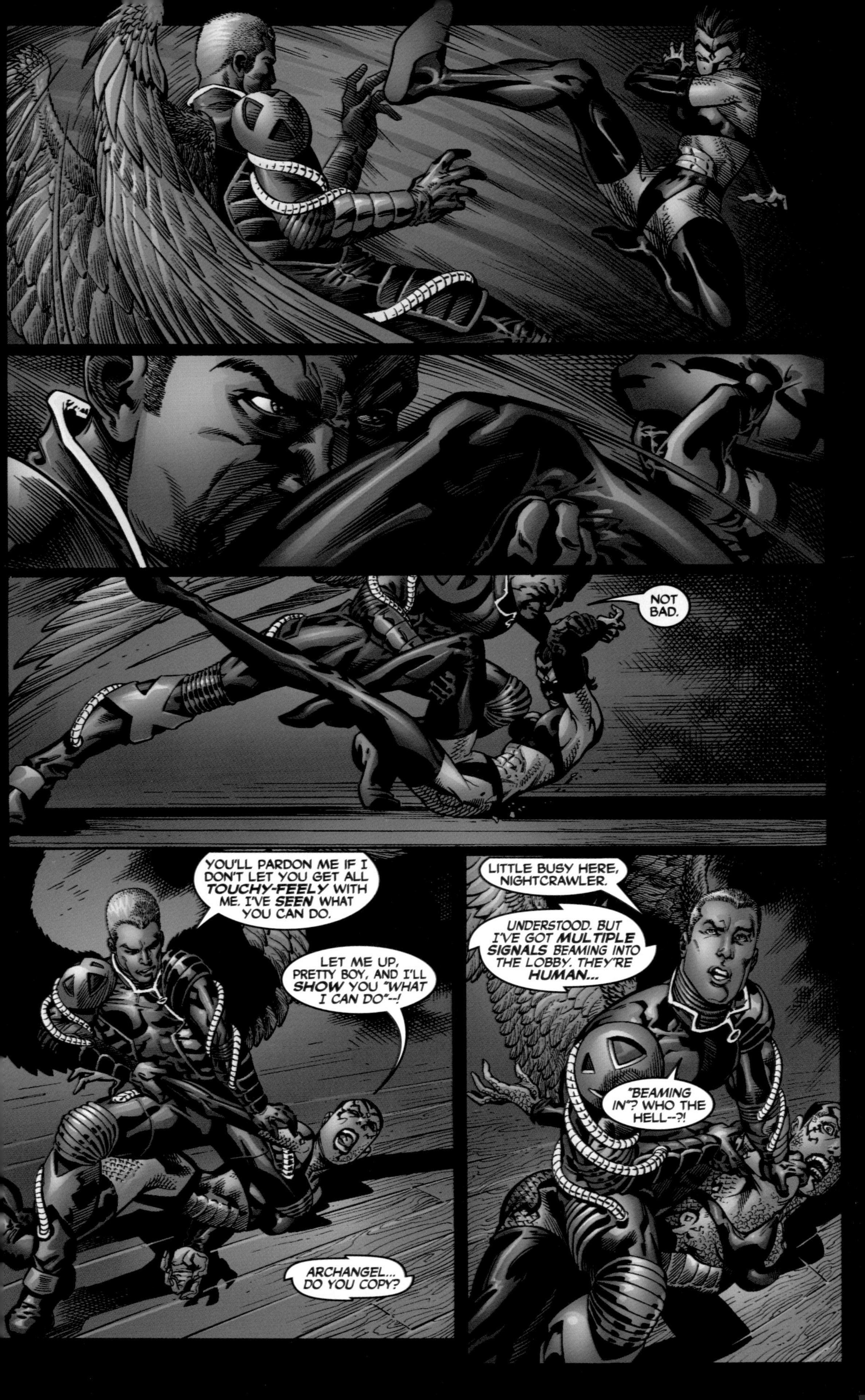
NOT BAD.
YOU'LL PARDON ME IF I DON'T LET YOU GET ALL TOUCHY-FEELY WITH ME. I'VE SEEN WHAT YOU CAN DO.
LET ME UP, PRETTY BOY, AND I'LL SHOW YOU "WHAT I CAN DO"--!
ARCHANGEL... DO YOU COPY?
LITTLE BUSY HERE, NIGHTCRAWLER.
UNDERSTOOD. BUT I'VE GOT MULTIPLE SIGNALS BEAMING INTO THE LOBBY. THEY'RE HUMAN...
"BEAMING IN"? WHO THE HELL--?!

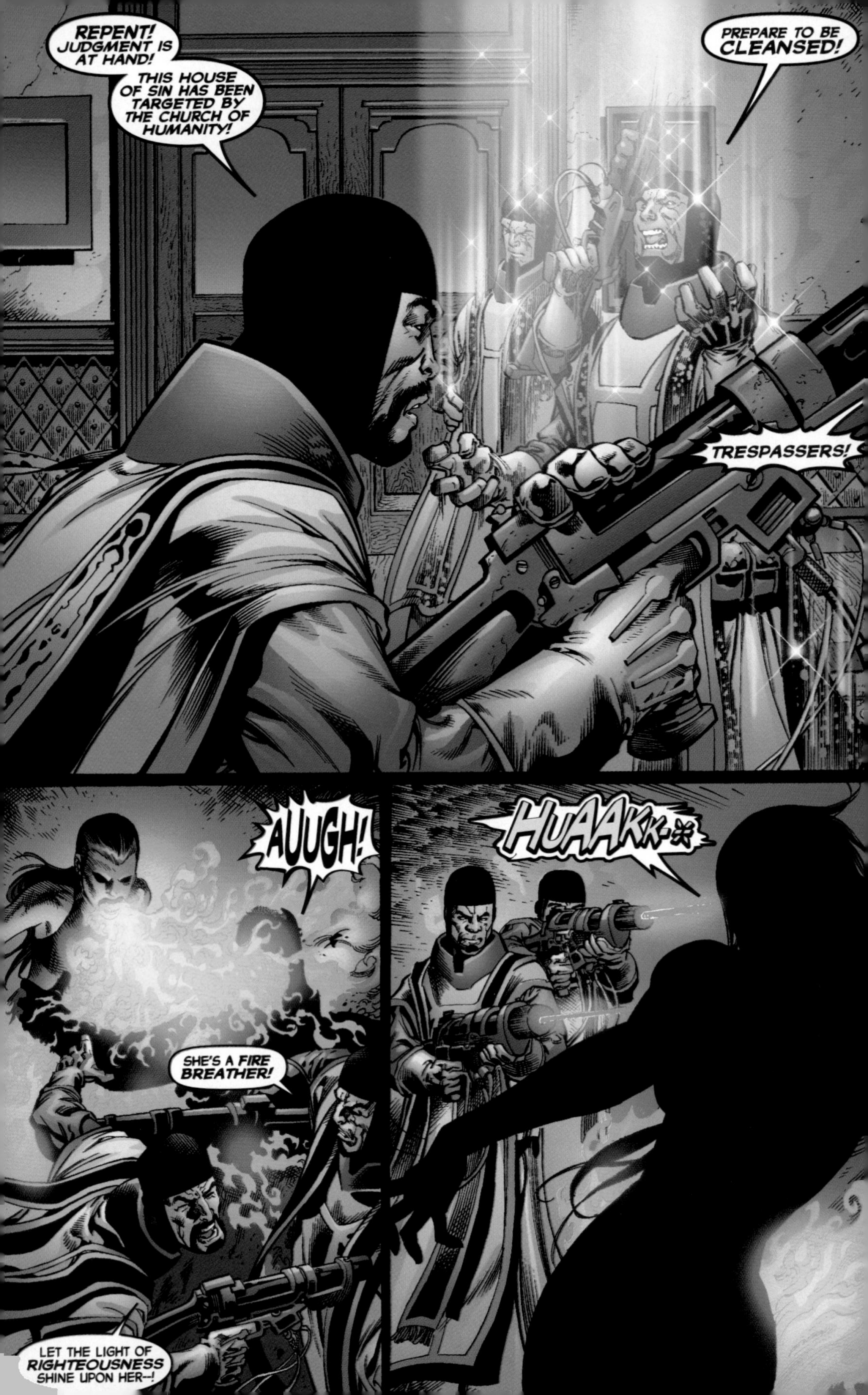
REPENT! JUDGMENT IS AT HAND!
THIS HOUSE OF SIN HAS BEEN TARGETED BY THE CHURCH OF HUMANITY!
PREPARE TO BE CLEANSED!
TRESPASSERS!
AUUGH!
SHE'S A FIRE BREATHER!
LET THE LIGHT OF RIGHTEOUSNESS SHINE UPON HER--!
HUAAKK--

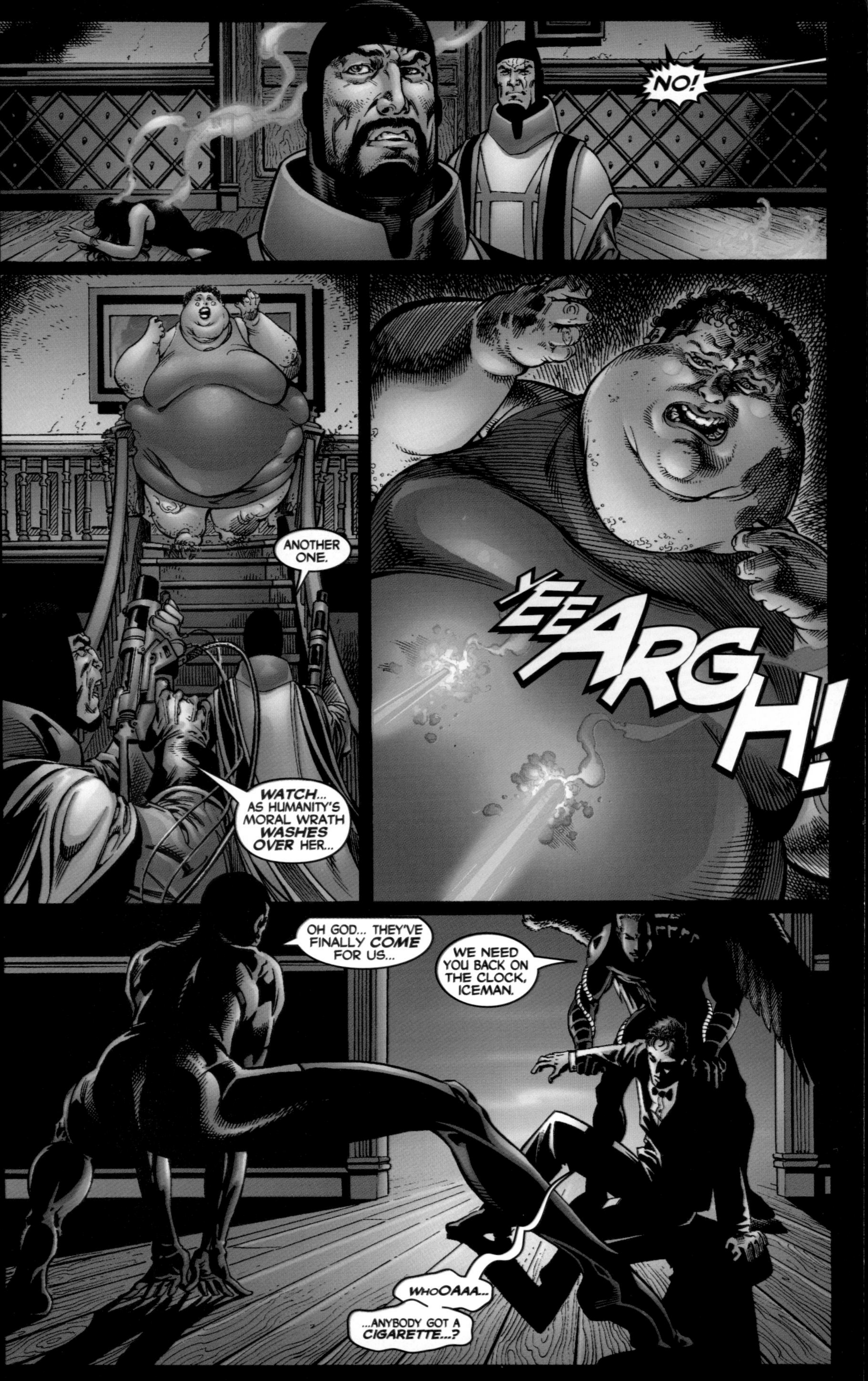
NO!
ANOTHER ONE.
WATCH... AS HUMANITY'S MORAL WRATH WASHES OVER HER...
YEEEARGH!
OH GOD... THEY'VE FINALLY COME FOR US...
WE NEED YOU BACK ON THE CLOCK, ICEMAN.
WHOOAAA...
...ANYBODY GOT A CIGARETTE...?

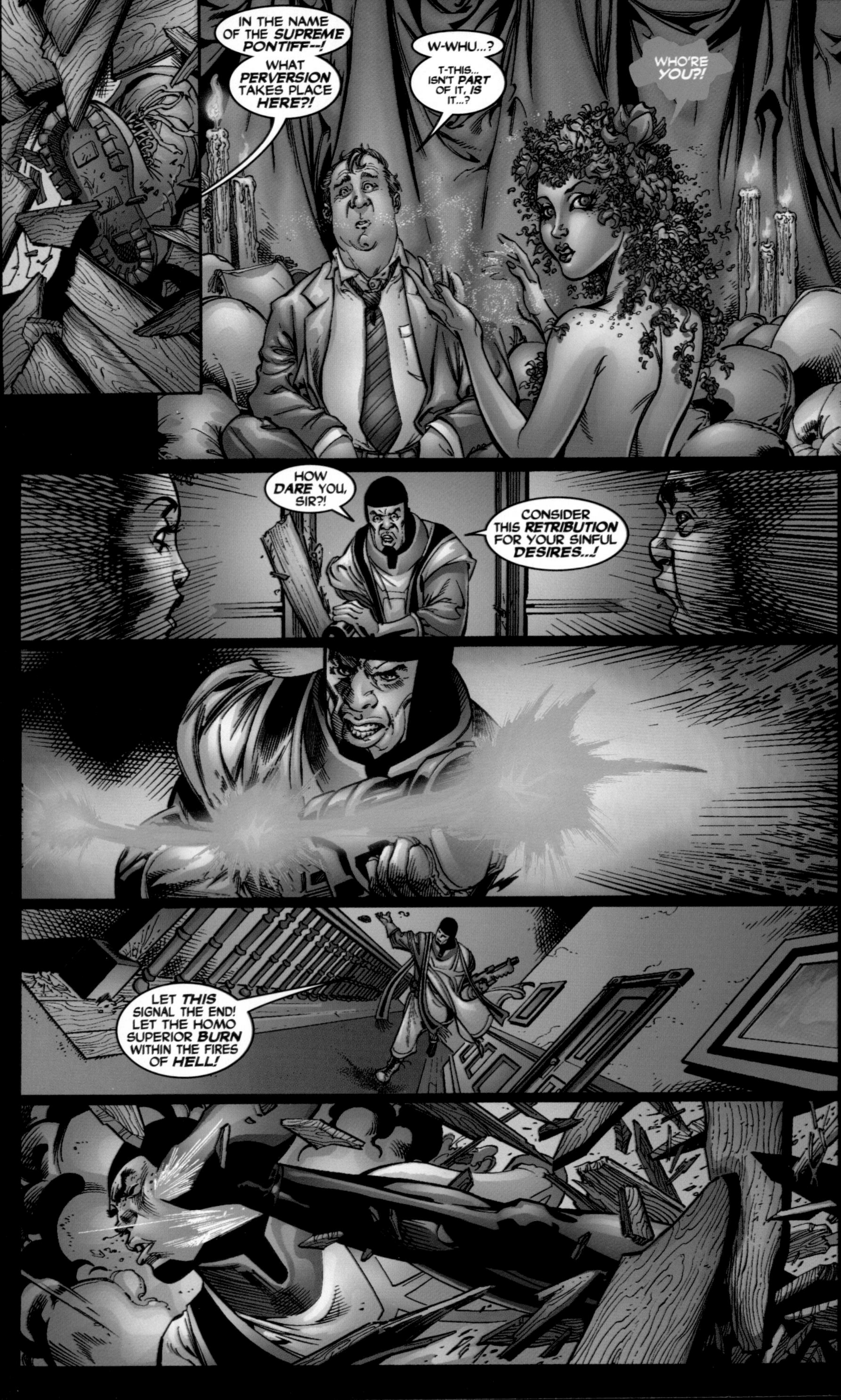
IN THE NAME OF THE SUPREME PONTIFF--! WHAT PERVERSION TAKES PLACE HERE?!
W-WHU...? T-THIS... ISN'T PART OF IT, IS IT...?
WHO'RE YOU?!
HOW DARE YOU, SIR?!
CONSIDER THIS RETRIBUTION FOR YOUR SINFUL DESIRES...!
LET THIS SIGNAL THE END! LET THE HOMO SUPERIOR BURN WITHIN THE FIRES OF HELL!

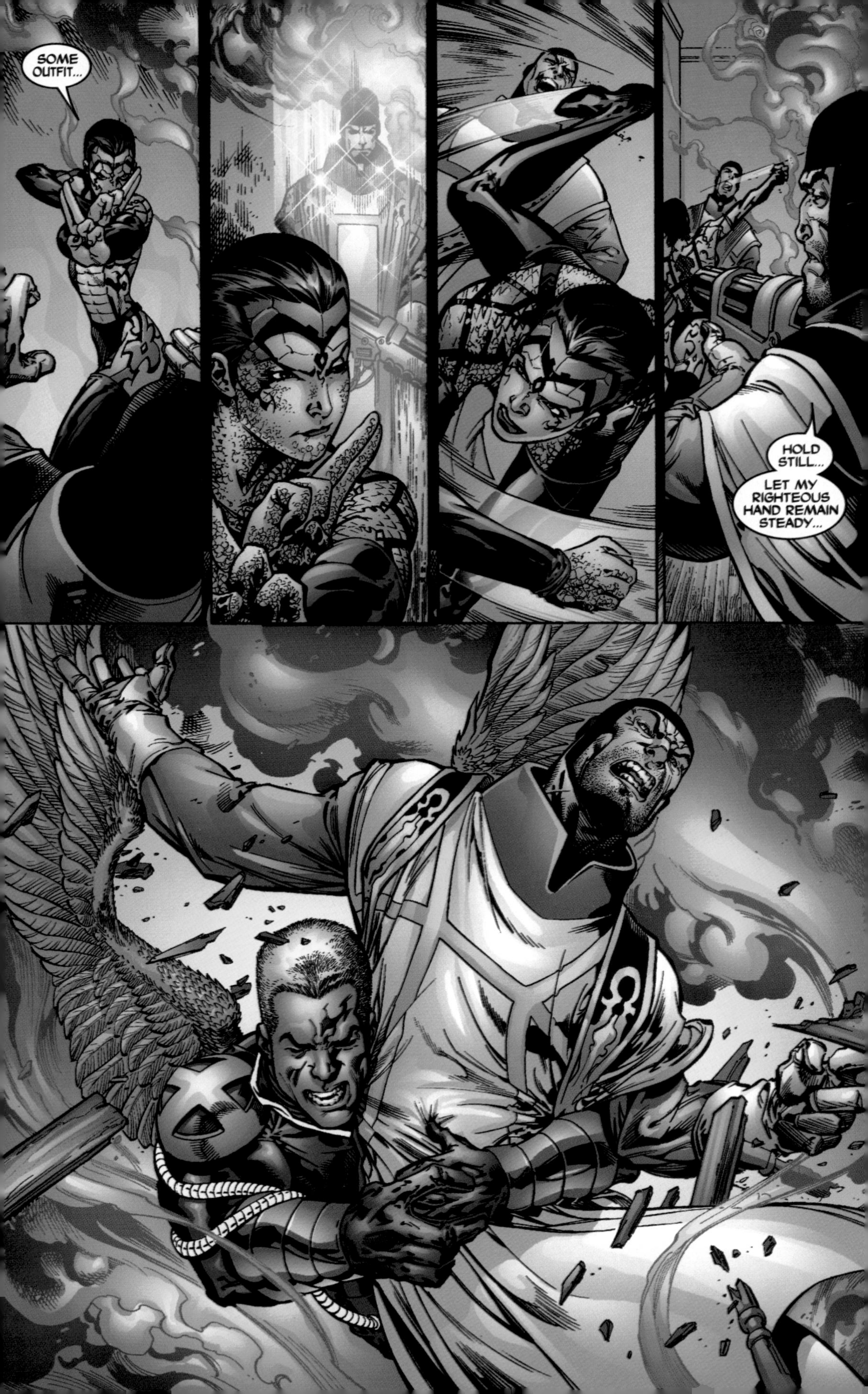
SOME OUTFIT...
HOLD STILL...
LET MY RIGHTEOUS HAND REMAIN STEADY...

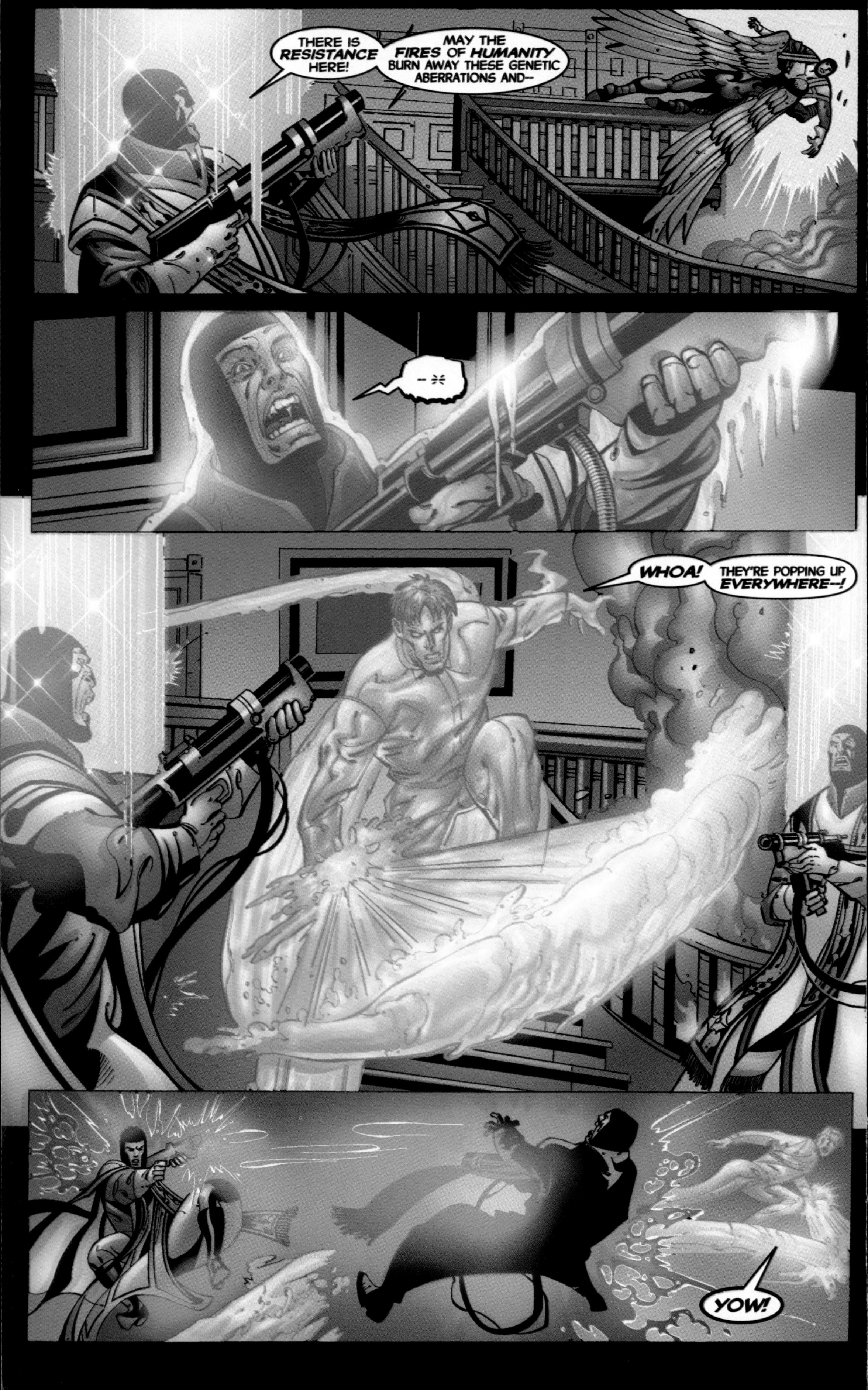

THERE IS RESISTANCE HERE!
MAY THE FIRES OF HUMANITY BURN AWAY THESE GENETIC ABERRATIONS AND--
--!!
WHOA!
THEY'RE POPPING UP EVERYWHERE--!
YOW!

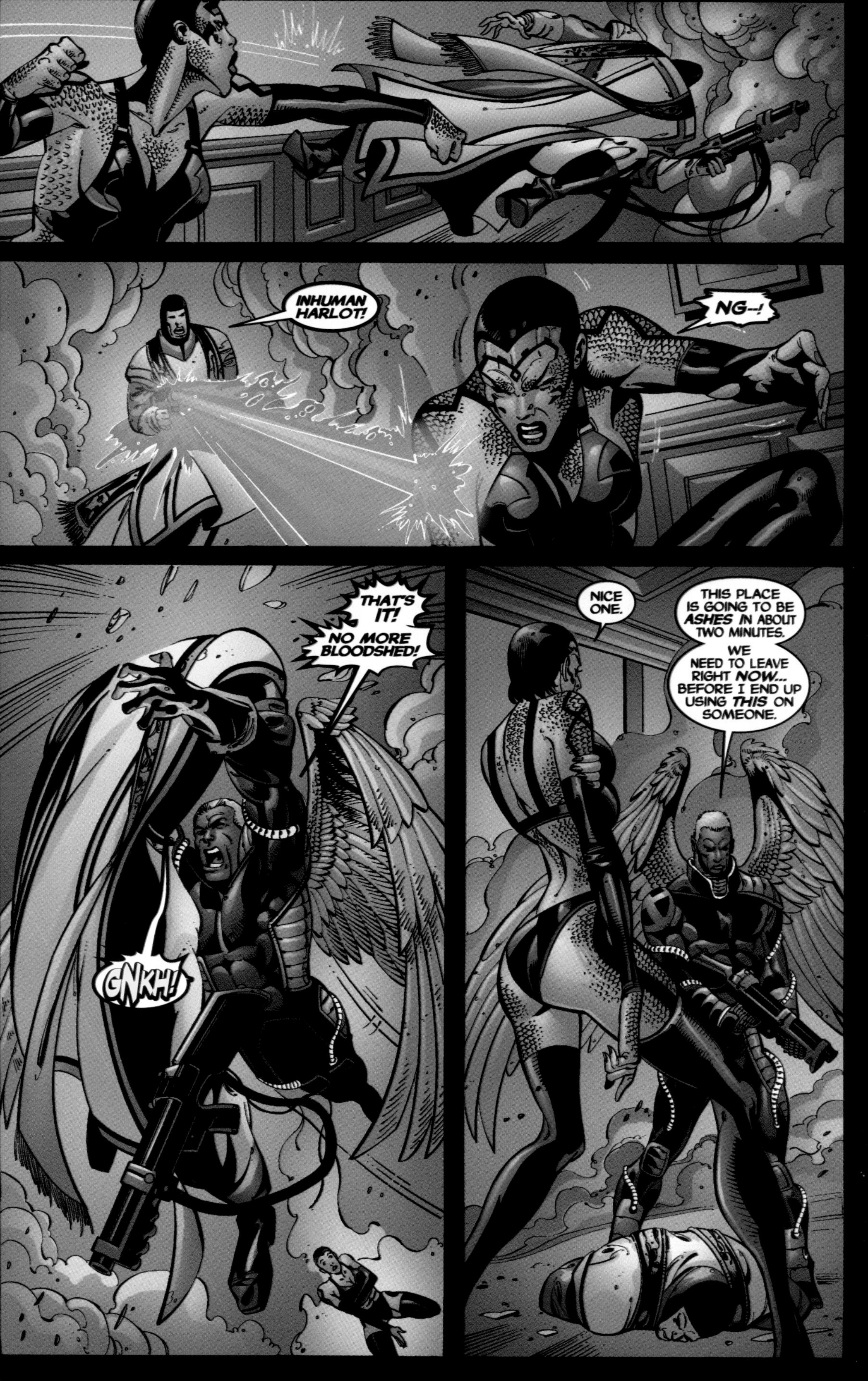
INHUMAN HARLOT!
NG--!
THAT'S IT! NO MORE BLOODSHED!
GNKH!
NICE ONE.
THIS PLACE IS GOING TO BE ASHES IN ABOUT TWO MINUTES.
WE NEED TO LEAVE RIGHT NOW... BEFORE I END UP USING THIS ON SOMEONE.

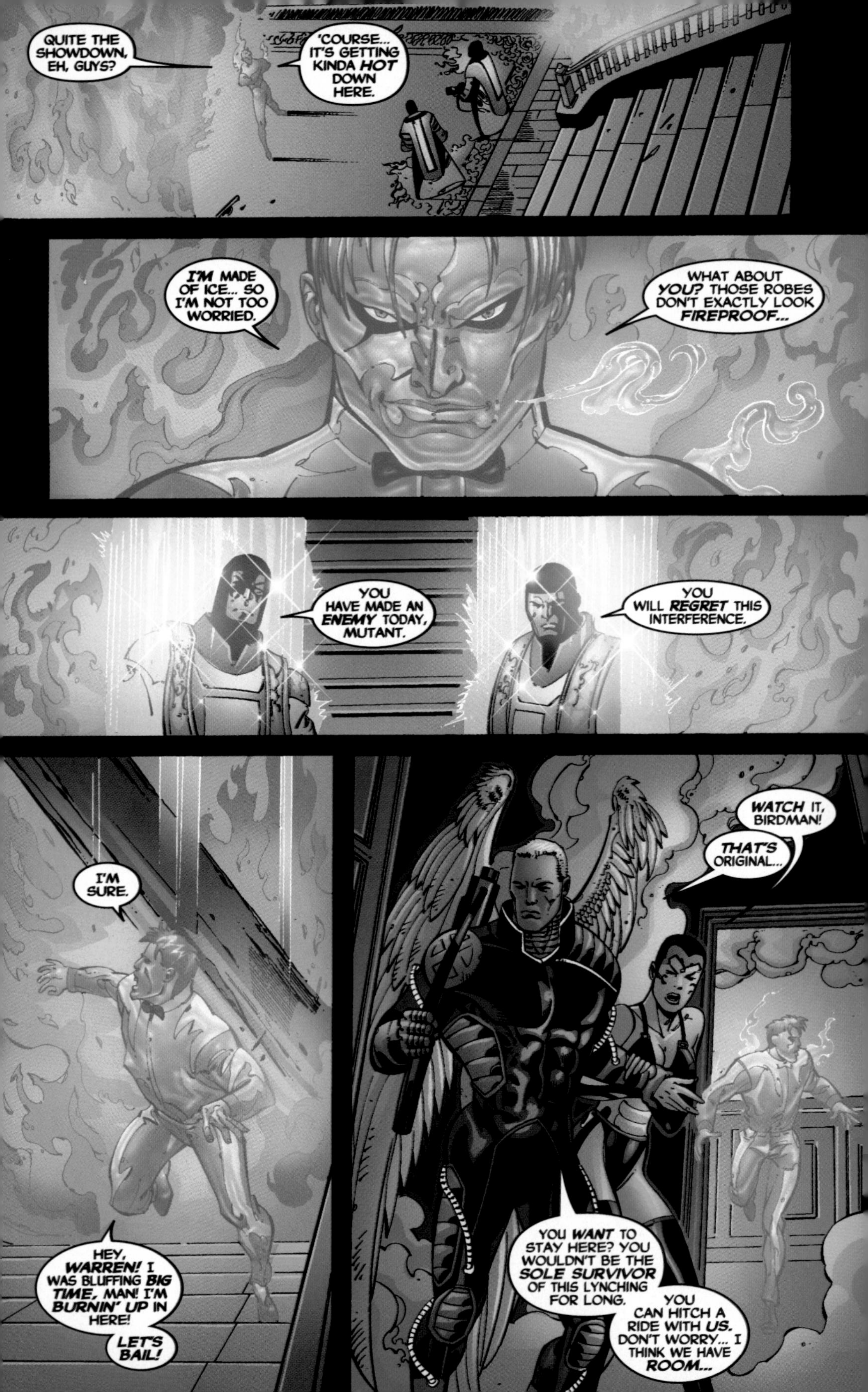
QUITE THE SHOWDOWN, EH, GUYS?
'COURSE... IT'S GETTING KINDA HOT DOWN HERE.
I'M MADE OF ICE... SO I'M NOT TOO WORRIED.
WHAT ABOUT YOU? THOSE ROBES DON'T EXACTLY LOOK FIREPROOF...
YOU HAVE MADE AN ENEMY TODAY, MUTANT.
YOU WILL REGRET THIS INTERFERENCE.
I'M SURE.
HEY, WARREN! I WAS BLUFFING BIG TIME, MAN! I'M BURNIN' UP IN HERE!
LET'S BAIL!
WATCH IT, BIRDMAN!
THAT'S ORIGINAL...
YOU WANT TO STAY HERE? YOU WOULDN'T BE THE SOLE SURVIVOR OF THIS LYNCHING FOR LONG.
YOU CAN HITCH A RIDE WITH US. DON'T WORRY... I THINK WE HAVE ROOM...

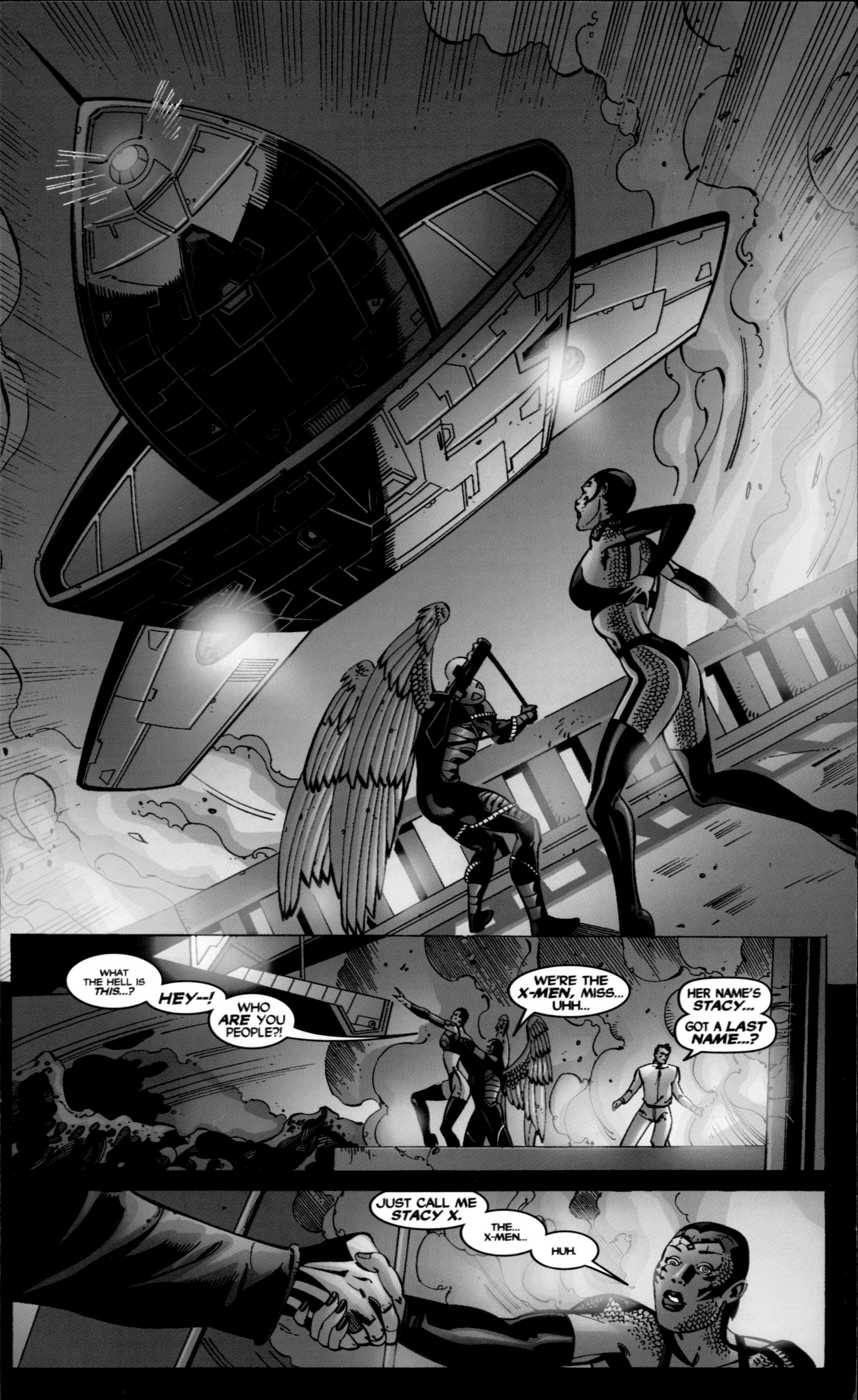
WHAT THE HELL IS THIS...?
HEY--!
WHO ARE YOU PEOPLE?!
WE'RE THE X-MEN, MISS... UHH...
HER NAME'S STACY...
GOT A LAST NAME...?
JUST CALL ME STACY X.
THE... X-MEN...
HUH.

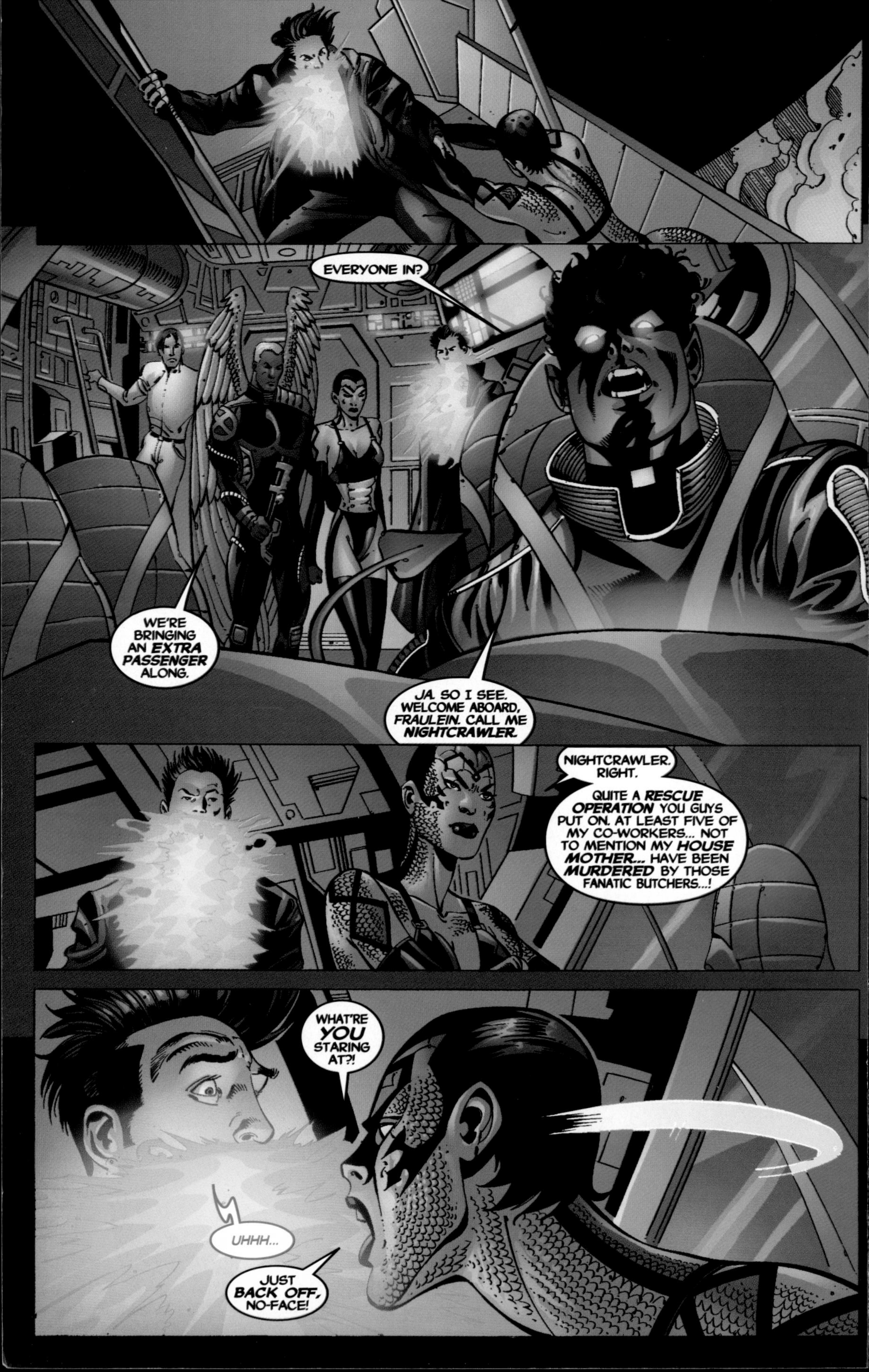
EVERYONE IN?
WE'RE BRINGING AN EXTRA PASSENGER ALONG.
JA. SO I SEE. WELCOME ABOARD, FRAULEIN. CALL ME NIGHTCRAWLER.
NIGHTCRAWLER. RIGHT.
QUITE A RESCUE OPERATION YOU GUYS PUT ON. AT LEAST FIVE OF MY CO-WORKERS... NOT TO MENTION MY HOUSE MOTHER... HAVE BEEN MURDERED BY THOSE FANATIC BUTCHERS...!
WHAT'RE YOU STARING AT?!
UHHH...
JUST BACK OFF, NO-FACE!